MEDALLION COLLECTORS' SERIES

edited by Gaby Goldscheider

Nursery Furniture

In the same series

Dolls
Gaby Goldscheider

Children's China
Pauline Flick

Cot in Arts and Crafts manner. Oak, carved, gilt and painted.
Design R. Norman Shaw 1867. H. 42 in. L. 42 in. W. 20¼ in.

MEDALLION COLLECTORS' SERIES

Nursery Furniture

Antique Children's, Miniature and Dolls' House Furniture

EDWARD GELLES

Constable · London

First published in Great Britain 1982
by Constable and Company Limited
10 Orange Street London WC2H 7EG
Copyright © 1982 by Edward Gelles
ISBN 0 09 463990 6
Photoset in 11 on 13 point Monophoto Ehrhardt by
Servis Filmsetting Limited, Manchester
Printed in Great Britain by
The Anchor Press Ltd
and bound by Wm Brendon & Son Ltd
both of Tiptree, Essex

To the memory of my parents

Contents

Foreword

I wish to thank the curators and staff of museums in this country and abroad, numerous dealers and collectors, and the staff of several London auction houses, in particular Mr Graham Child of Sotheby's, who have kindly provided me with photographs and information. I am also indebted to the editor of the Medallion Collectors' Series, Gaby Goldscheider, and to the publishers, for their help and encouragement.

Croydon, July 1980   E.G.

List of Illustrations

1. Painting of the children of James I, *c.* 1610

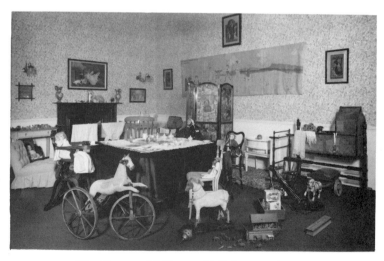

2. The Nursery, Wallington Hall, Northumberland

Introduction

'The child is father of the man.'
William Wordsworth

What is nursery furniture and how did it develop?
Where can one see it?
Where can one read more about it?
Where and how can it be bought and cared for?
The general reader and would-be collector will find
the answers to these questions in the following pages.

A charming painting of the children of James I (Fig. 1) shows
one of them sitting on a small armchair and another standing
behind a baby-walker. References to furniture specially made for
children occur in both art and literature from earliest times.
Much of this furniture has been lost through hard usage and
decay, but enough remains from the seventeenth century
onwards to make one wonder why so little has been written on
the subject. Not only are there fine collections, both public and
private, in this country and abroad, but enough material passes
through the antiques market to make nursery furniture an
interesting field for collectors.

A view of the nursery at Wallington, Northumberland (Fig. 2)
shows many of the items which come under this heading. On the
right we see a mahogany frame and caned swinging cot of the
type which became popular towards the end of the eighteenth
century. There are two late nineteenth-century high chairs at
either end of an adult size table, and also adult size chairs and
side tables. We can see a small child's country style armchair,
toys including a tricycle horse, push horse, and horse and cart,
and there is a wash-stand, towel rail, screen, fireguard, and

suitable wall decorations to complete the scene. To the above items might be added children's tables, chests, bureaux, playpens, rocking horses, push-carts and perhaps perambulators.

For the ubiquitous dolls special dolls' furniture was made. From very early days model or miniature furniture has been collected, and miniatures were also made as show pieces and travellers' samples. At the same time interest arose in the construction and furnishing of baby houses (later in the nineteenth century called dolls' houses). From being objects of interest to adult collectors, some miniature furniture found its way into the hands of children, for example for the use of dolls, and in the nineteenth century dolls' houses became children's playthings and an inevitable part of the furnishings of a nursery. For these dolls' houses tiny furniture was required and made, certainly from the sixteenth century onwards. In the nineteenth century and later, much of this furniture was produced in the styles of earlier periods.

We are therefore dealing with four categories of nursery furniture: (1) furniture made specifically for the use of children, which is the principal subject of this book (2) furniture of adult size relegated to the nursery, which will be referred to in passing (3) miniature furniture, which could be furniture for dolls – and in Catholic countries this would include pieces of devotional nature such as cradles and chairs for the Christ Child – and models made as collectors' pieces, show pieces, and travellers' samples, and (4) dolls' house furniture.

A very approximate indication of the scale of these categories of furniture would be in the order of half the adult size, going down to one-eighth to one-half size, and then to one-sixteenth to one-twelfth size.

American antique miniature furniture can be seen in museum and private collections, among the more important of which is the Henry Francis du Pont Winterthur Museum, a view of its miniature stair hall being shown in Fig. 3.

Nursery furniture on the smallest scale is shown in the dolls'

3. Miniature Stair Hall at Winterthur, Delaware, U.S.A.

nursery from a dolls' house in the Bethnal Green Museum (Fig. 4). Here we see a turn-of-the-century nursery with doll's bed, high chair, bassinet, baby-walker, rocking horse, a tiny dolls' house, as well as 'adult' size dressing table and wardrobe. The pink dotted wallpaper with a frieze of animals completes the Edwardian nursery decoration. The furniture has little quality of

4. Doll's Nursery in dolls' house (3 Devonshire Villas, Kilburn), *c.* 1900

craftsmanship, but it is of immense social interest to have an entire nursery of the period in match-box size miniature.

Dolls, dolls' houses, and their furnishings, toys and games are already flourishing collectors' fields, and all these belong to the nursery. Children's furniture, as such, is deserving of greater collectors' interest than it receives at present, firstly from the art historical viewpoint of stylistic development, and secondly for the social study of childhood through the ages.

There are a few books on English, American, and Continental antique miniature furniture (*see* Bibliography 1, 2 and 3).

As miniature furniture is therefore reasonably well documented, it is dealt with only briefly here. For children's furniture, a comprehensive bibliography is appended. In this connection it is important to note several exhibitions held in the past decade which are pointers to increasing interest in the subject (*see* Bibliography 4–8).

An exhibition of children's chairs was held in 1971 by Spink &

Son, the London art dealers. Chairs are by far the most numerous and varied of extant children's antique furniture. There are high chairs, low chairs, rocking chairs and many other designs, and it is particularly interesting to trace the designs through the centuries in parallel with the development of adult furniture styles. In earlier times, children were considered as miniature adults and this attitude was reflected in the furniture made for them, especially in the design of chairs. In the nineteenth century, when children began to come into their own, style and craftsmanship started to give way to utility. Children's furniture (1600–1900) shown at Towneley Hall, Burnley in 1977 included cradles, baby-walkers and chairs drawn mainly from sources in the North of England. Other exhibitions were at the Kunstmuseum, Aarhus in 1972, at the Kunstgewerbemuseum, Cologne in 1973, and at the Historisches Stadtmuseum, Munich in 1976. The German exhibitions were concerned with the development of children's furniture well into the present century. The emphasis at Cologne tended towards function and design, while the English exhibitions focused more on style and craftsmanship of the earlier period furniture.

Illustrations in this book are drawn from these exhibitions, from the records of auction houses and dealers, and from museum collections. Reference is made to examples of American nursery furniture, and a short list of relevant public collections includes some representative American, as well as European, museums. In London, the reader should certainly start with visits to the Victoria & Albert Museum in South Kensington and to the affiliated Bethnal Green Museum.

To the survey of children's furniture a brief note on accessories, including treen, metalware, and china is appended, to be dealt with more fully in separate volumes of this series. One of the most important collections of treen and wooden bygones is the Pinto Collection in the City of Birmingham Museum, formed by the author of the definitive work on the subject (*see* Bibliography 9).

Hints for collectors include suggestions on what to collect, a short list of antique shops and auction rooms, how to buy at auctions, and notes on the care and restoration of antiques. Looking at collecting in historical perspective, it appears that for hundreds of years the finest objects were made for the rich with emphasis on style and craftsmanship, but that at the present time design within the social context is becoming increasingly important. Nowadays, when the child is the centre of attention and interest, this must be even more relevant as far as nursery furniture is concerned. It follows that late nineteenth- and twentieth-century pieces will become increasingly collectable and valuable. Plain country pieces made for less affluent families in earlier centuries – not so stylish, but possessing charm and character – will, no doubt, be re-assessed and revalued.

History of the Nursery

An apartment for looking after babies, or for the exclusive use of young children, was rare in the medieval period.

Certain specific items of children's furniture, such as the cradle and baby-walker, go back to earliest times. Occasionally a Gothic cradle, stool, or child's coffer still turns up. For example, Christie's sold a fifteenth century child's chair last year (Sale 19.7.79. Lot 165 for £650). To all intents and purposes this study begins in the sixteenth century. From that time onwards we find references to children's nurseries and to inventories of their contents, and from the beginning of the seventeenth century an increasing number of furniture items survive.

In 1583 Sir William Ingilby had a nursery at his house at Padsidehead, and in 1613 the Shuttleworths of Gawthorpe are recorded as having bought twelve yards of frieze for cradle blankets (*see* Bibliography 15). In 1567 a nursery inventory lists a trussing bed, a trundle bed, featherbed and mattress, blankets, sheets, coverlets, covers and bolster, a chest, a little presser (wardrobe), and a chair (*see* Bibliography 27). In the sixteenth and seventeenth centuries the cradles and other children's furniture of the rich were dressed with costly silk and velvet hangings, and not infrequently with cloth of gold or silver. This was in keeping with their costly and voluminous clothes. Babies were buried under quantities of bedding; in 1658 Evelyn recorded in his diary that his young son was 'suffocated by ye women and maids that tended him and covered him too hot with blankets as he lay in a cradle near an excessive hot fire in a close room.' Early cradles were made in sizes to accommodate babies to their third or fourth year, and from this period cribs and beds for older children are rare. Many joined and carved oak cradles for the not so rich survive from the seventeenth century. These were generally mounted on rockers; the type of swinging cot known from Gothic times went out of favour until the later eighteenth century, when mahogany cots, often with caned sides, became fashionable.

From the seventeenth century or before, there survive not only cradles, baby-walkers or go-carts, play-pens, close stools with their little pewter or wooden pots, stools and small tables, but chairs, some being miniature versions of adult chairs of the period, and others being specially designed for babies to enable them to sit with adults at the dining table. These high chairs (see Fig. 29) later changed their style, when they became more portable and functional, for use other than as a dining chair.

The beginnings of a change in the attitude towards children might be detected in the so-called Age of Enlightenment, which followed the writings of Rousseau. Certainly, until that time children were dressed like adults, and apart from cradles, baby-walkers, and high chairs, which of necessity had to be specially designed for babies, children's furniture was designed to be a miniature version of adult furniture, and continued to be so until well into the nineteenth century. Indeed, this style of dressing children and furnishing their rooms tied in with attitudes towards education. The psychological need of the child for gradual development and self-expression was not really recognised; even in play children were expected to assume adult roles as speedily as possible. Therefore the rocking horse was not merely a toy at a time when the horse was a means of transport and when everybody who could afford a rocking horse would go on to ride a real horse in due course. Again, the Nuremberg kitchens were educational toys, and even the fine baby houses, which were at first largely adult amusements, would have been a special treat for the children and toys with a strong educational purpose.

In eighteenth-century England, children of the well-to-do were largely kept in nurseries with a varied staff of nannies, nurses and nursery maids, and this social arrangement persisted up until the First World War. In a bourgeois environment, as in America even in the eighteenth century, or in the *Biedermeier* period in Germany, children lived more *en famille* with obvious social consequences, and particularly with the result that fine furniture was made specifically for children's use. In America more good eighteenth-century children's and miniature furniture, such as chests, bureaux and cabinets, survived than in England. This is not to say that fine English period children's furniture was not made, but rather that both here and elsewhere it would have been made by cabinet-makers as special pieces for show or *en suite* with adult furniture, and as such was not to be hidden away in a remote nursery. As the Victorian age progressed, a certain loosening up of attitudes towards upbringing and education had its effect on the running of and the furnishings of the nursery. The nurseries for Queen Victoria's own children are the paragon for this period. Depending on wealth and social status, these would have extended from the more usual day and night nurseries to an entire suite of rooms with kitchen, laundry rooms, and so on. Apart from the principal children's furniture discussed in the following chapters, which included cradles, beds, and cribs, baby-walkers, and a variety of children's chairs and tables, as well as the rocking horse and the dolls' house, there were adult size pieces like wardrobes, cupboards, and a solid dining table and chairs. The essential furnishings also included a wash-stand, a bath-tub, fireguards, and screens to exclude draughts.

In some respects the nursery was in its hey-day in late Victorian and Edwardian times when it was described by

Muthesius (*see* Bibliography 13). He noted that a day and a night room were needed so that they could be aired, that the fires were not only for warmth but also for airing linen and clothes, and that they were suitably protected by fenders. Often there was a container from which hot water could be drawn, but occasional cooking and warming-up of dishes was done on a small gas or spirit cooker. The maid generally brought the food to the nursery, and nanny served it on nursery china which stayed in the nursery and was washed up there. The children usually visited their parents between tea and dinner-time when they were on their best behaviour. As for the furniture, he observed that the day room required cupboards for linen and clothes, a cupboard for toys and shelves for picture books, a small games table, and an adult size dining table with chairs to suit children of different ages, and also a low nursing chair. The little cot for the smallest baby in the day room had curtains of lace and muslin. The bedroom had beds for nurse and the children, and the former must have a wash-stand, dressing table, and wardrobes. The pram should not be brought into the nursery. The floors were covered with linoleum or cork, but there might be a fireside rug or two. The walls were emulsion painted or panelled, above which wallpaper could lend a decorative touch to the rooms.

In this period, wallpaper, rugs, and pictures specially designed and made for nurseries, became more generally available. Department stores like the Army & Navy, Story & Co., and particularly Liberty and Heal's were in the *avant garde* of taste. C.A. Voysey designed wallpaper with animals, birds, and fairy-tale figures and also fire-side rugs.

Cecil Aldin and John Hassall were noted for their designs of nursery wallpaper and pictures. Charles Rennie Mackintosh, the most famous Art Nouveau architect, designed a nursery in his unmistakable style. At this time, educational ideas had come a long way from Rousseau and Locke. In the era of psychologists such as Freud and educationalists such as Montessori, childhood was beginning to be recognised as having a claim to autonomy rather than being a mere preparatory phase for adulthood, and so the way was opened for the design of furniture suited to the special psychological as well as the physical needs of children, and this came about under the influence of the *Bauhaus* movement and its successors.

Styles of Furniture Design

Much of the finest nursery furniture tended to follow the prevailing fashions and styles of adult furniture, but a considerable proportion, particularly that made for the somewhat less affluent, was made for centuries to traditional designs in oak, ash, elm, pine and so on (Figs. 7, 21, 42, 49).

For those readers not familiar with the different styles and the fashionable woods of succeeding periods the summary in Table 1 may be of assistance. It shows that in the development of English furniture one can distinguish a number of periods called after the principal woods used, namely the periods of oak, walnut, mahogany, satinwood, and rosewood, which correspond roughly to the medieval Gothic and sixteenth-century Renaissance, the seventeenth- and early eighteenth-century Baroque, the mid-eighteenth-century Rococo, the late eighteenth-century neo-classical, and the turn of the nineteenth-century Regency styles. The art movements of the later nineteenth and early twentieth centuries show varied and conflicting trends, with the use of a variety of woods and differing treatments.

The carved oak pieces of the early periods (Fig 29) were succeeded by much lighter and more graceful furniture after the restoration of Charles II. This period saw the innovations of caning, veneering, marquetry, japanning, and the characteristic baluster turned supports on tables (Fig. 77) and chairs (Figs. 30, 33) including the barley sugar twist. The walnut period proceeded into the reigns of Queen Anne and George I with the development of the cabriole leg (Fig. 75).

The reign of George II saw the introduction of mahogany furniture (Figs. 34, 76, 81) and at mid-eighteenth century Thomas Chippendale's Rococo period (Fig. 35) was sometimes complicated by *Chinoiserie* and Gothic revival fantasies.

After 1760 and the accession of George III, in the period of the neo-classical revival of which Robert Adam was the leading British exponent, more delicate mahogany furniture was made, often inlaid or painted. Chippendale worked also in this style in his later career, and Hepplewhite's designs were influential in the last quarter of the century (Fig. 38). The final decade or two of the century were dominated by the designs of Thomas Sheraton (Figs. 12, 39), and this is the period when satinwood was most fashionable.

The Rococo and neo-classical designs of the George II and the later George III periods correspond to those of the Louis XV and Louis XVI periods in France (Fig. 40), just as the succeeding heavier classicism of the Regency corresponds to the French Empire style (Fig. 19). During the Regency, rosewood was fashionable (Fig. 43), but much mahogany furniture continued to be made.

The classical style became heavier and less refined in the early Victorian era, corresponding to the *Biedermeier* style in Germany and Austria (Fig. 88).

At the same time the neo-gothic style saw oak and other woods returning to favour (Fig. 45), while there was an eclectic revival of styles of the eighteenth and earlier centuries, in reaction to which and following on the neo-gothic revival William Morris and his friends turned back for inspiration to the medieval country craftsman. The Arts & Crafts Movement developed from their efforts.

From the latter movement (frontispiece), the Aesthetic movement, and the Anglo-Japanese style, the Art Nouveau style emerged at the end of the nineteenth century (see p. 44*f*).

Much late nineteenth-century design was utilitarian and orientated towards mass-production, one of the more successful innovations being Michael Thonet's bentwood furniture (Fig. 51).

The *Die Stijl* (see p. 45*f*) and *Bauhaus* (Fig. 56) styles, emanating from Holland and Germany, had great international influence on furniture design during the 1920s and 30s.

TABLE SHOWING FURNITURE STYLES AND PERIODS

STYLE and ORIGIN		PERIOD	WOOD etc.,	DESIGNERS, CRAFTSMEN, etc.
INTL. GOTHIC	15th century	Early Tudor	OAK	
RENAISSANCE	15th century	Late Tudor	OAK	
Italian	16th century	(Elizabeth I)	some walnut bulbous supports	
BAROQUE	17th century	Restoration (Charles II)	WALNUT caning, veneering, marquetry, japanning	Grinling Gibbons
Italian		(William & Mary)		Gerreit Jensen
		Queen Anne	cabriole leg, pad foot	Daniel Marot
PALLADIAN in England	c. 1720	George I	gesso, gilding	William Kent
ROCOCO French	1730–60	George II	MAHOGANY carving, cabriole leg with ball and claw foot, square leg	Thomas Chippendale
'GOTHICK'	1750–			
'CHINESE'	1760–			
NEO–CLASSIC		George III	MAHOGANY – inlaid, painted, turned fluted, then tapering leg	Robert Adam
			SATINWOOD 1780–1800 and 1820–	George Hepplewhite
				Thomas Sheraton

Style	Date	Period	Material	Designer
EMPIRE French	1800–20			
REGENCY English	1800–20	George IV	ROSEWOOD often inlaid and MAHOGANY	Thomas Hope
BIEDERMEIER German	1815–48			
NEO-GOTHIC	c. 1825–	William IV / Victoria	OAK etc.,	A.W.N. Pugin
ARTS & CRAFTS English	1860–	Victoria	ebonised, painted woods etc.,	William Morris / Norman Shaw / E.W. Godwin / C.A. Voysey / C.R. Mackintosh / H. van de Velde (Belgian)
ART NOUVEAU Intl.	1895–1914	Edward VII		
ART DECO French, German etc.,	1925–	George V		
De Stijl Dutch	1917–31			Gerrit Rietveld
BAUHAUS German	1919–32			M. Breuer

Children's Furniture

The illustrations which follow (pp 37–107) show clearly the great variety of design in every category of children's furniture, and particularly so for cradles and chairs. The emphasis is naturally on antique wooden furniture, but it should be remembered that much basket work was used and has perished, and that from certain periods there is children's furniture made of papier mâché, metal, and latterly of synthetic materials. In addition to the sheer variety of design, the illustrations show cheek by jowl examples of fine and elaborate craftsmanship and of the simplest and plainest kind. Compare, by way of example, the state cradle with superb gilt metal mounts by Thomire (Fig. 19) and a plain painted pine bed (Fig. 21). Some of the pieces illustrated here are great works of applied art, but all are of social interest.

1. Cots, Cradles, Beds

Wickerwork cradles were used since time immemorial but no early ones survive. Eighteenth and nineteenth century examples are illustrated in paintings by Joseph Highmore (*Pamela telling nursery tales*) and Sir David Wilkie (*Distraining for rent*). In the nineteenth century, a wickerwork cradle was called a bassinet, and is described by Loudon (*see* Bibliography 11), an example being illustrated (Fig. 5).

Wooden cradles from before the seventeenth century are rare. The two famous cots remaining from medieval times are the so-called 'cradle of Charles V' in the Musées Royaux in Brussels, and the 'cradle of Henry V' in the London Museum. Both are designed to swing between two uprights and are therefore designated as cots, the word 'cradle' referring here to examples mounted on rockers, and the word 'crib' being used for beds with guarded sides.

Penelope Eames (*see* Bibliography 28) analyses these two

5. Willow Cradle, nineteenth-century. H. 29 in. L. 38 in.

medieval examples and concludes that they are both essentially late fifteenth-century in date. The former was made for the father or aunt of Charles V. The original painting and gilding is now largely lost, but the arms of the grandparents, Maximilian of Austria and Mary of Burgundy, can be discerned. The latter comprises a rectangular box with rough reeded decoration and a stand with two chamfered posts to which it is attached by rings and staples. Each post is surmounted by a finely carved bird with long tail and folded wings. These were originally gilded. Previous writers (*see* Bibliography 1) have suggested that the posts were of a later date than the box.

Swinging cots went out of fashion in the sixteenth and seventeenth centuries, when cradles were generally made of oak, in the form of a rectangular panelled box, and mounted on rockers. Usually, there are wooden knobs at each corner, and more often than not there is a wooden hood which at different periods tended to be flat-topped, rounded, or canted. Cradles in warmer countries were shallower, as not so many bedclothes were required, and hoods were not needed. Even so, English cradles of this period sometimes have a headboard or turned rails, instead of a hood. These hoods were often hinged, and less frequently so was the end of the cradle for easier removal of baby, bedding, and utensils. The finial knobs at the corners were useful as convenient handles and for winding wool. Small knobs were often provided on the sides of the cradle for fastening coverlets. In seventeenth- and eighteenth-century cradles, the end posts of the body part project downward and have slits made in them at their extremities into which the rockers are fixed with pegs. In later cradles, the rockers are fastened to the bottom of the cradle itself, a few inches from each end.

The panelling tended to be carved in seventeenth-century cradles, fielded but devoid of carving in the eighteenth, and plain in later examples. The carving of the earlier cradles was of stylised flowers, leaves, or lozenges, and often included initials and date.

Among early cradles illustrated in Ralph Edwards' *Shorter Dictionary of English Furniture (see* Bibliography 15) are a carved oak example of the late sixteenth century, said to have been used by James I, which has turned rocking posts, sides inlaid with a chequer pattern of holly and boxwood, the hoodless back with a carved semi-circular headboard, the base carved with bold gadroons, and mounted on shaped rockers. Iron staples replace the usual turned knobs at the sides of the cradle.

Another example in R. Edwards' Dictionary said to resemble the cradle of Charles I sold after his death for £3.10.0, is a hooded cradle entirely covered with crimson velvet fringed and panelled with galon, studded with gilt nails. Pommels covered with velvet replace the turned wooden rocking posts.

A late seventeenth-century oak cradle in the Victoria & Albert Museum (Fig. 6) has a carved hinged hood bearing the date 1691 and incorporating turned rails, turned end finials and side knobs, panelled sides, rockers let into slits in the end posts, and an opening beneath the hood giving access to the interior. A plainer

6. Cradle. Carved oak, hinged hood, turned finials, dated 1691. H. 30 in. L. 36 in.

7. Cradle. Oak, early eighteenth-century. L. 36 in. Sold 1979 for £300

example (Fig. 7) could be of a somewhat later date, as this style was continued well into the eighteenth century. Even in the nineteenth century, the seventeenth-century tradition with the shaped hood and wooden rockers is still preserved (Fig. 10) in a cradle made of pine painted to simulate mahogany, although the panelled sides have been replaced by solid planks, there are no finials or carving, and the rockers are now fixed directly on to the underside of the body.

Such cradles continued in use for a long time, but the second half of the eighteenth century had seen the suspended swinging cot return to popularity.

Four elegant early nineteenth-century examples are illustrated here. Fig. 11 shows a George IV mahogany cot, with turned posts surmounted by finials, between which the box swings, and with four uprights supporting a tester.

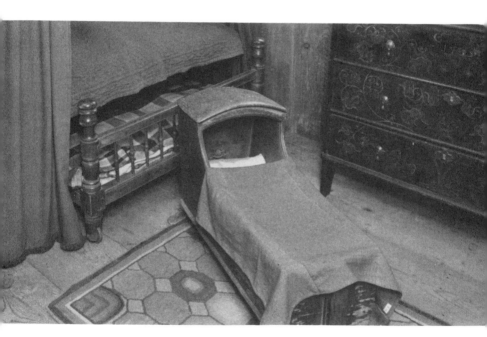

8. Cradle. Pine, arranged to rock on stationary trestles. American, eighteenth-century

9. Cradle. Painted wood. Dutch, *c.* 1800. Sold 1978, for £620

10. Cradle. Pine painted to simulate mahogany, nineteenth-century. H. 25 in. L. 35 in.

11. Cot. Mahogany swinging cot with elegantly turned posts and tester, early nineteenth-century. H. 62 in. W. 37 in. Sold 1979, for £640

A most interesting design in Sheraton's *Cabinet Dictionary* (*see* Bibliography 20) corresponds to the swinging mahogany cot illustrated in Fig. 12. This incorporates a clock spring, and was made by William Hollinshed, Bedstead Maker, of 56 King Street, Long Acre. Another attractive mahogany cot (Fig. 13) has metal hoops attached to the body for supporting a draped hood.

12. Cot. Mahogany, swinging between turned posts and fitted with clock spring. Wm. Hollinshed, ill. Sheraton. H. 38 in. L. $45\frac{1}{2}$ in. early nineteenth-century

13. Cot. Swinging mahogany cot, early nineteenth-century. H. 39 in. L. 38 in. W. 20 in.

Fig. 14 shows a mahogany swinging cot with cane panels and a slatted base on turned posts with an ogee-shaped caned hood. In other examples, the base of the cot is variously secured with woven tape instead of wooden slats.

Later in the nineteenth century, metal beds, cots, and cribs came into use. Such a suspended metal cot is illustrated in Fig. 15.

For the slightly older child, a bed with a hinged or otherwise secured side or sides has found favour right up to the twentieth century. Such a crib from the Chippendale period, but made in Philadelphia and reputed to have been used by Benjamin Franklin's grandson, is illustrated in Fig. 16. Cribs with caned

Children's chairs including (on right) Art Nouveau high chair
by H. van de Velde (Belgian, 1896)

Baby buggy in De Stijl manner. Dutch. Designed by Gerrit Rietveld, 1918, but made later. H. 23 in. L. 47 in. W. 25 in.

14. Cot. Mahogany swinging cot with cane panels and slatted base on turned posts with ogee-shaped hood, nineteenth-century

15. Cot. Suspended metal cot, late nineteenth-century. H. 41 in. L. 39 in.

16. Crib. Mahogany child's crib with hinged side. American (Philadelphia), *c.* 1770. H. 42½ in. L. 47 in. W. 22¼ in. Reputedly used by Benjamin Franklin's grandson

sides within a mahogany framework were common in England in the late eighteenth and nineteenth centuries.

Mention should be made of 'trundle' or 'truckle' beds, which were low beds on wheels and which could be stored under a higher bed. Originally variants used by servants who 'truckled' to their masters (cf. *Concise Oxford Dictionary*), they were conveniently adapted for the use of children.

The carved Flemish Rococo bed by Pierre Delvaux (Fig. 17), dating from about 1730, is a work of art. The plainer style of the late eighteenth century distinguishes the American pine bed with a tester borne by delicately turned supports (Fig. 18), while three further illustrations of children's beds which could not be more diverse (Figs. 19, 20, 21) are of the sumptuous French State

17. Bed. Flemish Rococo carved oak bed by Pierre Delvaux, *c.* 1730. H. 34½ in.
L. 64½ in. W. 41½ in. Sold 1980, for £1,400

18. Bed. Pine. American (Mid-Atlantic States), *c.*1790. H. 58½ in. W. 35½ in.

19. Bed. Cradle of the King of Rome. Design Prudhon and Percier. Ormolu mounts by Thomire, French Empire, 1811

20. Bed. Iron bed with adjustable hood. German, eighteenth-century

21. Bed. Painted pine. American, possibly Pennsylvania, early nineteenth-century. H. 19 in. L. 46 in. W. 36 in.

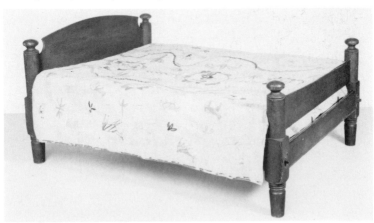

bed made for Napoleon's son, the King of Rome; a German iron bed with adjustable hood; and a plain American child's bed in painted pine.

Referring to the frontispiece, this unique cradle, in the Arts and Crafts manner, was designed by R. Norman Shaw, in 1867 for Julian, son of Alfred Waterhouse. The box-like body is mounted within a stand which remains stationary, while the cradle rocks on a treadle. The hinged hood may be lifted. The cradle is made of oak, carved, gilded, and painted. There are fourteen decorative panels on the hood, painted with birds, and inset with three farthings of the year 1861. Six panels on each side of the cradle are painted with the signs of the zodiac in red, black and gold and there are two panels painted with birds and insects on the base at the front, and a further two panels low down on the back of the cradle.

2. *Baby-walkers*

Contraptions of different kinds made to train babies to walk, as well as to serve the functions of support and protection, have been used since the Middle Ages, and have been variously called walking cradles, walking cages, go-carts, go-gins, baby-walkers, baby-cages, baby-minders, and baby-runners.

A baby-walker is illustrated in a German woodcut of the early fifteenth century which is in the British Museum, another is shown in a Rembrandt etching, and they appear to have been in common use in England from the beginning of the seventeenth century. They are frequently shown in contemporary paintings, such as *The children of James I* (Fig. 1) and *Boy with Coral* (Fig. 22), or the Flemish family group of 1640 by Gonzalez Coques. They are generally believed to have been introduced to England via the Low Countries.

A number of designs can be distinguished. Most have the common feature of securing and supporting the child, generally round the waist. Some are fixed in place permitting a limited movement within certain confines, while others may be propelled either on non-pivoted rollers in one direction only, or on

22. Painting. *Boy with Coral, c.* 1650. 42¾ in. × 33 in.

pivoted wheels or castors, which allow movement in any direction.

An illustration from the Cambridge and County Folk Museum (Fig. 23) shows, besides various other interesting items of nursery furniture, three types of baby-walker. Hanging on the wall is a pole-type runner, part of a long walking-cage can be seen and in the foreground is a circular baby-walker on wheels.

Another example of the pole type (Fig. 24) belongs to the Sussex Archaeological Society. An upright wooden pole is fixed between the ceiling and the floor, and a side arm projects horizontally and supports at its end a ring which can be opened and secured round the child's waist, with a hook and eye, or similar device. The vertical pole is pivoted so that it can revolve, the side arm may be morticed into this pole and wedged, and the

23. Collection showing three types of baby-walker. Pole type hanging on wall, playpen type walker, and circular baby cage on wheels.
(1) eighteenth-century. Extending arm L. 26 in. diameter of aperture 7 in. (2) eighteenth-century pine. H. 17 in. L. 60½ in. W. 15½ in. diameter of aperture 6½ in. (3) nineteenth-century. H. 20 in. diameter of aperture 8¼ in. and of base 24½ in.

24. Pole type baby-walker, seventeenth century. Length of side arm $29\frac{1}{2}$ in.
Diameter of ring aperture 9 in. (outer), 6 in. (inner).

ring would generally have been padded with leather, or other
material. These two examples date from the seventeenth and
eighteenth centuries, and other contemporary ones are known,
including Scandinavian varieties known as *Gangstol för barn*.

Also used in the seventeenth and eighteenth centuries was a
fixed play-pen type of baby-cage. This has an open rectangular
framework supported on four splayed legs, and a ring to hold the
child can slide along grooves in the top side rails, from one end of
the frame to the other. The cage may be 4 to 7 feet long, and

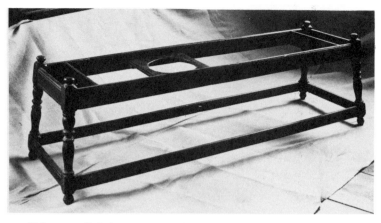

25. Baby cage. Oak, late seventeenth-century. Four turned splayed legs with sliding frame supporting child. H. 18 in. L. 59 in.

examples in oak, ash, pine, etc., are known. A fine late seventeenth-century oak cage of this kind is in the Hereford City Museum (Fig. 25), while other examples are in Strangers' Hall Museum, Norwich, and in the Musées Royaux at Brussels, where it is described as a '*glissière pour apprendre à marcher aux enfants*'. Abacus type strings of coloured beads on wires, or toy trays, were sometimes fitted at the ends of the frames.

Earlier in date than the two types of baby-walker already described and surviving them in one form or another, is a cage on non-pivoted wheels. This took the form of a framework with a ring to hold the child; alternatively, a simple open go-cart in which the child could hold on to the rails and push it along at the same time. An early example of the latter type (Fig. 26), in turned beech, is from the Victoria & Albert Museum.

A more refined variant of the baby-walker, introduced in the seventeenth century and changing a little in design through the eighteenth, had a circular, rectangular, or hexagonal base, with four or six pivoted wheeled castors, and joined to a circular or otherwise shaped ring, at waist height, by four or six turned supports. The ring would have a suitable opening and fastening device to hold the child. These baby-walkers would have been made in beech, walnut, mahogany, etc., at different periods. A particularly fine late seventeenth-century example, sold at Christie's in 1978, is illustrated (Fig. 27). An eighteenth-century baby-walker in ash and mahogany, with hexagonal frame, six pivoted castors, and a hexagonal tray top, is in the Victoria & Albert Museum, while a similar one in yew wood is illustrated in Ralph Edwards' *Shorter Dictionary of English Furniture* (*see* Bibliography 15). A very elegant, later eighteenth-century

26. Go-cart. Turned beech, *c.* 1700. H. $17\frac{1}{4}$ in. W. $13\frac{1}{2}$ in.

27. Baby-walker. Beech and walnut, late seventeenth-century. Sold 1978, for £1,050

example, on a rectangular base with four castors and slender simulated bamboo uprights and base stretchers, is at Sulgrave Manor; its circular hinged top has a small semi-circular tray attached. Examples are known in which the height of the ring can be adjusted. Continental walkers of this type and period are of very similar design (*see* Bibliography 7); for example, the baby-walker in the Germanisches Nationalmuseum, Nurnberg, exhibited at the Kunstgewerbemuseum, Cologne in 1973, known as *Laufstall auf Rollen*.

In 1828 baby-walkers were sold by 'toy' shops all over London, but particularly in the turners' shops of Spinning Wheel Alley, Moorfields, as mentioned by J.T. Smith in *Nollekens and his Times*. Later writers (*see* Bibliography 11 and 12) refer to them, and they continued to be made throughout the nineteenth century (*see* Fig. 23; also Bibliography 5: Cat. No. 12).

Willow baby-cages, documented as having been common in earlier centuries, have not survived. Metal examples still exist from the later Victorian and Edwardian eras.

3. Chairs

Among children's chairs which are mentioned in early inventories, there is one belonging to Robert Sidney, Earl of Leicester, 'a little chair for a childe of carnation and greene clothe and tinsell' valued at 20 shillings in 1588. From the beginning of the seventeenth century, a great many wooden varieties survive, but not those of wicker and other perishable materials which were once in common use.

Early 'nursery' chairs had a low box seat, often with a drawer beneath, no arms, and were generally on rockers (*see* Bibliography 25). Children's chairs were mostly with arms, and at this same early period, high chairs were made. These were sturdily built, frequently with splayed legs for stability and with a foot-rest, and occasionally with a holding bar. Since they were primarily for seating the baby against the dining table, a holding bar was not general, although as the painting by Matthys van den Bergh (Fig. 28) shows, these were sometimes provided in seventeenth-century examples. Simple stools would of course have been used, and close stools provided with wooden or pewter pans. A primitive child's chair, said to be found primarily in Wales and the border counties, was made simply by attaching spindles and a top rail to a thick wooden base. It could then be stood on a table or on another chair (*see* Bibliography 25); a further example can be seen at Hall i' th' Wood, Bolton.

More early joined chairs have survived than turned ones, perhaps because the mortice and tenon joints are more durable than the weaker dowel joints of turned chairs. Rare, early seventeenth-century turned or 'thrown' high chairs of ash and oak are illustrated by Symonds and Edwards (*see* Bibliography 27 and 15).

However, these early high chairs were also made of joined oak with a panelled back, sometimes carved with a date and initials (Fig.29). The position of the foot-rest shows that these chairs were made very wide to allow for the babies' voluminous clothes. In the late seventeenth and eighteenth centuries, high chairs became lighter and more movable, and were not used solely for

28. Portrait of Nicolaus Heinrich Ritter by Matthys van den Bergh, d. 1658. Illustrates seventeenth-century high chair with bar. Sold 1974

seating the child against a heavy dining table. Consequently, they were then generally provided with some form of holding stick or bar.

The extra height of high chairs is usually achieved by having longer legs, but examples still exist in which a small chair is attached to a full size chair base, which projects at the front to form a foot-rest. Fig. 32 shows such a chair which is dated 1680. However, the date may be a later addition, as the decoration is of an earlier type. Another chair of such design, being a Queen Anne walnut high chair with cabriole legs, is illustrated by Jane Toller (*see* Bibliography 1, Plate 42).

High chairs continued to be made in the prevailing adult styles, as shown in two fine walnut examples from the Restoration period (Figs. 30, 33). An eighteenth-century high chair, with elongated cabriole legs and paw feet (Fig. 34), and an

29. High chair. Carved oak, early seventeenth-century. Chair on left H. 40½ in. W. 19½ in.

30. High chair. Walnut. Charles II period. H. 40½ in.

31. Child's chair with foot rest. Oak. North Country, *c.* 1675. Sold 1970, for
£180

32. Child's high chair. Oak with inlaid holly and bog-oak. Carved initials and date: RW. 1680. H. 46 in. W. 18½ in. D. 16¾ in.

33. Child's armchair, Charles II period. Walnut. Carved with spiral supports, turned and spiral legs. Caned back and seat. Sold 1974, for £620

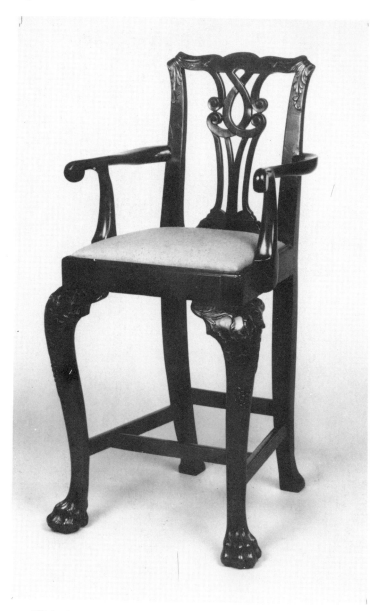

34. High chair. Mahogany, mid-eighteenth-century. Cabriole legs with paw feet.

35. High chair. Mahogany, mid-eighteenth-century. Pierced splat and decoration in Chippendale style

36. Child's side chair. Walnut, tulip. American, Philadelphia. Benjamin
Daniel or Joseph Trotter, *c*.1770. H. 29 in. W. 17½ in. D. 16 in.

interesting but awkward looking chair with double cabriole legs (*see* Bibliography 15), are noteworthy examples from the succeeding period. There are no designs for children's furniture in Thomas Chippendale's published drawings, but high chairs were made in this style. Fig. 35 shows a fine high chair of that period, and Wenham illustrates a Chinese Chippendale high chair, with shaped top rail and fretwork stretchers (*see* Bibliography 24). A mahogany high chair of pure Hepplewhite style may be seen in Fig. 38. A design which became popular in the

37. Child's Windsor chair. Carved and turned yew and elm, *c*. 1770. II. 24¾ in. W. 17¾ in. D. 16 in.

38. Hepplewhite high chair with foot rest, *c.* 1780.

last quarter of the eighteenth century was a low arm-chair
mounted on a small table to form a high chair. Generally, the legs
of the chair end in an X-shaped stretcher, in the middle of which
is a brass screw hole and, with a similar screw hole in the centre
of the table top, the two may be joined by means of a brass thumb
screw.

A good example of the Sheraton period is illustrated (Fig. 39).
A very similar one belongs to the Victoria & Albert Museum, and
other late eighteenth- and early nineteenth-century examples are

to be found. The two parts can be used as a low chair and table, and unfortunately, no doubt, many have become separated and lost. An early nineteenth-century mahogany and cane *bergère* chair on a carved stand (Fig. 50) is a superb example of a style which remained popular during the Victorian era.

From the seventeenth century onwards, Windsor chairs were

39. Child's chair on stand. Mahogany, late eighteenth-century. Converts to chair and table

40. Child's *fauteuil*. Stamped de Gay. Louis XVI period. Carved and gilded

made in various sizes, as both low chairs (*see* Fig. 37) and high chairs (*see* Fig. 46). From the eighteenth century, they were made also as rocking chairs and as variants, such as the smoker's bow chair (Spinks Exh. No. 8), in the nineteenth century. American examples tend to have more slender and emphatically splayed legs than the English ones (*see* Fig. 63). Ladderback chairs, with rush seats, are also found from the seventeenth century onwards as both high and low chairs, often painted.

Wing rocking chairs are very common from the end of the seventeenth to the end of the nineteenth century. They come in

41. Astley Cooper chair, late eighteenth-century

42. Ash chair, French, provincial, eighteenth-century, also high back oak commode chair, eighteenth-century, and ash chair. Sold 1976, for £160, £180, £240

all sizes to suit children of different ages, and are in oak, walnut, cherry, pine, etc., as well as in mahogany. The wide skirts of the chairs generally formed the rockers. Often they were of the commode variety; sometimes the pot-holes were provided with lids, and very occasionally, the original pewter pots may be found. Frequently there are decorative holes cut at the top and sides of the chairs for picking them up or hanging them on wall-hooks (*see* Bibliography 1. Plate 35). Some pretty cherrywood examples are shown in Fig. 48. Other kinds of rocking chairs, from the eighteenth and nineteenth centuries, include ladder-back and spindleback varieties. An American early nine-teenth century rocking chair, with neo-gothic decoration, is illustrated in Fig. 45.

Turning now to other low chairs: these were generally made with arms to contain the child. Side chairs without arms are much rarer. An inventory from Ham House of 1683 refers to 'two chayres for children the one black and the other jappanned' (*see* Bibliography 15). R.W. Symonds illustrates several children's chairs from the Percival Griffiths Collection (*see* Bibliography 27). These include armchairs and a side chair in walnut, with caned seat and back, from the period 1680–1700, and also a beautifully balanced upholstered walnut chair, with curved arms, cabriole legs, and scroll feet, from about 1720. A very fine American mid-eighteenth-century side chair, with a low seat, has crisply carved cabriole legs, ending in claw-and-ball feet, a solid vase-shaped splat, and carved shell decoration (Fig. 36). A mahogany armchair of the Hepplewhite period, with a

43. Regency child's side chair. Rosewood, caned seat

44. Child's easy chair. Mahogany. American, probably New England, *c.* 1810.
H. 35½ in. W. 25¼ in. D. 25½ in.

'gothick' splat, is illustrated in Edwards' dictionary (*see* Bibliography 15). A rare small Regency side chair in rosewood (Fig. 43) was probably made en suite with a set of adult furniture. An unusual mahogany child's armchair, called a 'Mendlesham' chair after its place of origin, dates from the mid-nineteenth century (Fig. 47). From that time onwards, children's versions of the popular bentwood furniture are to be found (Fig. 51).

Upholstered wing and easy chairs of child size are not often seen. E. Wenham illustrates a small leather-covered wing chair with carved cabriole legs from the first half of the eighteenth century (*see* Bibliography 24), while Fig. 44 shows one of several

45. Child's rocking chair. American, Pennsylvania. Maple, etc., with neo-
gothic decoration, *c.* 1830–1840

46. Windsor high chair. Ash and elm, early nineteenth-century. Bar and foot rest missing

later American examples from the H.F. du Pont Winterthur Museum. A fine child's *fauteuil* of the Louis XVI period, carved and gilded and with original tapestry, is in the Louvre (Fig. 40).

In contrast to these chairs, made as small-scale versions of adult designs, is the deportment or correction chair called after its designer – the 'Astley Cooper' chair (Fig. 41) – examples of which date from the late eighteenth to the middle of the nineteenth centuries.

47. Child's Mendlesham armchair. Mahogany, mid-nineteenth-century

48. Child's commode rocking chair and small companion. Cherrywood, nineteenth-century

Most of the pretty papier mâché chairs date from around 1840, and among the child-size versions the little spoon-backs, with cane or upholstered seats, are most attractive.

Cane and wicker chairs were very popular for children throughout the nineteenth century. The Army & Navy Stores Catalogue for 1898 advertises such armchairs for 2/6d (12½p).

In late Victorian and Edwardian times more complicated chairs, designed specifically for children, began to be made. An example is an armchair with tray, foot-rest, and rocker, which

49. Child's commode armchair, nineteenth-century

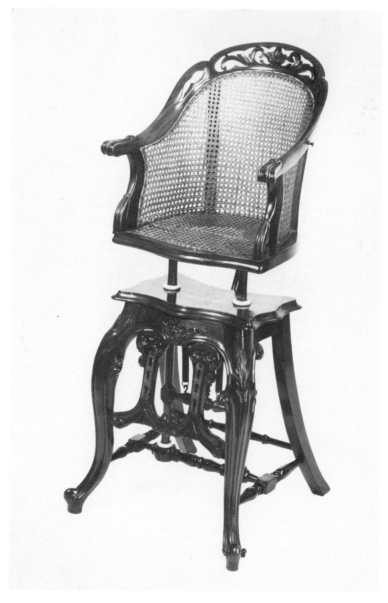

50. Child's chair on stand. Mahogany and caned chair on carved stand with spring action, *c*.1840. H. 40in. W. 17in. D. 18½in.

51. Bentwood child's chair. Beech with cane seat, late nineteenth-century. H. 26in. After Michael Thonet (1796–1871)

can be converted into a high chair (Fig. 52). One such chair was advertised as a 'convertible child's chair, available stained light or dark, four positions with playboard, and forming go-cart'. This was priced at 15/9d (79p). In Gamage's Christmas Catalogue for 1913, such a chair is described as a 'Kindergarten Chair', available in walnut finish at 11/9d (59p) or with a pan at 14/6d (72½p). The chair in Fig. 52, from the Victoria & Albert Museum, is similar to item No. 50 in the Towneley Hall Exhibition (*see* Bibliography 5).

52. Child's convertible chair – armchair with tray, rocker, foot-rest/high chair, end nineteenth-century

There is a child's chair designed by C.A. Voysey en suite with adult furniture at the Geffrye Museum, and a high chair by H. van de Velde is illustrated facing p. 44. Marcel Breuer's designs for children's chairs and tables are exemplified in Fig. 56.

4. Tables, Chests, Desks

By contrast to chairs which had to be custom-built for children, tables and chests of adult size could be used as such, or adapted for nursery use. This is not to say that special child-size tables, chests, and desks were not made. But they are relatively rare, even from the seventeenth and eighteenth centuries, and more so in Europe than in America. While not many examples have been preserved, references to them do occur in early documents. To quote from the will of Roger Elmesley of London in 1434 'also a litel tabel peynted trestelwise: also a litel joyned stool for a child: also a litel cofur to putte in his small thynges'.

Early children's tables looked like stools of the period and could be mistaken for them. However, there is no doubt that they are tables when en suite with child-size armchairs of similar design and decoration (*see* Bibliography 27, Ill. 1 & 7). Later in the seventeenth century, gate-leg tables were made for children following the adult style, and from the eighteenth century, rare examples of little side tables or drop-leaf tables may be found. An eighteenth-century American child's table in walnut is illustrated in Fig. 53. A little cricket table (Fig. 55) may be compared with cricket and tavern tables from America (*see* Bibliography 2, pp. 250–1). A nineteenth-century child's mahogany drop leaf table on turned legs is shown in Fig. 54. In the present century, specially designed nursery furniture in-

53. Table for child. Walnut. American. New England, *c*.1790. H. 21¼in. W. 22¼in. D. 16½in.

54. Drop-leaf table. Mahogany. American, nineteenth-century. H. 18¾in. W. 22¾in. (open), L. 19⅞in.

55. Cricket table for child compared with stool on left. Sycamore with ash legs, nineteenth-century

56. Table and two chairs by Marcel Breuer. German, 1927

cludes tables of course, and from the most influential twentieth-century style, we have an example of *Bauhaus* design by Marcel Breuer (Fig. 56).

There are many examples of small coffers and blanket chests from the sixteenth to the eighteenth centuries (*see* Bibliography 1, 2), but children's chests-of-drawers from the eighteenth and nineteenth centuries are rare, at least in England, for reasons referred to in an earlier chapter. Among the more numerous American examples, there are some of such quality and proportions that it is difficult to decide whether they were made on commission for a child, or as models.

A fine mahogany chest-of-drawers from New England, dating from the end of the eighteenth century, has a rare reverse serpentine front to four graduated long drawers, and is about 26 in. in height and width (Fig. 57). This is but one example from many in American museums. An eighteenth-century cherry-wood chest of drawers, also from New England, having a straight front to four graduated long drawers, flanked by spirally carved quarter round stiles on ogee feet, with a height of $23\frac{1}{4}$ inches and width of $20\frac{1}{2}$ inches was in the sale of the Garbisch Collection carried out by Sotheby's in America (on 24.5.1980 as lot 1043).

57. Chest of drawers for child. Mahogany. American. New England, probably Massachusetts, *c*.1800. Reverse serpentine front. H. $25\frac{3}{4}$in. W. 26in. D. $16\frac{1}{2}$in.

58. Bureau for Child. Pine painted red with gilt and gilt gesso decoration, *c*.1730. H. 28¼in. W. 23½in. D. 14½in.

Children's desks follow the development of adult styles. In the sixteenth and seventeenth centuries, table desks were generally used. These had a lid hinged at the top to be raised to give access to the box-like interior, which might be arranged in compartments. Such was the early merchant's desk of which child-size versions are extant.

The table desk developed by having a drawer let in beneath the writing compartment, at the bottom of its well. Towards the end of the seventeenth century, the lids of these desks were hinged at the bottom. The lid was now brought forward instead of being raised, and it could then rest in a horizontal writing position on two lopers situated at either end of the drawer beneath the desk, which could be pulled out to act as supports. From a desk on a table or stand, the bureau developed. With the lid hinged at the bottom, a compartment containing pigeon holes and drawers above a well, and with a drawer underneath, the desk was now placed on a chest-of-drawers. These two were at first made separately, but when they were of matching size, a piece of moulding was put around the front and sides to conceal the join. Early in the eighteenth century, bureaux were made in one piece with a case of drawers, often two short, side by side, above several graduated, long ones. The shaped interior of the writing compartment, with a well and secret drawers, gave way later to a plainer interior. Bureaux generally stood on bun feet up to about 1700, then bracket feet were used, and splay feet became fashionable around 1800. In the early and mid-seventeenth century, English desks would be of oak. Later, in the seventeenth century until about 1730, the favoured wood was walnut, and after that it was the turn for mahogany.

A very rare English japanned bureau, dating from about 1730, is at the Greenfield Village and Henry Ford Museum (Fig. 58). It is japanned in red and gold. The interior has pigeon holes, drawers, and a well. There are two short above two long drawers, and it stands on bracket feet. A height and width of about 28 in. and 23 in. respectively indicate that it was made for an older child. Examples of American antique children's bureaux – or slant-front desks, as they are called in America – are to be found in the Colonial Williamsburg and Metropolitan Museum of Art collections, among others. Two examples were in the Garbisch collection sold on 24.5.1980, being lots 1044 and 1050. The first was a mahogany bureau, 26 in. high, 22 in. wide; the interior containing pigeon holes, cupboards, and little serpentine drawers, two upright document drawers with fluted fronts, and a well with a sliding cover below. The case had two short above two long drawers on a base with bracket feet. This piece is of early eighteenth-century design. The second Garbisch item was an eighteenth-century cherrywood child's bureau with the usual interior, the case with just two long drawers, and standing on bracket feet. The height and width are both about 24 in. (Fig. 59).

59. Bureau for child. Cherrywood. American. New England, late eighteenth-century. H. 24in. W. 23⅞in. D. 12in. Sold 1980, for $2,300

From a slightly later period, around 1800, we have an English child's bureau in mahogany. The sloping front encloses pigeon holes and drawers and the case has one long and six short drawers, on splay feet, with a height of 26 in. and width of 21 in. (Fig. 60). Next there is a rare late eighteenth-century mahogany pedestal desk for the older child (Fig. 61). It is less than 2 feet wide, and has a pull-out slide beneath a long drawer, with five little drawers down either side. There is a small shelf half-way between the table top and the plinth. Finally, Fig. 62 shows a beautiful American desk and bookcase, dating from the end of the eighteenth century, and probably from Pennsylvania. It is 49½ in. high, 22⅝ in. wide, and 12⅝ in. deep, and is shown by courtesy of the Greenfield Village and Henry Ford Museum.

60. Bureau for child. Mahogany, *c.*1800. H. 26in. W. 21in.

61. Pedestal desk for older child. Mahogany, late eighteenth-century. W. *circa* 20in.

62. Child's secretaire-bookcase. American. Pennsylvania, *c.* 1790. Walnut. Mahogany finials and maple inlay. Top drawer pulls out to reveal desk interior. H. 49½in. W. 22⅝in. D. 12⅝in.

The desk, or as we would call it, the secretaire-bookcase, is of walnut, with mahogany finials inlaid with maple. Starting at the top, it has a broken swan pediment, three finials, with the central one flattened and inlaid, above an inlaid patera. The flat band of alternate light and dark inlay suggests dentil decoration around the cornice, the mitred doors to the bookcase are decorated with stringing and with a darker band round the cock-beaded edges. The lower overhanging part gives the impression of having four graduated long drawers decorated with similar stringing, but the top drawer pulls out to reveal a fitted secretaire, i.e. desk, interior. The shaped apron merges into splay feet. While it is essentially of Hepplewhite design, the woods used, and some details like the pediment for example, differ from what one might expect to find in an English piece of this period. Please note that the table showing furniture styles on page 34–5 applies only in a general way, even to English furniture. American period furniture, while very much under the influence of the great English eighteenth-century designers such as Chippendale, Hepplewhite, and Sheraton, demonstrates a time lag in adult styles, and even more so, in children's furniture design. Furthermore, it does not conform too closely to the guide lines on fashionable woods used in England at different periods, and it exhibits characteristic national and regional features in construction and decoration.

While the bureau was the most common form of writing desk in the eighteenth century, a sloping desk with lift-up lid might still have been used by clerks in offices and by children in schoolrooms. Around 1790, this design became fashionable again in the shape of the 'davenport' – a small writing desk above a set of drawers set at right angles to the desk. This also continued in popularity for a large part of the nineteenth century.

On the subject of school desks, examples of a narrow bureau-bookcase – the Etonian 'burry' – have been described by Jane Toller (*see* Bibliography 32). The Museum of London has a display based on the Board Schools of the late nineteenth century, as described in E. Robson's *School Architecture*, 1874.

It includes a school desk and bench, a teacher's desk and high stool, a blackboard, a large mid-century mahogany standing abacus, and various other accessories, such as wooden dumbbells, and geometrical shapes. Some individual mid-century mahogany desks with slanting lids on curved and scrolled front and straight back supports, carved with the City of London crest, can also be seen in the Museum of London, as well as a late nineteenth-century School Board style desk for six children, with ink wells and slots for their slates on cast iron supports. It may be of interest to students of social history that the latter was removed from the Great Synagogue Talmud Torah class in Brick Lane, Spitalfields.

5. Other Nursery Furniture

Of the various children's settees, sofas, day-beds and chaiseslongues which are still to be found, American and Continental examples are decidedly more numerous than English ones. They turn up at furniture auctions, and are generally in the adult style of the period. A German eighteenth-century suite of settee, chair and small table was exhibited in Munich (*see* Bibliography 8). The Geffrye Museum has a child-size late Regency sofa. An American Windsor type settee is shown in Fig. 63. Another and also an *Empire* style settee is illustrated by the Schiffers (*see* Bibliography 2), who describe several cupboards, corner cupboards, and bookcases.

One of the most interesting and unusual wardrobes is undoubtedly that made for Edmund Joy, which is inscribed with his name and the date 1709. This is in the form of a dolls' house, painted, and made in the style of William and Mary. It has a central portion and two projecting wings, and there are doors with locks to each of the three sections. The dimensions are 64 in. height, 56 in. width, and 26 in. depth. The left-hand side has four shelves and the right-hand one is fitted with four drawers. The central portion encloses a hanging space with hanging pegs of late seventeenth-century design (*see* Bibliography 45).

Every nursery had wash-stands; one of the more noteworthy is

63. Windsor type bench for two children. American. New England, *c*. 1810–40. Birch and Pine. Black paint and gilt decoration. Foot-rest missing. H. 33¼in. W. 24¾in. D. 11¾in.

the diminutive version of a period mahogany corner wash-stand, *c*. 1780, as illustrated by the Schiffers (*see* Bibliography 2, ill. 272). Another essential requisite would have been the towel rail, generally quite utilitarian, but antique Continental ones may be found with a carved polychrome figure as a towel holder. A

64. Child's sedan chair. Mahogany. European. L. 62½in. Sold 1976, for £150

partial view from the Cambridge and County Folk Museum Collection (Fig. 23) includes a wash-stand, as well as an interesting early nineteenth-century push-cart, baby-walkers, a correction chair, a Noah's Ark and numerous other toys. An early example of a play-pen is shown in Fig. 65.

Essential nursery requisites would have included bath-tubs, fire-guards, brass or wire-mesh fenders, and screens. Many of the latter would have been more utilitarian than decorative. However, the Victorian scrap screens can be attractive as well as amusing, and a good example from Pollock's Toy Museum is shown in Fig. 66.

Wallpaper, pictures, and rugs specially designed for children did not become general until late Victorian times. Mid-nineteenth-century examples of wallpapers are to be found in the collection at the Victoria & Albert Museum, but not until the period of the Arts & Crafts Movement did well-known designers turn their attention to this subject. Of these, Walter Crane was pre-eminent. In the Art Nouveau period which followed many artists designed nursery furnishings, and particularly wallpapers. Designs by C.A. Voysey, Cecil Aldin and John Hassall have already been referred to briefly (p. 31). Other wallpapers from this period in the Victoria & Albert Museum include examples designed by Kate Greenaway, 1893 (illustrated in Fig. 67), by Mabel Lucy Attwell, *c.* 1910 (illustrated in Fig. 68) and by Jessie M. King. There followed a proliferation of designs for nursery wallpapers, bed and cushion covers, and for rugs which were influenced by the prevailing Art Deco and Bauhaus styles. Reference should be made in this connection to the recent exhibition of the Silver Studio Collection at the Museum of London, which is permanently housed at the Middlesex Polytechnic.

6. *Rocking Horses*

The hobby-horse, which in its simplest form is merely a stick with a horse head, has been a child's plaything since earliest

65. Child's play-pen. American, eighteenth-century. Painted red

66. Scrap Screen. Height 62in. Width of each panel 27in. Nineteenth century

times, being mentioned by Classical authors and illustrated in medieval texts. Coins issued to celebrate the ending of the Thirty Years War (1618–48) show a hobby-horse in reference to a large gathering of children riding hobby-horses, who paid tribute to the Imperial Emissary at the peace conference (*see* Bibliography 8). A different kind of hobby-horse is the Morris dancer's,

67. Nursery Wallpaper. Designed by Kate Greenaway, 1893

which is a draped wicker cage with an opening near the front; it can be fastened round the dancer, who wears a horse-head mask. Later elaborations of the child's hobby-horse include examples in which the stick at the back is fitted with a cross bar and two wheels.

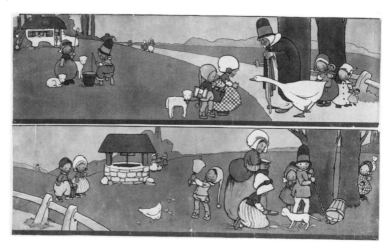

68. Nursery Wallpaper. Designed by Mabel Lucy Atwell, *c.*1910

The rocking horse probably dates from the end of the sixteenth century. At first it was merely a box type seat mounted on a wooden rocker with a horse-head fitted in front, as can be seen in a number of collections including that of the Museum of London (Fig. 69). One of the earliest rocking horses, reputedly used by Charles I, is in the possession of Kay Desmonde at her private museum. There are also some interesting antique rocking horses and sleighs at the Sonneberg Toy Museum in East Germany.

At a later date there followed the more or less realistically figured horse with a flat seat or saddle, mounted on a rocker (Fig. 70). The nineteenth-century development of a horse which was mounted on a fixed platform and moved on two parallel pivots, gave a more stable and secure plaything, retaining pride of place in many a nursery. The Bethnal Green Museum has a number of examples.

The chamber horse was not a horse at all, but a kind of eighteenth-century exercise chair which simulated the up and down motion of horse-riding. Such a chamber horse is recorded to have been made for the off-spring of George III. It could carry four children, had a mahogany frame with spring seats covered all round with morocco leather, and was provided with four holding-handles and four footboards.

Tricycles which incorporate horses may be seen in many collections. A Victorian example from the Bethnal Green Museum is illustrated in Fig. 71. Models of horses to pull, or horses and carts of various descriptions, come into the category

69. Rocking horse, early seventeenth-century. Pine, originally painted

70. Rocking horse, late nineteenth-century. Wood painted dapple grey with padded seat and support for girl's side saddle, on green painted rocker. L. 45in. Sold 1979 for £250

71. Tricycle horse, *c.*1875–80

of toys and are outside the scope of this volume. The Bettenham Manor Collection of baby carriages has an interesting push cart, embodying a pair of little horses which gallop as the carriage is pushed along from behind.

7. *Baby Carriages*

Long before the modern perambulator came into existence, children were carried in a variety of carts. A simple board on two wheels with a handle to push or pull gave way to different forms of box-like vehicle on four wheels. Eighteenth- and early nineteenth-century illustrations show examples of a 'stick-wagon', like a hay-cart with sides made of sticks several inches apart, with two front wheels and two slightly larger back wheels, without springs, drawn by a single shaft or handle. Other typical baby carriages of this period are shown in paintings of the Wedgwood family by George Stubbs, and of the children of George III by Benjamin West. These might have some sort of seat for one or more children, with two small front and two larger rear iron-shod wooden wheels with wooden axles. They could be pulled on a single shaft either by hand, or by a small animal, as these carriages were used outdoors as well as indoors, in the spacious mansions of those days. One of the earliest known baby carriages was made around 1730, for the children of the 3rd Duke of Devonshire. This was a fine carriage of advanced design, shaped like a scalloped shell, on four wheels and equipped with springs, upholstered, and with a retractable hood. In the age of elegance, the children of the rich were also sometimes provided with miniature versions of adult carriages. Some fine examples of the coachbuilder's craft from the eighteenth and early nineteenth centuries include chaises, a landau, and a curricle from the collections formed by Charles Wade and A.E. Richardson (*see* Bibliography 34).

Around 1820 we find precursors of the perambulator in the form of a three-wheeled carriage, with a deep well suitable for one or two older children, sometimes provided with a parasol, but still drawn by a shaft or handle.

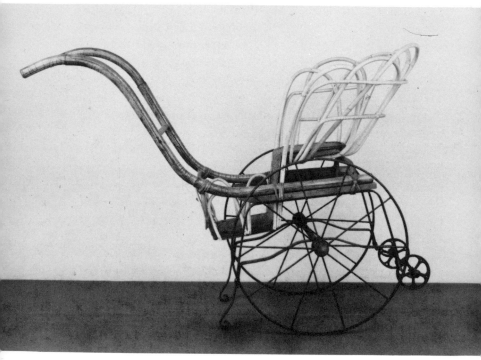

72. Push chair. Cane and wicker, nineteenth century

A kind of mid-Victorian push-chair for older children to sit up in (Fig. 72) later developed into the four-wheeled mailcarts of the Edwardian era. But the major change towards the modern pram took place in the 1840s. Like its predecessors, the carriage was for a slightly older child rather than a baby. It had three wooden wheels, iron tyres and was shaped like a bath-chair, and it had a handle at the back, which distinguished it from the earlier drawn carriages. It was now pushed and the child could be kept in view (Fig. 73). The name 'perambulator' for the actual carriage became current in the following decade. Light wire-spoked wheels and rubber tyres were first used on perambulators around 1875, and the four-wheeled pram superseded the three-wheeled carriage, when it was no longer classed as a road vehicle, and one was therefore allowed to push it along the pavements. At this period, perambulators were hammock-sprung with handles at both ends, and with a retractable hood which could be reversed. This design did away with the need for turning the carriage, which, as they generally had no brakes, could be dangerous on the narrow pavements of those days. A fine papier mâché and mother-of-pearl inlaid pram of about 1875 is shown in Fig. 74.

Very soon after this time, wicker-work cradles called 'bassinets' were imported from France and fixed on to wheeled undercarriages. At first, these carriages were quite flat and only suitable for babies, until a well was introduced so that children could sit up in the perambulator.

Towards the end of the century, several firms produced a considerable variety of perambulators and mailcarts. In America also, the baby carriage, or buggy, became for a time a status

73. Early perambulator, *c.*1845–50

symbol. A Sears Roebuck catalogue of 1897 illustrates many baby carriages. These are generally provided with a deep well, either hooded, or with a parasol, on a sprung four-wheel carriage with push-handle, and with the seat facing in the direction of motion. The carriages were priced from $8.50 to $11.50 and are beautifully upholstered in a variety of materials. The Army and Navy Stores catalogue of 1907 advertises models called 'The Ideal Landau', 'The Cheltenham', 'The Windsor', 'The Canoe', 'The Cornwall', and 'The Sandringham'.

'The Cheltenham', for example, is described as of wooden body, panelled, mounted on Cee springs (in the shape of a letter C), fitted reversible jointed hood, upholstered in American leather cloth, £4.4.0d, or in extra large size for two infants to lie down, £4.14.6d.

Firms which have been associated particularly with the development and manufacture of the modern perambulator in England include Simpson, Fawcett & Co., of Leeds; Simmons & Co., of Tanner Street, London S.E.; the Wilsons of Leeds, makers of the Silver Cross perambulator, and the Lines Brothers, who first made prams with steel bodies in the 1920s and who introduced the famed Pedigree range.

The use of springs goes back to the Cavendish baby carriage of 1730, but numerous patents for springing date from the mid-nineteenth century onwards, as do developments in wheels, brakes, and so on, and there have also been a great number of amusing innovations and more or less transient modifications which are recounted by Min Lewis (*see* Bibliography 35). Her book and the forthcoming monograph by Jack Hampshire (*see* Bibliography 36) include many curiosities such as the Dunkley motorised pram and will tell you more about the detailed development of the modern pram, such as the many changes in the shape and design of the body and the improvements in wheels and suspension. The latter author has a remarkable collection of baby carriages at Bettenham Manor, near Biddenden in Kent, which may be seen by appointment. There are also many fine examples at the Bethnal Green Museum, one of

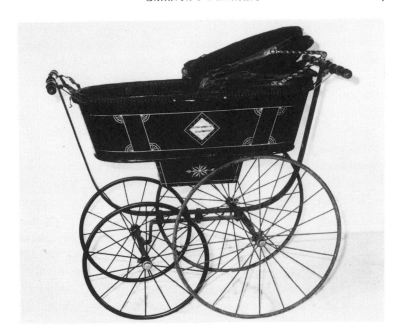

74. Perambulator, *c.* 1875. Papier mâché body with mother-of-pearl inlay. Hammock-slung with handles at both ends

which is the baby buggy (see p. 45*f*) designed by Gerrit Rietveld in 1918 in the *De Stijl* manner.

A similar development in the design of antique baby carriages took place in Europe (*see* Bibliography 8), except that in colder countries sleighs were additionally used from early times onwards.

8. Accessories: Treen, Metalware, China

The hundred and one objects used in the daily routine of nursery life – for eating and drinking, toilet and ablutions, for study and play, for reading, writing, drawing, and all the other childish activities – come under this heading. The kind of objects, other than dolls, that spring to mind are rattles, feeding-bottles and pap boats (*see* Bibliography 35), plates, cutlery, wash basins, ewers, chamberpots, blackboards, slates, drawing boards, portable desks, writing boxes, ink-pots, pencil boxes, alphabets, abacuses, money boxes and, of course, a variety of small toys. Reference to those made of turned wood may be found in one or other of the several works on treen and wooden bygones (*see* Bibliography 9, 37).

There are no books dealing specifically with juvenilia made of brass, pewter or silver, but reference to them may be found in literature on the relevant adult subjects. Charles Oman, among others, has written on silver 'toys', but there is very little on nursery silver as such (*see* Bibliography 35 and 38). Pauline Flick has written a monograph on *Children's China* in the present series (*see* Bibliography 39). The perennial antique toy for a baby, of course, is a rattle, and for the somewhat older child, a hoop.

The Pinto Collection of treen contains examples of most of the just mentioned items. Among the more unusual are horn-books – used in olden times for teaching children the alphabet – being of wood and protected by a thin sheet of horn, but leather, ivory, and rarely silver ones, are known. Alphabet sticks, copying sticks, educational boards, and slates are illustrated, also deportment boards to be held behind the back for a certain time each day, clickets for calling pupils to attention, and finger stocks for punishment (*see* Bibliography 9, Plates 445–450).

One of the most sought-after collector's items of nursery silver is the rattle. This was often attached to a stick of coral from which the early rattles took their name. Rattles and teething-sticks, separate or combined, have been discussed by Arnold Haskell (*see* Bibliography 35). Frequently, they were suspended from a chain around the child's waist or neck (Figs. 1 and 22).

Rattles generally incorporated a whistle, and little silver bells were usual attachments, though these became rarer as the eighteenth century progressed. Early records of nursery silver most frequently mention christening spoons – which might be Apostle spoons or later, seal-top spoons – and two-handled porringers. The latter were in more general use, and more examples of seventeenth and early eighteenth-century porringers survive than do little children's mugs. Some examples of the so-called brandy saucepan, that is a little wooden-handled silver saucepan and cover, would have been made for nursery use. There were also skillets which are covered saucepans with a handle and generally on three feet. An inventory of 1688 lists the nursery silver provided for the young Prince of Wales; it includes skillets, basins, dishes, plates, saucers, a warming pan, chamber pots, porringers, a sugar box and spoons, a chafing dish, cups, candlesticks and snuffers. In the early eighteenth century, shallow oval dishes called 'pap boats' were introduced, which were made in large quantities, and in varying styles, from that time to the middle of the nineteenth century. They are still reasonably priced and quite collectable. In Victorian times, silver christening sets included a spoon, knife and fork, and a mug. This kind of mug, which was mostly plain and cylindrical in the late eighteenth century, perhaps with two or three bands of horizontal reeding, became more ornate and often baluster-shaped as the nineteenth century advanced, but it tended to become plain again in Edwardian times.

Most nursery objects for everyday use have been made of different materials – either at one and the same time or in succeeding periods – for the rich, not so rich, and the poor. For example, armorial silver-gilt chamberpots date from the seventeenth and eighteenth centuries, when pewter and wooden ones were usual. In the nineteenth century, innumerable chamberpots, wash basins, ewers, and of course, every kind of eating and drinking utensil, were made in chinaware. At this time, many of the famous porcelain factories began to make mugs, plates, cups and saucers, and decorative items specially designed for children.

In addition to museum collections, much interesting material is to be found in houses open to the public, and in particular in the Royal collections. For example, the Swiss Châlet at Osborne House, in the Isle of Wight, built for Queen Victoria's children in 1853–4, contains domestic accessories and children's tools, as well as nursery furniture in its original setting (*see* Collections to Visit, p. 152).

Miniature Furniture

'Man is the measure of all things'
Protagoras

Some children's furniture is, of course, a miniature version of adult pieces. But by miniature furniture one generally understands either furniture of dolls' house size, that is one-sixteenth or one-twelfth full size, or occasionally larger, or miniatures of one-eighth to one-half size which, as we shall see, may have been made as models, show pieces, travellers' samples, apprentice or 'master' pieces, or as dolls' furniture.

Such furniture was made in the past both for children and adults, and indeed, it has fascinated adults through the ages. In the seventeenth century, particularly in Holland, there was a craze for collecting miniatures of every description. Not only furniture, but toys of silver, china, and so on, were displayed in collector's cabinets and in 'baby houses', as the dolls' houses of the earlier period were called.

The fascination miniature and the nostalgia for childhood are illuminated in literature and may be analysed by psychologists, but are never fully explained.

But obviously, through the 'magic' of the world in miniature we break the time barrier which separates us from childhood. The miniature may be a symbol; it may also be a model; models have been made for a variety of practical purposes and also just for themselves. Miniatures represent one's tangible possessions, but scaled down to size, so that one can fondle and play with them.

Miniature objects were made and recorded long before the

seventeenth century, and were indeed made for children not only to play with, but for instruction, as, for instance, the famous Nuremberg kitchens. Examples are known from the sixteenth century and were imported from the Low Countries and from Germany, and also made in England soon after. Every conceivable article found inside a house, or associated with it, has been reproduced in miniature at one time or another: furniture in wood and other materials, iron or brass fireplaces, grates, fenders, carpets, tapestries, pictures and silver or brass chandeliers. There are the finest miniature silver 'toys', china, glass, ornaments of every description; all cooking and eating utensils, miniature food, dolls' clothes, books, musical instruments; even miniature money, work-tools, carpenter's tools, gardening tools, and so on, all in a variety of sizes, made as objects for collectors' cabinets and for furnishing miniature rooms and 'baby' houses, or the more modern dolls' houses. In the late seventeenth and the eighteenth centuries miniature furniture was made by estate carpenters, on commission by craftsmen, or imported and sold by 'toy'-men. Early in the nineteenth century, adult interest in the baby house, which one kept in the drawing room or on the landing, faded, and the child came more into its own with its dolls' house in the nursery. There was then a vast increase in the manufacture of dolls' house furniture, particularly in Germany, which supplied the whole of Europe.

Whatever may have been the original purpose of the intermediate size of miniature, some of these pieces found their way eventually into the nursery. A fine-scale 'model' might come to serve as a dolls' chest, and a table, which started life as a show piece or travellers' sample, might have spent several generations in a dolls' house before turning up as a desirable antique in a shop or auction. The origin and purpose of intermediate size miniatures have been discussed by several authors, who have generally concluded that the apprentice or master piece is a myth as far as period furniture is concerned. Some have even questioned whether travellers' samples had a widespread use and have suggested that show pieces were rare, and that most intermediate size miniatures were models, pure and simple. Certainly, there are many fine American and European period miniatures which fall into the latter category. However, there is no doubt that English craftsmen did make miniatures of different sizes and for different purposes. Particularly they made show pieces – that is, samples to show to customers – and dolls' house furniture on commission, as the great Chippendale is supposed to have done for Nostell Priory and Cane End House.

Miniature apprentice pieces of period furniture may indeed be rare, but they do exist. However, a piece of miniature furniture should be judged on its own merits, that is its size, proportions, quality of construction, condition and provenance, before any conclusions are reached regarding its origin and purpose.

A sample should accurately demonstrate the function of a full size piece, while it may or may not be fully finished in every detail. If the proportions are perfectly to scale, then we have a true model. Dolls' furniture, on the other hand, will show more regard for strength and utility, than for perfect proportions.

The following chapter on intermediate size miniatures supplements existing accounts of American and European miniature furniture (*see* Bibliography 2 and 3). The short chapter on dolls' houses and dolls' house furniture is an introduction to several monographs on these subjects, the most inspiring of which is by Vivien Greene (*see* Bibliography 45).

9. *Models, Show Pieces, Dolls' Furniture*

The following illustrations should demonstrate some of the points just made about intermediate size miniatures.

The Queen Anne walnut armchair shown in Fig. 75 has a back with a solid bent vase-shaped splat, outscrolled arms, a D-shaped drop-in seat with a leaf-carved seat rail and cabriole legs headed by leaves and ending in pad feet. It is of good quality and proportions, and its overall height is 12 in. – in other words, about one-third of the normal size chair, of which it is clearly a model.

75. Queen Anne miniature armchair. Solid bent vase-shaped splat, drop-in
seat with leaf-carved seat rail, cabriole legs with acanthus carving ending in pad
feet. H. 12in. Sold 1974, for £950

76. George II miniature table. Mahogany. H. 8in. W. 10in. D. 7in. Sold 1974 for £650

The George II mahogany table shown in Fig. 76 has a banded rectangular top and is raised on slender lappeted cabriole legs ending in pad feet. It has a single long drawer and is 8 in. in height. It could be a commissioned piece made by a craftsman, or a travellers' sample.

The oak gate-leg table in the William and Mary style shown in Figure 77 has a hexagonal top and finely turned baluster legs and supports. Its proportions are very good and the height of $5\frac{1}{2}$ in. indicates that it might have been made specially for a baby house, or possibly, it might be a sample. The drawer is missing, as it is on many of these tables.

The eighteenth-century chest with a height of 18 in. in Fig. 78 is a piece of unusual size and proportions.

The early nineteenth-century chest of drawers in satinwood, mahogany and rosewood, 9 in. high shown in Fig. 79 is small enough to have been used in a dolls' house, but of the quality of a craftsman's sample.

A late eighteenth-century Dutch walnut cylinder bureau shown in Fig. 80, 15 in. high and $27\frac{1}{2}$ in. wide, may be described as a model.

The three-tier mahogany dumb waiter on a shaped turned column with a tripod base ending in pad feet shown in Fig. 81 dates from the second half of the eighteenth century, and with a

77. Miniature gate-leg table, late seventeenth-century. Oak. H. $5\frac{1}{2}$in. Drawer missing

78. Miniature chest of drawers. Mahogany, eighteenth-century. H. 18in. W. 14in. D. 9in. Two short and three long drawers. Bracket feet

79. Miniature chest of drawers. Satinwood, mahogany, and rosewood. H. 9in. early nineteenth century

80. Miniature cylinder bureau. Walnut. Dutch, *c*.1770. H. 15in. W. 17½in.

81. Miniature three-tier dumb waiter. Mahogany. Tripod base with pad feet, mid-eighteenth-century. Displaying miniature pewter set. H. 12in.

82. Miniature bureau-bookcase. W. 9¾in. Miniature upright piano. W. 14¼in.
nineteenth-century. Signed W.A. Whittseley. Sold 1973, for 330 and 70 gns

height of 12 in. and outstanding quality, is clearly a sample or
show piece. It bears a fine display of miniature pewter.

The bureau-bookcase in the Georgian style, but dating from
the nineteenth century, is 9¾ in. wide (*see* Fig. 82). It is not of the
same fine quality as the previous items, the overlarge brasses
spoiling the illusion of a full scale piece. The Victorian upright
piano in the same illustration, 14¼ in. wide, is a better and more
interesting object. It can be described as a model, and so can the
Biedermeier cabinet, 24¾ in. in height, shown in Fig. 88. Both
these miniatures exhibit craftsmanship and attention to detail.
The piano has fine inlay and brass attachments, and again the
Biedermeier cabinet, which some may consider a stodgy piece of

83. Miniature lowboy. Carved walnut. American eighteenth-century. H. 18in.
W. 21¼in. D. 12¾in. Sold 1980, for $2,100

furniture, is extremely well made, as is apparent from the
photograph.

There is more fine period miniature furniture in America,
where models of outstanding quality may be seen in museums
and other collections. Some turned up at the recent auction of
the Garbisch Collection, from which a few examples are taken.

A miniature lowboy of the Chippendale period in carved
walnut shown in Fig. 83 has a rectangular top with notched
corners. There is a long frieze drawer above three small drawers,
the central of which is shell-and-vine carved on a punchwork
ground, the whole flanked by fluted quarter columns. The apron
having central shell decoration, continues to shell carved cabriole

legs, ending in claw and ball feet. The height is 18 in. and as with many of these fine American miniatures, the dimensions are compatible with use by a child.

A miniature tall chest of drawers made of walnut in Pennsylvania in the last quarter of the eighteenth century shown in Fig. 84 is 29 in. high and 20 in. wide. It has a moulded

84. Miniature tall chest of drawers. Walnut. American. Pennsylvania, *c.*1770–1800. Three small drawers above two drawers above three graduated long drawers. H. 29in. W. 20in. D. 14in. Sold 1980, for $24,000

rectangular top above a case with three short drawers, above two short drawers. Three graduated long drawers are flanked by fluted quarter columns. This elegant piece stands on ogee bracket feet.

A small mahogany bookcase from Massachusetts, or New York, made around 1800 in the Federal style, is in two sections. The upper section has a cornice above a bell-flower inlaid frieze, and glazed double doors opening to an interior with an adjustable shelf above two small inlaid drawers. The projecting lower section has an inlaid drawer and double cupboard doors between inlaid tiger maple stiles. The arcaded apron has a central inlaid fan device and continues to splay feet. The height is $33\frac{3}{4}$ in. and the width is 19 in. (*see* Fig. 85).

A diminutive walnut highboy in the William and Mary style, $24\frac{1}{2}$ in. high and $13\frac{1}{2}$ in. wide, is constructed in two parts. The upper part has a rectangular top. There are two short and three graduated long drawers, and the sides are panelled. The lower part has a long drawer above a shaped apron and stands on baluster and ball turned legs, joined by turned and rectangular stretchers, and ending in ball feet. This rare piece is believed to come from Pennsylvania (*see* Fig. 86).

A very fine carved mahogany highboy from Philadelphia and the Chippendale period is $46\frac{3}{4}$ in. high and 23 in. wide (*see* Fig. 87). Again, it is in two parts, the upper part with moulded cornice ending in florally carved rosettes, and in the middle a pierced ornament which is carved at the centre with a peanut. The scrollboard, with central applied carved shell device surrounded by scrolling grasses, is above a pair of moulded cupboard doors which open to an interior fitted with thirteen small drawers. The lower section has four small drawers above a shaped apron, with central shell continuing to acanthus carved cabriole legs, and ending in claw and ball feet.

85. Miniature bookcase. Inlaid mahogany. American. Massachusetts or New York. In Federal Style, *c.*1790–1810. H. 33¾in. W. 19in. D. 9¾in. Sold 1980, for $4,250

86. Miniature highboy. Walnut. American. Pennsylvania. William and Mary style, but *c.*1740–60. H. 24½in. W. 13½in. D. 9¼in. Sold 1980, for $33,000

87. Miniature highboy. Carved mahogany. American. Philadelphia. Chippendale style and period 1760–80. H. 46¾in. W. 23in. D. 13in. Sold 1980, for $36,000

88. Miniature *Biedermeier* cabinet. German, *c.*1840. H. 24¾in. Sold 1973 for 75 gns

89. Six miniature pieces of upholstered furniture covered with crimson silk, *c*.1870. About 7in. – 8in. H.

The three pieces of dolls' furniture illustrated here are a William and Mary caned walnut armchair in Fig. 90 which does not aim at the delicacy of a model but suits the accompanying doll; a nineteenth-century walnut doll's crib shown in Fig. 91, and an early nineteenth-century American doll's four-poster bed in Fig. 92.

10. Dolls' Houses and Dolls' House Furniture

Baby houses were built as early as the sixteenth century. The earliest surviving ones date from the seventeenth century and from the eighteenth, hundreds of English examples have been

90. Doll and Doll's chair, *c.*1690

91. Doll's crib. Walnut, *c.*1850

92. Doll's Bed. American, early nineteenth century. Four-poster with turned posts, arched tester of two side pieces and four cross pieces. H. 19½in. L. 20¼in. W. 13½in.

preserved. Some famous ones such as Westbrook, Uppark, and Nostell were made for the young daughter of the house, but generally in the eighteenth century, they were adult amusements, with which the children might only be allowed to play under supervision. They housed precious 'toys' and invariably they were fitted with locks. They had a façade with windows and a front door, and sometimes an indicated staircase. At the beginning of the eighteenth century, they were generally in the form of an oak cabinet on a stand, flat-topped, and without chimneys. They were quite small – of the order of 2 to 3 ft. in height and width – and had a central panel and wings on each side, opening outwards. These were followed by mahogany houses, also on a stand, with glass panes in the windows on the sides, as well as the façade. Around 1760, they became more substantial and heavy, 5 ft. or more in height and width. These are frequently of pine with painted brickwork, and often stand on simulated brick arches. Some have fine mahogany staircases, and panelled doors, or sometimes void doorcases. Generally, the ground floor represents the basement, containing kitchen and servants' hall. The front door may stand on a single or double flight of steps, with simulated windows below (Fig. 93). The roof may be pedimented and balustraded, or if sloping, may be painted to simulate the roof tiles. These houses exhibit a great variety of opening devices. In addition to those with wings which swing outwards, examples are known where the centre portion of the front is hinged or where the façade opens horizontally for part of the house. Some are found with a front which slides apart or where it rises on sash-cords like a window. Other fronts lift off completely, as in many mid-Victorian houses, and some have a fixed front, combined with an open back. Some houses have beautiful staircases; these are mainly mid-eighteenth century. In some houses the staircase is merely indicated; others have none. Windows and their glazing, doors, chimney-pieces, fireplaces, grates, and the general proportion of rooms, all relate to the period of the baby house or dolls' house in question. So does the manner in which the walls are painted or papered, and other methods of internal and external decoration. Many were made with an existing house – possibly of a slightly earlier period – in mind. Hence, there are a relatively large number of Queen Anne style houses, but few are close enough in proportion, or even in appearance, to be called 'models'. However, it should be noted that some, like Nostell Priory, were designed by distinguished architects – a tradition carried into the twentieth century with

93. Tate Baby House, *c.*1760

94. *Mrs. Bryant's Pleasure.* Dolls' House detail, nineteenth-century

Queen Mary's dolls' house at Windsor Castle. Baby houses tended to become smaller towards the end of the eighteenth century. Generally, they had three storeys without side windows, boldly painted simulated brickwork, and chimneys. The transition from the baby house to the nursery dolls' house as we know it today, cannot be precisely dated. But by the early nineteenth century one finds larger houses, about 4 ft. or so in height and width, with no staircase, and generally with three large rooms, one above the other. The elegant style of the early baby houses, containing their rare miniature treasures, had disappeared. English-made dolls' houses soon followed, which were of a flimsier and lighter type. Later, in the nineteenth century, dolls' houses were imported in quantities; these vary enormously in style and quality. Among those in the London Museum dating from the second half of the nineteenth century, is Princess May of Teck's dolls' house. It has six rooms and a central staircase and a well-finished façade with two wings opening outwards. Some wonderful dolls' houses were constructed in the present century, including Queen Mary's dolls' house at Windsor Castle, and Sir Nevile Wilkinson's 'Titania's Palace', which, after passing through the London auction rooms, now graces Legoland in Denmark (Fig. 95). Among the most interesting collections of dolls' houses are the museums of Vivien Greene at the Rotunda, Oxford; Flora Gill-Jacobs' in Washington, D.C., which is now under the aegis of the Smithsonian Institution; and a collection at the Margaret Strong Museum in Rochester, N.Y.

Antique dolls' houses can be bought at auction or from a

95. Titania's Palace. Dolls' House Interior. The Morning Room

number of specialised dealers at prices ranging from around £150 upwards. Quoting from a recent sales catalogue of Christie's, South Kensington: on 27.6.1980, lot 42 was a painted, wooden dolls' house, the roof of printed paper tiles with two chimneys, the house on two floors with bay windows on either side of the front door and with narrow balconies to the upper storey, the front opening in the middle to reveal four rooms and staircase with interior fireplaces, kitchen dresser, and original floor coverings and wallpaper, secured by a hook and eye, the width of the house $24\frac{1}{4}$ in; dating from the end of the nineteenth century – that is, just about 'antique' – and the price it fetched was £160.

Miniature rooms and their furnishings go back even further than baby houses, to the Nuremberg kitchens of the sixteenth century, and possibly earlier. Unlike the distinct transition which took place from the baby house to the dolls' house in the nineteenth century, miniature rooms have always been of at least two kinds: adult amusements or 'toys', and playthings for children, generally with an educational purpose, as indeed were the Nuremberg kitchens. In the tradition of the adult toy is the work in miniature of Cornelis Bavelaar, who carved in a variety of materials including wood, ivory, and bone (*see* Bibliography 42). Rather different are the miniature rooms which are furnished with small scale models after a certain style. Such is the collection of rooms at the Phoenix Art Museum in Arizona, which includes English and French as well as American, period and modern rooms (*see* Bibliography 41). Here there is less interest in furniture as works of art than as historical models.

A remarkable collection of German children's miniature rooms was recently exhibited (*see* Bibliography 8), demonstrating that these playthings reached their greatest degree of diversity at the end of the nineteenth century.

From the eighteenth century onwards, through the *Biedermeier* period, right up to the nineteenth century and on to Art Nouveau and modern times, there is an impressive assembly of rooms and dolls' house furniture. It ranges from dolls' kitchens, a dolls' schoolroom and a fire-station, to a variety of dolls' shops mainly from the later nineteenth and the twentieth centuries. These include such rarities as a large department store built as a dolls' house. About 6 ft. in height and width, and dating from about 1880, it has three floors, a lift, and telephone, and is fully furnished, with 900 bales of cloth and a large range of clothes and haberdashery. Of a slightly later date are a toy-shop, an antique shop, and a pub. A dolls' bathroom, with shower and flushing W.C. complete with water tank and receptacle, dates from about 1920. Among separate items of furniture there are musical instruments, spinning wheels, lamps, candlesticks, bed-warmers, suitcases, baskets, and dinner, tea and coffee services in porcelain and pottery. Also there are utensils in wood, ivory, and brass; cutlery, kitchen utensils in copper and iron, sets of weights, coffee grinders, foods modelled in wood and metal, desk and writing sets, and many other interesting exhibits. These minia-ture playthings are of the greatest sociological interest in so far as they cover every aspect of the middle-class housewifely rôle over a period of 150 years. Some of the items are such period pieces that their full size equivalent is unobtainable today, and their very function practically forgotten.

Period dolls' house furniture may be seen in museums as separate items, or *in situ* in baby or dolls' houses. But occasionally one can still find a piece such as the cock-fighting chair in the possession of Mr. Graham Child. This early eighteenth-century chair, a version of what is often described in books as a reading chair, reveals its true purpose in the drawer let into the skirt of the seat, which contains two tiny spurs. At one end of the curved arms is a little candle-slide and at the other a little slide for counters; an upholstered stool is en suite with this very rare piece, which is less than 3 in. in height.

In addition to furniture specifically commissioned from cabinet makers or made by estate carpenters, slightly larger show pieces and travellers' samples will have found their way into baby houses. And, as already mentioned, from the late seven-teenth century onwards, the 'toy' shops sold imported Dutch

96. German dolls' house furniture in oak and softwood with metal and china accessories, nineteenth century. Sold 1978, for £90

miniatures. At the same time much furnishing was home-made, of card or feathers, particularly beds and upholstered chairs and settees. From quite early times, paper furniture was used in dolls' houses, some of it in the form of designs on sheets to be cut out and pasted on card. In the nineteenth century much dolls' house furniture was mass-produced, including basketwork, wire-mesh cradles and beds, metal grates and chimney-pieces, and much other painted filigree metal furniture. From various sources came painted wood, gilt metal, and papier mâché. Particularly noteworthy is the imitation rosewood furniture, in the late *Empire* style, made in Germany in large quantities, and in different sizes, for over half a century. This *Biedermeier* 'Waltershausen' furniture, which Vivien Greene calls 'dolls' house Duncan Phyfe', will now command prices in three figures for individual items. Some miscellaneous items of German wooden dolls' house furniture, in oak and softwood, with various

97. A.B.C. Collection of dolls' house furniture made by Fred Early. Twentieth-century. Sold 29.11.1979, lots 71–92. Some walnut, others in mahogany, and satinwood. Sizes 1½in. to 6in.

accessories, are shown in Fig. 96. The lot was recently sold at Sotheby's for £90. Dolls' house furniture continues to be made in all the earlier styles, but the quality varies enormously, as examples from two recent auctions illustrate: Fig. 97 shows

98. Collection of dolls' house period style furniture. Twentieth-century. Sold 1979 for £140

furniture made by Fred Early, one of the cabinet-makers who worked on the furnishings of Titania's Palace in the first two decades of this century. These are pieces of dolls' house size made in walnut, mahogany, and satinwood in the early eighteenth-century, Chippendale, Hepplewhite, and Sheraton styles. A satinwood suite of drawing room furniture about 4 in. high made £1,100 and a pair of knife-urns on plinths about 5 in. high fetched £1,000. Altogether twenty-two lots totalled £13,000. These were record prices for miniatures of quality, though of no great age. Fig. 98 shows a collection of period style furniture made more recently, which sold for £140 – a very reasonable price for a lot of serviceable pieces of a more mundane quality.

Hints for Collectors.
Dealers and Auctions

Period children's furniture and miniature pieces turn up quite often in antique furniture shops and in good furniture auctions. Victorian nursery furniture, and particularly items like rocking horses, push carts, and such like, also treen and other accessories, may be found in the more general type of antique shop, while dolls, dolls' houses, and dolls' house furniture have a more specialised market.

A tour of some of London's leading antique shops made earlier this year, indicated that material worth collecting is readily available – at a price! Starting at the top end of the market, I saw a beautiful early eighteenth-century walnut veneered bureau, 22 in. wide, at Malletts in Bond Street; once upon a time, bureaux were common enough. Now, eighteenth-century adult size examples often run into four figures. Malletts also had a miniature chest of the same period, with a height of 18 in. and a child's Louis XVI *fauteuil*. Two fine chairs from Barling of Mount Street and from Mallett at Bourdon House, are illustrated in this book (*see* Figures 30 and 50). From the numerous shops in the Fulham Road, mention may be made of Melvyn Lipitch who had two pretty chairs of a size suitable for children, three to four years old – a charming seventeenth-century yew and elm low Windsor chair, and a Sheraton period inlaid high chair with foot rest. He had just sold a 15 in. high mid-eighteenth-century mahogany bureau, a rare sample. Richard Courtney, next door, had a very good small child's mahogany ladderback armchair, attached by the original metal rod to the matching table base. Together these make a high chair; separate, a low chair and table. This chair is characteristic of the late eighteenth century; it has its original adjustable foot-rest, and the filled-in holes inside the arms indicate that once there has also been a holding bar. In the same shop there were several miniature travellers' samples, of the order of 8–12 in. in height, including a gate-leg table and a chest of drawers. Further up the Fulham Road, Baxter showed me a charming little early nineteenth-century papier mâché spoon-back chair, which he was keeping for his grandchild. One of the many items which had passed through his hands was an eighteenth-century mahogany chest of drawers, about one-third normal size, with a straight front of graduated drawers and bracket feet on one side, and with a serpentine front and ogee feet on the other side – the drawers meeting in the middle of the carcase. This example is exceedingly rare and interesting, as it is so obviously a show piece. Kensington Church Street also has some good shops, mostly on the expensive side, but bargains can be found. Murray Thomson had several children's Windsor chairs at reasonable prices. Speaking of country furniture, Charles and Jane Toller at Datchet in Berkshire, are specialists in this field and often have items of nursery furniture, particularly early cradles, coffers, and chairs. Most furniture dealers get interesting pieces from time to time, and regular visits to local dealers, where some rapport can be established, will often prove more rewarding than a haphazard search.

In the United States, dealers who might occasionally have high quality children's and miniature antique furniture include Stair, Ackermann, and Levy in New York. Their standard would correspond to that of the London dealers in Bond Street, Mount Street, and Fulham Road, just mentioned.

Antique miniature furniture tends to be more difficult to come by than children's furniture. One reason is that many furniture specialists like collecting models and samples because there is always room for one more piece, in contrast to adult size ones, which take up too much space. The rarity of well-made miniature period models has put them into the same price range as the full size furniture.

Dolls and accessories are really quite a separate and flourishing collectors' market. One of the leading dealers in dolls and dolls' house furniture is Kay Desmonde of 17 Kensington Church Walk, London. But there are, in fact, a considerable number of shops, all over the country, which specialise to some extent in dolls, dolls' houses and furniture, accessories, toys, juvenilia, ephemera, and so on. Much publicity for, and information on this field, is provided by magazines and journals. Some are specialised, like the *International Toy and Doll Collector*, edited by Constance Eileen King and published bimonthly, and some are of a more general nature, like *Antique Collecting* – the monthly journal of the Antique Collectors' Club of Woodbridge, Suffolk. Specialised fairs are also being more frequently organised, for example, those on dolls and juvenilia run by the Historic and Heritage Antique Fairs. The many antiques markets that have sprung up in London and elsewhere are a happy hunting ground for collectors. Among the more long-established are the Kensington Antiques Hypermarket and Antiquarius in the King's Road, Chelsea. With the increasing scarcity of good antiques, quite a number of specialists in dolls, dolls' houses, and dolls' house furniture now sell both antique and modern items, for example, The Singing Tree in the New King's Road, S.W.6, and The Dolls' House Toys Ltd., in Lisson Grove, N.W.1. Some of the museums with important collections of nursery furniture also have toys, but of those specialising in the latter, including such toys as rocking-horses and dolls' houses discussed in this book, Pollock's Toy Museum at 1 Scala Street, London, W.1. is a good example. The new Covent Garden development houses several shops devoted to toys, dolls, dolls' houses, and so forth.

The three largest London auction houses, mentioned below, regularly offer nursery furniture. Forthcoming sales are advertised in the press, once a week in the *Daily Telegraph* for example, and also in journals, magazines, and trade papers. Some of the auction houses send out notification of sales on a subscription list. Christie's in King Street off St James's,

Sotheby's in New Bond Street, and Phillips' in Blenheim Street off New Bond Street, have regular antique furniture sales on a more or less weekly basis, in which children's furniture such as cradles, chairs, chests, and bureaux occasionally appear (*see* pp. 36–93).

Sotheby's in New Bond Street have a dolls department but related items are handled by Sotheby's Belgravia in Motcomb Street where they have a special collectors' department. Phillips' run dolls and dolls' house sales about every quarter and a similar number of toy sales. At Christie's South Kensington in the Brompton Road they have fortnightly sales of dolls, dolls' houses and furniture, and there are also sales of toys every three months in which such items as rocking horses and push carts might appear, and they also sell children's clothes such as smocks, baby robes, and quilts. Children's silver and china items such as rattles, mugs, plates and flatware are generally included in regular silver and porcelain sales.

Would-be collectors should contact these salerooms to find out what sales might be of most interest. It is advisable to preview a day or two before the sale, and to study catalogues and prices. The New York branches of these auction houses should be approached for information on American sales.

The field sketched out in this book is so wide that the intending collector can specialise in many different areas. Some obvious points to make are that one should always buy the best quality one can afford. If at all possible, items should be in perfect and complete condition with no heavy or obvious restoration, but some concession may be made to age and rarity. For example, I personally would buy an attractive seventeenth, eighteenth or even nineteenth-century high chair if the holding bar or foot-rest were missing or replaced, or an early chest or bureau with replaced handles or restored feet. But under no circumstances would I touch a piece which has been radically altered or cut down; it might then still serve a practical furnishing purpose but it would no longer be a collector's piece. One should be on particular guard against adult size tables which have had their legs shortened, and small chests which have been made up, or cut down. Many tripod tables have been reduced to a height more convenient for use with modern seating arrangements, commodes have been converted, and Victorian and Edwardian dressing tables have been vandalised by having the little sets of drawers at either end removed and made up into 'miniature' chests. With a little experience, the tell-tale signs of conversion will be spotted; a good original antique miniature has the right balance and proportions which are quickly recognised by the initiated collector. Even if the size is not immediately discernible, one can get a good idea of quality from photographs, that is, if the proportions including handles, finials, etc., are perfectly correct (*see* Figs. 75–77, 81 and 88).

Period nursery furniture is scarce and antique miniature furniture is even scarcer. Any good quality piece is therefore worth buying. If one has interior decoration in mind, cradles can be used other than for their original purpose, for instance, for flowers or plants as indeed can little children's wheel-barrows. Children's high and low chairs make an attractive contrast with adult size furniture, while small tables and chests are exceptionally useful and practical in any setting, as side pieces against a wall or by the side of chairs and settees. Sedan chairs, rocking horses, push carts and so on, are interesting conversation pieces but require a larger setting. The serious collector could still assemble a representative collection of children's chairs from the seventeenth to the twentieth century, or perhaps a representative group of children's furniture from a chosen period. Genuine little children's tables such as the seventeenth-century gate-leg variety are extremely rare and highly desirable, and so are antique children's chests and desks. One could specialise in miniature models, show pieces and travellers' samples. Clearly, furniture for dolls is a closely related field, while dolls' houses and dolls' house furniture are already widely studied and collected.

A limited amount of damage and restoration has sometimes to be accepted. Restorers are difficult to find, but the London auctioneers, for example, will advise on these problems. Caning, upholstery etc. on seat furniture may be replaced, unless it is valuable early tapestry work. Distressed looking-glasses should certainly be retained, even if regilding of frames may be acceptable. In general, one should look for items that appeal to the eye in every way, which have pleasing proportions, good quality construction and finish, good colour or patination, and are therefore better than average examples of their particular kind.

Useful Addresses

Mallett & Son (Antiques)
40 New Bond Street, London, W.1
Telephone: 01-499-7411

Mallett at Bourdon House
2 Davies Street, London, W.1
Telephone: 01-629-2444

Barling of Mount Street
112 Mount Street, London, W.1
Telephone: 01-499-2858

Melvyn Lipitch
120 Fulham Road, London, S.W.3
Telephone: 01-373-3328

Richard Courtney
114 Fulham Road, London, S.W.3
Telephone: 01-370-4020

H.C. Baxter & Sons
193 Fulham Road, London, S.W.3
Telephone: 01-352-9826

Murray Thomson
141 Kensington Church Street, London, W.8
Telephone: 01-727-1727

Charles and Jane Toller
20 High Street, Datchet, Bucks.
Telephone: 75-42903

Kay Desmonde
17 Kensington Church Walk, London, W.8
Telephone: 01-937-2602

The Singing Tree
69 New King's Road, London, S.W.6
(old and new dolls' houses and accessories)
Telephone: 01-736-4527

The Dolls' House Toys Ltd.
116 Lisson Grove, London, N.W.1
Telephone: 01-723-1418
29 The Market, Covent Garden, London, W.C.2
Telephone: 01-379-7243
(old and new houses and accessories)

Christie's (Christie, Manson & Woods Ltd.)
8 King Street, St. James's, London, S.W.1
Telephone: 01-839-9060

Christie's South Kensington
Old Brompton Road, London, S.W.7
Telephone: 01-581-2231

Christie, Manson & Woods International Inc.
502 Park Avenue, New York, N.Y. 10022
Telephone: 212-826-2888

Phillips' (Phillips, Son, & Neale)
Blenstock House
7 Blenheim Street, London, W.1
Telephone: 01-629-6602

Sotheby's (Sotheby Parke Bernet & Co.)
34 and 35 New Bond Street, London, W.1
Telephone: 01-493-8080

Sotheby's Belgravia
19 Motcomb Street, London, S.W.1
Telephone: 01-235-4311

Sotheby Park Bernet Inc.
980 Madison Avenue, New York, N.Y. 10021
Telephone: 212-472-3400

Bibliography

1 Jane Toller, *Antique Miniature Furniture in Great Britain and America*. Bell & Sons, London, 1966
2 H.F. Schiffer and P.B. Schiffer, *Miniature Antique Furniture*. Livingston Publishing Co., Wynnewood, Pennsylvania, 1972
3 Georg Himmelheber, *Kleine Moebel*. Deutscher Kunstverlag, 1979
4 *Spink & Son Exhibition of Children's Chairs*. London, 1971. Review: Frank Davis, *Chairs for Children*. Country Life, 18.11.1971
5 Towneley Hall Art Gallery, Burnley. *Exhibition of Children's Furniture*. Catalogue 1977.
6 Kunstmuseum, Aarhus, Denmark. *Exhibition of Children's Furniture*, 1972
7 Kunstgewerbemuseum, Cologne. Exhibition *Kindermoebel und Spielobjekte*. Catalogue 1973
8 Historisches Stadtmuseum, Munich. Exhibition *Aus Muenchner Kinderstuben 1750–1930*. Catalogue 1976
9 Edward Pinto, *Treen and other Wooden Bygones*. Bell & Sons, London, 1969
10 James Mackay, *Nursery Antiques*. Ward Lock Ltd., London, 1976
11 J.C. Loudon, *Encyclopedia of Cottage, Farm & Villa Architecture and Furniture*, 1833. Reprint S.R. Publishers Ltd., London, 1970
12 J.H. Walsh, *A Manual of Domestic Economy suited to Families spending £150–£1500 a year*. G. Routledge & Sons, London, 1879
13 Hermann Muthesius, *The English House*, 1904. Reprint, Granada Publishing Ltd., London, 1979
14 Heal & Son Ltd., *The Nursery Book being some attempt to deal with the problem of the furnishing and equipment of the modern nursery*. London, 1915
15 Ralph Edwards, *Shorter Dictionary of English Furniture*. Country Life, 1972

16 E. Joy, *Pictorial Dictionary of British Nineteenth Century Furniture Design*. Antique Collectors' Club, 1977

17 Thomas Chippendale, *The Gentleman and Cabinet-Maker's Director*. Reprint of 3rd Edition. Dover Publications Inc., New York, 1966

18 George Hepplewhite, *The Cabinet-Maker and Upholsterer's Guide*. 3rd Edition, 1794

19 Thomas Sheraton, *The Cabinet-Maker and Upholsterer's Drawing Book*. Reprint, Dover Publications Inc., New York, 1972

20 Thomas Sheraton, *Cabinet Dictionary*, 1803

21 Thomas Hope, *Household Furniture and Interior Decoration*, 1807

22 George Smith, *A Collection of Designs for Household Furniture and Interior Decoration*, 1808

23 George Smith, *The Cabinet-Maker and Upholsterer's Guide*, 1826

24 Edward Wenham, *Children through the Ages*. Review of Exhibition at Chesterfield House. Connoisseur, May 1934, p. 330

25 Jane Toller, *Nursery Furniture*, Antique Collector, Nov. 1973, p. 83

26 Margaret Macdonald-Taylor, *Nursery Furniture of Bygone Days*. Country Life, 1.12.1960, p. 1323

27 R.W. Symonds, *Furniture of the Nursery*. Antique Collector, May 1949, p. 97

28 Penelope Eames, *Furniture in England, France, and the Netherlands from the Twelfth to the Fifteenth Centuries*. The Furniture Historical Society, London, 1977 (Cradles, pp. 93–107)

29 R.W.P. Luff, *Three Centuries of Cradles*, Country Life, 21.12.1961

30 Thomas W. Bagshawe. *Baby-cages*. Apollo, Dec. 1937, p. 326

31 Anon., *Child taught to walk by Go-cart*. The Times, 7.10.1967

32 Jane Toller, *Children's Desks*. Antique Collector, May 1974, p. 51

33 S.J. Sewell, *The History of Children's and Invalids' Carriages.* Journal of the Royal Society of Arts, Vol. 71, 7.9.1923

34 A.E. Richardson, *A Disquisition on Perambulators.* Country Life, 9.11.1940, p. 408

35 A.L. Haskell and M. Lewis, *Infantilia: the Archaeology of the Nursery.* D. Dobson, London, 1971

36 Jack Hampshire, *Prams, Mailcarts, and Bassinets. A Definitive History of the Child's Carriage.* Midas Books, 1980

37 Jane Toller, *Treen and Other Turned Woodwork for Collectors.* David & Charles, London, 1975

38 Judith Banister, *Nursery Silver.* Antique Collector, July 1974, p. 52

39 Pauline Flick, *Children's China.* Constable, in preparation

40 Edward Pinto, *The Fascination of Miniature.* The Times, 7.10.1967

41 J.W. Thorne, *Miniature Rooms.* Collection Phoenix Art Museum, Phoenix, Arizona, 1962

42 R. van Mesdag, *Life in Miniature: Work of Cornelis Bavelaar.* Country Life, 23.8.1979, p. 544

43 Mary Hillier, *Lord and Lady Clapham.* Connoisseur, Feb. 1976

44 Flora Gill-Jacobs, *A History of Dolls Houses.* Charles Scribner's Sons Ltd., London and New York, 1953

45 Vivien Greene, *English Dolls Houses.* B.T. Batsford Ltd., London, 1955. New Edition, Bell & Hyman, London, 1980

46 L. von Wilckens, *Das Puppenhaus.* Georg D.W. Callwey, Munich, 1980

47 Marian Maeve O'Brien, *Collectors' Guide to Dolls' Houses and Dolls' House Miniatures.* Hawthorn Books, New York, 1974

48 Bernard and Therle Huges, *Collecting Miniature Antiques.* Heinemann, London, 1973

Collections to visit

Great Britain
Bath American Museum in Britain, Claverton Manor, Bath, Avon
Biddenden Bettenham Manor, near Biddenden, Kent (Baby Carriages)
Birmingham City Museum & Art Gallery, Chamberlain Square, Birmingham
Bolton Hall i' th' Wood, Bolton, Lancs
Bradford Bolling Hall Museum, Bolling Hall Road, Bradford, West Yorkshire
Bristol Blaise Castle House Museum, Henbury, Bristol
Burnley Towneley Hall Museum & Art Gallery, Burnley, Lancs
Cambridge Cambridge and County Folk Museum, 2/3 Castle Street, Cambridge
Cardiff Welsh National Folk Museum, St. Fagans, Cardiff
Cheltenham Toy and Doll Museum, Sudeley Castle, Winchcombe, nr. Cheltenham, Glos.
Edinburgh Museum of Childhood, 38 High Street, Edinburgh
Ipswich Christchurch Museum, Christchurch Park, Ipswich, Suffolk
Hereford Hereford City Museums, Broad Street, Hereford
Lancaster Museum of Childhood, Judge's Lodgings, Church Street, Lancaster
Leeds Temple Newsam, Leeds (5 miles S.E. of Leeds. Bus 22)
Lewes Anne of Cleves House, High Street, Lewes, Sussex
   Sussex Archaeological Society, Lewes, Sussex
London Bethnal Green Museum, Cambridge Heath Road, E.2
   Geffrye Museum, Kingsland Road, Shoreditch, E.2
   Gunnersbury Park Museum, Gunnersbury Park, W.3
   Museum of London, London Wall, Barbican, E.C.2
   Pollock's Toy Museum, 1 Scala Street, W.1
   Victoria & Albert Museum, South Kensington, S.W.7

Luton　Museum and Art Gallery, Luton, Beds
Menai Bridge　Museum of Childhood, Water Street, Menai Bridge, Anglesey
Morpeth　Wallington Hall, Morpeth, Northumberland
Norwich　Strangers' Hall Museum, Charing Cross, Norwich Castle Museum, Norwich, Norfolk
Oxford　The Rotunda, Grove House, 44 Iffley Turn, Oxford
Tunbridge Wells　Municipal Museum & Art Gallery, Mount Pleasant, Tunbridge Wells, Kent
Wakefield　Nostell Priory, nr. Wakefield, West Yorkshire
Isle of Wight　Osborne House, East Cowes, Isle of Wight
York　The Castle Museum, Tower Street, York

United States of America
Greenfield Village & Henry Ford Museum, Dearborn, Michigan
Metropolitan Museum of Art, 5th Ave. and 82nd Street, New York
The Henry Francis du Pont Winterthur Museum, Winterthur, Delaware
The Abby Aldrich Rockefeller Folk Art Center, 307 South England Street, Williamsburg, Virginia
The Smithsonian Institution, 12th and Constitution Ave., Washington D.C.
Phoenix Art Gallery, 1625 N. Central Ave., Phoenix, Arizona
Margaret Strong Museum, Rochester, New York

Europe
Belgium　Musées Royaux d'Art et d'Histoire, 10 Parc du Cinquantenaire, Brussels, 6
France　Musée National du Louvre, Palais du Louvre, Place du Carrousel, Paris, 1
Musée de Cluny, 6 Place Paul Painlevé, Paris
Musée National de Malmaison, Château de la Malmaison, Rueil Malmaison, Hauts de Seine, 92
Château de Compiègne, Compiègne, Oise, 60
West Germany　Cologne, Kölnisches Stadtmuseum, Overstolzenhaus, Rheingasse 8–12
Cologne, Kunstgewerbemuseum, Eigelsteintorburg 5000, Köln, 1

Frankfurt, Museum fur Kunsthandwerk, Schaumainkai 15, 6000 Frankfurt-am-Main 70

Munich, Stadtmuseum, St. Jakob's Platz 1, 8000 München 2

Munich, Bayerisches Nationalmuseum, Prinzregentenstrasse 3, 8000 München 22

Nürnberg, Germanisches Nationalmuseum, Kartausergasse 1

East Germany Sonneberg, Spielzeug Museum, Beethovenstrasse 10, Sonneberg 1

Holland Amsterdam, Rijksmuseum, Stadhonderskade 42

Sweden Stockholm, Nordiska Museet, Djurgarden, Stockholm

Switzerland Zürich, Musée Bellerive, Höschgasse 3, (Sammlung des Kunstgewerbemuseums)

Glossary

Acanthus Carved leaf ornament found particularly on eighteenth-century mahogany furniture

Apron Decorative carved or shaped member below seat rail of chair or settee sometimes extending to junction of legs with the rail; also below the frieze of cabinet stands and tables

Arcading Ornamentation on case furniture in the form of a series of arches (or columns or pillars) found particularly on early chests and on apron pieces

Ball Foot Round terminal particularly to late seventeenth-century case furniture

Baluster Turned support of different shapes including straight, twisted, and vase-shaped

Banding Decorative border in contrasting woods; when the band of contrasting wood applied to a veneered surface is cut across the grain this is termed cross-banding

Barley Sugar Twist turning reminiscent of barley sugar

Beading Decorative moulding resembling string of beads

Bell Flower Ornament of carved or inlaid flower pattern

Bentwood Wood steamed and bent to form members of chairs, settees, etc.

Bergère Deep easy chair with upholstered sides; also used later for caned armchair with enclosed sides

Bracket Foot A foot with mitred corners and unjoined sides which may be straight or scrolled, found on case furniture such as chests, bureaux, and cabinets from about 1690 onwards

Cabriole Leg Carved outwards at the knee and inwards at the foot, which may be hoof, pad, claw and ball, or scroll. Favoured during first half of eighteenth century

Canting Surface which is bevelled, chamfered, or obliquely faced, as in canted corners of case furniture

Carcase The body of case furniture to which veneers are applied

Cartouche   Carved tablet imitating scroll with rolled up ends decorating centre of pediments or apron pieces

Chamfer   Bevelled or cut away surface, as on chamfered legs of some Chippendale and Hepplewhite furniture

Claw and Ball Foot   Dragon's or bird's claw clutching a ball, particularly as terminal to cabriole leg in the period 1720–60

Cock Beading   Plain semi-circular moulding; for example as applied to edges of drawer-fronts 1730–1800

Cornice   Uppermost horizontal section of an entablature in furniture, as on cabinets, bookcases, etc.

Dentil   Series of small equally spaced rectangular blocks or 'teeth' forming a decoration, as under a cornice

Dowel   Headless wooden pin for joining two pieces of wood

Dovetail   Tenon shaped like dove's tail or reversed wedge fitting into corresponding mortise to form joint

Fan   Decoration carved on early oak, inlaid or painted on eighteenth-century furniture (also lunette)

Feather Banding   Two strips of veneer laid together at an angle so as to form herring-bone or feather pattern against ground veneer

Fielding   See *Panelling*

Finial   Terminal ornament, in neo-classical furniture generally vase or urn-shaped, often found on top of cabinets and at the intersection of stretchers on tables

Fluting   Concave semi-circular shaped grooves used particularly on legs of Adam period furniture

Fretwork   Open or pierced lattice-work decoration or in relief (as in blind fretwork, see Fig. 35) found on all manner of furniture, for example in the mid-eighteenth-century Chippendale period

Frieze   Carved or otherwise decorated band below cornice on case furniture or tables

Gadrooning   Form of carved repetitive ornamental edging

Galon   A braid woven of silk, gold, or silver thread

Gate-Leg   As in gate-leg tables, they fold against the frame of the table when closed, but may be drawn forward to support drop-leaves when these are raised to open up the table

Gesso   Composition material made of whiting (chalk), linseed oil, and size, applied particularly to mirror-frames and side tables in the period 1690 to 1730, and later. Used as base for gilding

Highboy American chest on chest with table-like legs. The tallboy is a chest on chest with small feet, such as bracket feet

Hipping Decoration on seat furniture where carving on knee of legs extends and merges with carving on seat rail

Inlay Wood or other materials let into the solid surface; used decoratively since the sixteenth century. Contrast the later marquetry

Japanning Decorative treatment, particularly European imitation of Oriental lacquer-work since the seventeenth century, in which several coats of coloured varnish were applied to a gesso base to form the ground on which the design was painted in colours mixed with gum arabic. Raised details were added by dropping a paste of whiting and gum arabic onto the surface. The raised detail was then shaped, coloured, and gilded. Black is the most usual ground colour, red was also used, other colours are much rarer. A variant of japanning imitated the Chinese incised lacquer- or Bantam-work

Lappet Overlapping decorative piece, as on early to mid-eighteenth century table and chair legs

Linenfold Carved decoration particularly on fifteenth- and sixteenth-century furniture, for example on the panelling of chests, which in its principal form gives the impression of folded linen

Lowboy Flat-topped dressing table with drawers. Eighteenth-century examples would according to period be in walnut or other woods or mahogany, and on cabriole legs with pad feet or claw and ball feet, or later, on square chamfered legs. See *Highboy*

Lozenge Diamond-shaped figure employed both in carving and inlay particularly on seventeenth-century furniture

Marquetry Development of veneering from the second half of the seventeenth century onwards. A decorative pattern of various exotic woods in thin slices of veneer fastened on to a common wood. Most frequently as floral patterns, or as spiky and scrolling patterns closely spaced and interwoven, which is called 'seaweed' marquetry. A form of marquetry using simple geometrical patterns is known as parquetry

Mitre Joint in a moulding formed by the two pieces of wood meeting at right angles so that the line of junction bisects the angle

Mortise and Tenon Joint of two pieces of wood, one of which has a cavity called a mortise into which the other having a part or end called a tenon is inserted. First used by sixteenth century 'joiners'.

Moulding Decorative band obtained by a continuous projection or incision applied to a surface

Ogee Foot Shaped in a double continuous curve, concave below passing into convex above, as in a form of shaped bracket foot

Pad Foot Resembling small club foot and associated with cabriole legs on chairs, tables, etc., from the beginning of the eighteenth century

Panelling Panels set in a framework and held together by mortise and tenon joints, as on chests and other case furniture. A fielded panel is a panel in which the edges are bevelled, having a flat field in the centre.

Papier Mâché Paper pulp mixed with chalk and glue. Also made from sheets of paper and a paste formed of flour, water, and size, pressed and shaped in moulds. Invented in the seventeenth century, used in the eighteenth, for example, in the japanned articles made by Henry Clay, and for large-scale production of furniture in the early nineteenth century particularly by Jennens and Bettridge of Birmingham, who also exported to America. A variety of decorative processes and inlays were employed, for example, mother-of-pearl inlay, and furniture made included chairs, settees, tables, beds, cabinets, as well as innumerable small objects

Patera Small oval or round, carved, inlaid or painted neo-classical ornament

Paw Foot Particularly associated with cabriole leg around 1730–45 and also used in the Regency period

Pediment Decorative part of cabinets, bookcases etc., placed on top of cornice. Different shapes were favoured at various times, such as unbroken and broken pediments, e.g. broken swan-necked pediment

Plinth Base for urns, vases, and statues, or base supporting case furniture not provided with feet

Rail   Horizontal member of framework, as in seat rail

Reeding   Convex raised decoration found for example on turned legs of late eighteenth- and early nineteenth-century furniture

Sabre Leg   Sharp outward curved leg found on neo-classical seat furniture in the Regency period

Scroll Foot   Terminal to chair and table legs occasionally favoured, for example in third quarter of the eighteenth century

Shell   Interior or exterior of shell often with dependent husks was a popular carved decoration on eighteenth-century furniture.

Splat   Piece between uprights of chair back, differently shaped, as in Queen Anne period solid vase-shaped (Fig. 75) or in Chippendale period pierced ribbon back (Fig. 35) splats

Splay Foot   Favoured in Regency period for chests, bureaux, cabinets, generally indicating later date than bracket foot

Stile   Upright side support in a chair back. Any vertical section of a framework, as in panelled chests

Stretcher   Member connecting legs of chairs, tables, etc., H-shaped, X-shaped, and in other forms at different periods

Stringing   Decorative inlay in form of narrow lines

Tester   Canopy particularly over a four-poster bed

Turning   Process of working on a rotating surface with appropriate cutting tools. Furniture or members thereof made in this way; as in baluster, ball, barley sugar twist turning

Veneering   Process dating from second half of seventeenth century in which thin decorative slices or leaves of a fine wood are applied and fastened on to a common wood

Index

THE INSIDER'S GUIDE TO
CHINA

THE INSIDER'S GUIDES

JAPAN • CHINA • KOREA • HONG KONG • BALI • THAILAND • INDIA • NEPAL • AUSTRALIA
HAWAII • CALIFORNIA • NEW ENGLAND • FLORIDA • MEXICO
THE SOVIET UNION • SPAIN • TURKEY • GREECE
KENYA

The Insider's Guide to China

Moorland Publishing Co Ltd
Moor Farm Road, Airfield Estate, Ashbourne, DE61HD, England
First Published 1987
1989 revised edition published
by arrangement with CFW Publications Ltd

© 1987, 1989 CFW Publications Ltd

ISBN: 0 86190 263 7

Created, edited and produced by CFW Publications Ltd
130 Connaught Road C., Hong Kong. Fax (852) 543 8007
Editor in Chief: Allan Amsel
Design: Hon Bing-wah/Kinggraphic
Text and artwork composed and information updated
using Xerox Ventura software

Printed by Samhwa Printing Co Ltd, Seoul, Korea

THE INSIDER'S GUIDE TO

CHINA

by Derek Maitland

Photographed by Adrian Bradshaw
and Nik Wheeler

MPC

Contents

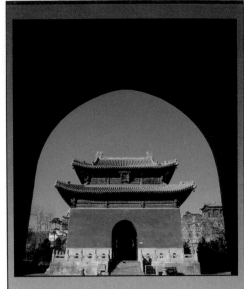

CHINA

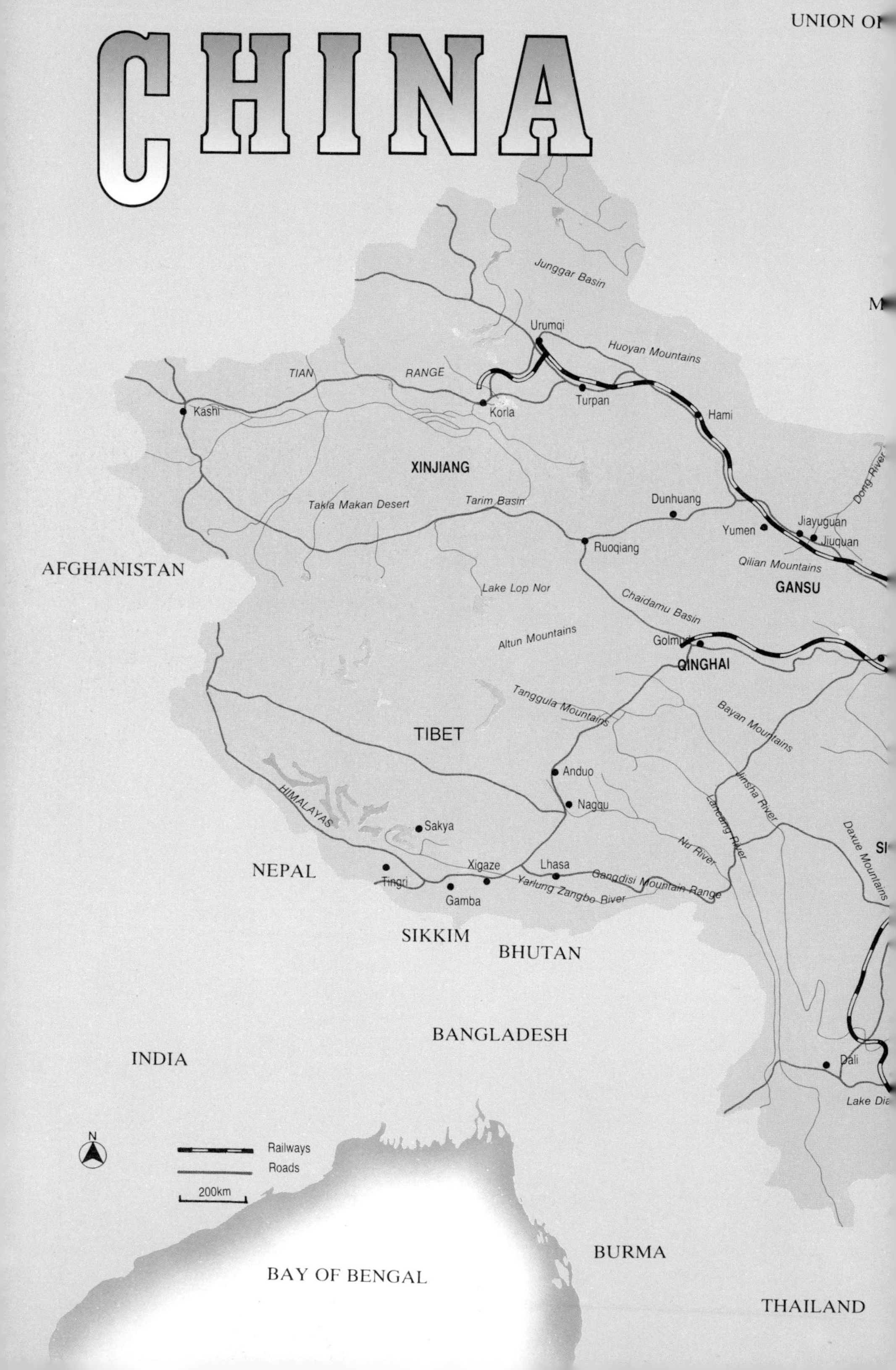

UNION OF

M

Junggar Basin

Urumqi

Huoyan Mountains

TIAN   RANGE

Kashi

Korla   Turpan   Hami   Dong River

XINJIANG

Takla Makan Desert   Tarim Basin   Dunhuang   Jiayuguan

Yumen   Jiuquan

Ruoqiang   Qilian Mountains

AFGHANISTAN   GANSU

Lake Lop Nor   Chaidamu Basin

Altun Mountains   Golmud

QINGHAI

Tanggula Mountains   Bayan Mountains

TIBET

Jinsha River

Anduo

HIMALAYAS   Naggu   Lancang River

Daxue Mountains

Sakya   Nu River   SI

Xigaze   Lhasa   Gangdisi Mountain Range

NEPAL   Tingri   Yarlung Zangbo River

Gamba

SIKKIM   Dali

BHUTAN   Lake Dia

BANGLADESH

INDIA

N

Railways
Roads

200km

BAY OF BENGAL   BURMA

THAILAND

The Middle Kingdom

A tour of China is more than just a tour, it is a grand pilgrimage through a civilization that has kept its basic structure and philosophy intact for nearly 5,000 years. And its cultural heritage is so vast, its monuments, relics and other wonders stir the imagination so evocatively, that it is one of the most fascinating and rewarding travel experiences on earth.

China's cultural attractions are every bit as astonishing as the textbooks and tour literature would have us believe. Its present-day society is as strange, as interesting and even as bizarre as one would expect of a people who have triumphed over resounding social collapse, terrible warfare and civil conflict, violent revolution and almost complete isolation for more than three decades from the rest of the human race. And in a certain sense, it is this society that is China's biggest wonder, and the China tour a pilgrimage to the soul of its people too.

China is also a challenge. Not only is it physically huge – the third largest country in the world – but all those years of political turmoil and radical social experiment, the mass rallies and red revolutionary flags and banners, have left their mark on the society. Its isolation and its noble but thoroughly dogmatic drive for total economic self-sufficiency may well now be just another twist in the complicated tangle of its long history – the future another complex economic twist altogether – but it means that the society is still pulling itself up out of an era in which there was very little development of all the services and amenities that make a modern society work; and for the modern tourist, this means a certain amount of frustration together with fascination along the China trail. But this can also be an integral part of the China experience, for there was never a more interesting time to visit China than now. Not only is it throwing the door to tourism wide open, meaning that there are now very few places in China where foreigners cannot go, but it is encouraging tourism whilst it is in a heady state of change, stepping from Mao to Mammon, one colossal foot still planted in the principles of the revolutionary era, the other reaching along a new liberalizing, modernizing but thoroughly unpredictable capitalist path.

Its tourist industry reflects this gradual, heavy shift of policy. On one hand, the official hand, there is still a definite preference for organized group tours, operated inside China mainly by the national tourist authority CITS (China International Travel Service), allowing foreigners in by all means, but in very controlled circumstances, on strict itineraries and segregated to a great extent from the ordinary people. On the other hand, China is now open to growing hordes of business travelers involved in foreign investment and the modernisation programme – an influx which is triggering a boom in international-class hotels and a major improvement in the standards of older properties. While the organized tour means comfort and convenience and CITS protection from the more arduous and less attractive aspects of the society, it is at the price of open contact with the masses. At the other end of the travel spectrum lies tight-budget backpacking, but this can mean the misery of being too close to the society's bottom rungs – dingy and even squalid hostels and guesthouse dormitories, a continual competition for the cheapest "Chinese-price" seats on trains, a struggle in the awful crush that occurs on the overcrowded and often dilapidated public buses, bad food in very unhygienic conditions and so much time and attention spent searching the ground at the feet that much of the grand physical and cultural panorama of China can be missed.

In between these extremes there is a good compromise, the Middle Way – a path that the new legions of individual business travelers have found. It offers comfort when you most need it, the

freedom to rough it when circumstances call for it, and, most important of all, complete immersion in Chinese society. It is the way I traveled China – as an individual traveler depending only on my own arrangements, wits and initiative to get through. But with enough money to enjoy China, not endure it.

ONE IN A BILLION

Of my own lone nine and a half week tour, I can honestly say that it rewarded me with the most physically challenging, frustrating, sometimes despairing yet exciting, enlightening and even amusing experience I have had in some 20 years of international travel as a journalist. I trudged aboard the *MV Jinjiang* in Shanghai at the end of the long odyssey, bound for Hong Kong, having visited 20 cities and 30 major tourist locations, lost seven kilos in weight, filled four notebooks with information, anecdotes and observations, shot more than 120 rolls of film and felt that I had touched, or at least got very close to, the human soul of China. And I am convinced that I was able to accomplish this

because of the Middle Way of individual budget travel.

I had neither succumbed to the segregated and relatively costly comfort of the organized tour, nor had I allowed the trip to become an endurance test, which it can be if you travel with very little money at all. I found that I was able to buy my own train and bus tickets, check into hotels and guest houses of my own choice as I came to them, buy my own food and choose at all times where I wanted to go. I learned Chinese as I went along, walked or bicycled around most of the cities and moved so freely amongst the ordinary working people that I felt at times that I had become one in a billion, and in both senses of the term – accepted and certainly approved of by them for striking through their society on my own, yet competing directly with them for space, food, shelter, transport and all other daily essentials. And I would submit that that's as close as you can get to any society.

ABOVE Light blanket of snow softens imperial architecture and mood of the Ming dynasty's most dramatic legacy, the Forbidden City in Beijing.

I had no fixed itinerary when I started out, and no travel or hotel reservations. I had only a tentative route, a clockwise trail taking me across the southern provinces to Kunming, swinging up through western China and Tibet, crossing over the north to Beijing and then descending through the east-central region for a final run down the Yangtze River cities to Shanghai.

It proved to be an ideal itinerary for any grand tour, and one that I can quite justifiably recommend to any China traveler. It also provided me, and this guidebook, with a series of radial centers – major cities

from which shorter regional tours can be taken to the most interesting, accessible and worthwhile cultural attractions.

My route meant that I moved through the easier, warmer, wealthier and more accommodating southern cities at the start of the tour, when I needed easy travel. I traveled the tougher regions of the west, Tibet and the arid northwest when I was still fresh enough to cope with them. After

ABOVE Picturesque Sky Lake lies in the Tian Range near Urumqi – revered as heaven by ancient Xiongnu nomads.

the excitement of Lhasa I was able to build up to a second cultural peak on the swing across the north to the monumental splendor of Beijing. And when I was tired and feeling the full strain of the journey I was able to wind down and relax again on the relatively refined river ferry and train trek down the eastern Yangtze.

The cost of all this? The whole nine and a half weeks came to a total $2,400, and I can't say I really stinted on anything. I could have tightened up on the spending here and there and enjoyed it all just as much for less than $2,000. I would warn, though, that prices have increased considerably since then, partly due to a national 20–40 percent rise in inflation – the price China has already begun to pay for switching to the capitalist path.

It wasn't always easy. Nothing in China really is. You take one billion energetic, industrious people and an infrastructure – transport, accommodation and communication – that has been seriously neglected in a decade of controversial and violent social upheaval called the Great Proletarian Cultural Revolution, and you can take it for granted that daily life is going to be something of a grind. A CITS group tour will remove you from it, a threadbare backpack existence could make you a possibly very begrudging victim of it. The Middle Way will throw you right into it, but on terms that are your own.

In the final analysis, anyone's chosen form of travel in China is going to be decided on personal and financial grounds – age, stamina and the amount of money available for the trip. To any elderly person or anyone who doesn't feel up to the rigors of individual travel, I would thoroughly recommend a package tour, and again, on the principle that the paramount consideration on any visit to China should be to enjoy it, not endure it.

If I am not personally attracted to the tour group syndrome it is because it appeared to me to be a sophisticated form of apartheid. I studied several groups on the Yangtze River section of my tour and found that they were cut off not only from the Chinese people but from other groups as well.

In the luxurious Swan Hotel in Guangzhou I met a German tourist who was literally in a state of rage at having been rushed across the country on a CITS tour and had little contact with the Chinese beyond desk-clerks and dining hall staff. "I now have to come back on my own to see everything I missed," he complained bitterly. This segregation went to absurd lengths in a half-empty soft-seat compartment on a train from Suzhou to Shanghai when a member of an Australian tour group approached a Japanese party and complained that "some of your group are sitting in my group's seats." You can backpack through China for a few dollars a day, and I've no doubt that if you're young enough and willing to put up with the discomfort at that level of travel it can be a thoroughly adventurous and possibly noble way to do it. For one thing, it is a slap at the notorious two-tiered pricing system that operates throughout China – one price for the Chinese and another for "foreign guests" – and about which I'll explain more in the TRAVELERS' TIPS section.

But one man I met, an American who'd traveled for three months on about $7 a day, had also nearly frozen to death hitchhiking on a truck across the Tibet-Qinghai Plateau. Another backpacker, an American girl, was airlifted out of the Xishuangbanna minorities zone in southern Yunnan with hepatitis. In Beijing it occurred to me that anyone undecided about real tight-budget travel should, before they make up their mind, go along to the backpacker's hotel, the Qiaoyuan, on the city's outskirts south of the Temple of Heaven, take a good look at its dormitory accommodation and try to picture an environment like that every night right across China.

As for the Middle Way, it means bringing enough money to China to travel sensibly, freely and in some comfort. It means budgeting for hotels and older guesthouses that are not high-priced but have clean rooms, linen, toilets and baths and adequate heating in winter.

The Middle Way means having enough funds to upgrade to a soft-berth compartment on the trains when you need a good rest or are so socially over-stimulated that you simply crave peace and some solitude for a while. It means having enough to eat decently, and this cannot be regarded too importantly for good food can be scarce at certain times of the year in some regions, and the proletarian Chinese diet can be so debilitating that a tourist I met in Datong near the Inner Mongolia border suggested I call this book THE WEIGHT-WATCHER'S GUIDE TO CHINA. "You'll have everyone in America signing up for a China tour," he laughed.

The Middle Way allows you to rough it for a while if you want to, but comforted by the thought that you have enough money to treat yourself to a bit of luxury when you need it – a clean, warm bed, a good bath, a good meal and a chance to have your clothes laundered and feel reasonably human again.

The Middle Way gave me many memorable moments in China, and not just the moments of awe that any visitor feels in the vast, historic presence of Tiananmen Square, the Great Wall, the Grand Buddha of Leshan, the magnificent Buddhist grottoes of Baoding and Dunhuang, the Potala Palace in Lhasa, the terra-cotta army of Emperor Qin's tomb in Xi'an and all the other great cultural monuments. There were moments amongst the people, too, that I will remember forever – playing pool on the roadside with industrial workers in Guilin, reading an English-language primer to a doctor and two nurses in a temple near Kunming, my first fiery experience of Sichuan hotpot in Dazu, awakening to the lusty, unlikely bellow of the "Eton Boating Song," of all things, from a Tibetan classroom in my hotel in Lhasa, filming amazingly colorful Spring Festival carnivals in Xining, Ta'er and Lanzhou, presenting an impromptu lecture on the Western media to an advanced

English class at Tongjie University in Shanghai, and so on... .

If all that can be called getting close to the soul of Chinese society, then the aim of this guidebook is to provide a blueprint that will do the same for you.

THE COUNTRY AND ITS PEOPLE

THE SWEEPING EVES

Just as China is physically vast, it is also a land of vividly contrasting terrain and climate. It is the third largest country on earth after the USSR and Canada, its territory covering seven percent of the world's total land surface, an area of nearly 10 million square kilometers (3.8 million square miles) including Tibet. It stretches 5,500 km (3,410 miles) from its northern to southern borders and almost the same distance from east to west.

Dotted around its 14,000 km (8,680 mile) eastern and southern coastline are nearly 5,000 islands, some of them, such as Hainan off the southwestern coast, large enough to support substantial farming and fishing communities. The island of Taiwan, where the Nationalist Guomingdang forces fled in the revolution of 1949, is considered by the Beijing leadership to be part of China and reasonably free to make up its own mind on when it wants to take the inevitable step back under mainland control. The tiny Portuguese-administered enclave of Macau is earmarked too. The British colonial possession of Hong Kong, that remarkable capitalist industrial and trading center which has thrived and fattened over the years as the communist giant's principal source of foreign exchange, returns to full Chinese sovereignty in 1997.

The terrain within all this territory is so variable and contrasting that, for the relatively casual visitor, it needs to be approached in its simplest terms. In one sense it has the same basic architecture as its traditional man-made temples and pavilions with their sweeping, multi-tiered eaves. If you take Tibet in the far west as the tip of the roof (and Tibet is, in fact, popularly termed the "Roof of the World"), the rest of the terrain sweeps and falls away to the east in a series of descending plateaus and plains, arriving finally at sea level along the eastern seaboard.

The landscape is dominated by two great river systems, the Yellow River in the north and the mighty Yangtze to the central south. Both originate in the upper reaches of the Tibet-Qinghai Plateau and surge downhill toward the eastern coast and both have acted as the landscape's principal sculptors. Over many thousands of years the Yellow River has deposited and then carved its way through a vast plain of soft loess soil, creating a dramatic and sometimes bizarre pattern of winding canyons, rounded bluffs and strangely shaped outcrops where harder soil and rock have resisted its knife. To the south, the Yangtze has carved the narrow, precipitous Yangtze Gorges of Sichuan Province, and beyond that its southern tributaries have rushed and seeped through a wide belt of limestone to form a similarly dramatic landscape of karst – geological formations in which erosion has left pinnacles, underground caverns and abruptly shaped mounds and hills that have given the city of Guilin and its Guangxi-Zhuang Autonomous Region its fairyland character.

These river systems have been both life-giving and death-dealing over the many centuries of recorded Chinese history, both unleashing terrible floods which have periodically destroyed croplands and wiped out whole communities, killing countless numbers of people. The Yellow River, known in the past as "China's Sorrow," has breached its banks and dikes more than 1,000 times and changed its course on at least 20 occasions, and during the 2,000 years from the Han to Qing dynasties, the Yangtze has gone on the rampage in more than 200 disastrous floods.

Elsewhere, the landscape sprawls and soars through climatic zones that range from frigid-temperate with permafrost in the far north to temperate, sub-tropical and tropical as it sweeps south. In winter the far northern reaches, lashed by bitterly cold winds from the Siberian steppes, are bleak and forbidding, either dry and frozen or, as one of Mao Zedong's many poems depicted them, "a thousand miles sealed with ice, ten thousand miles of swirling snows." Meanwhile, in the far south, the sun beats down upon lush rain-forests, bamboo groves and rice paddies below the Tropic of Cancer. In summer the entire country boils in the south and bakes in the drier north, with the temperature at a national average of 25°C (77°F).

The western mountains of Yunnan, Sichuan and Qinghai provinces rise majestically to heights of 7,000 m (23,000 feet) or more to form the foothills of the awesome Himalayas; the deserts and dust-bowls, including the dreaded Taklimakan and the harsh Turfan Depression – more than 150 m (500 feet) below sea-level, one of the lowest dry-land surfaces on earth – are moonscapes of relentlessly shifting sands under which the homes, temples and bones of the fabled Silk Road and the frontiers of Chinese civilization lie buried. And in between these stark physical contrasts there lies a wide diversity of prairies, jungles, "green seas" of bamboo, spectacular rivers – some 1,500 of them – 370 large lakes, gentle streams and jagged coastlines.

GAZELLES AND GINKOS

For all this huge land-space, only about 15 percent of China is suitable for agriculture and extensive human settlement, and this means that in some areas there is an abundance and similar diversity of vegetation and wildlife. In all, China claims to have some 32,000 species of higher plants and more than 4,500 species of animals and birds, including more than 400 species of mammals, or 10 percent of the world total.

ABOVE Three faces of China's minorities – Kazakh (Cossack) girl from Xinjiang TOP, old woman of Tibet CENTER and Turkic-speaking merchant from Urumqi.

Some of this natural heritage, including the giant panda and the ginko tree of Sichuan province, is native only to China. And as the near-arctic forest wildernesses of the north give way to sweeping grasslands and the lush tropical river plains of the south there are tigers, bears, moose, deer and gazelle, wild horses and camels, wolves and foxes, snow leopards, yaks, antelopes, monkeys, civet cats and even elephants.

However, that's not to say that the country is one vast and flourishing natural zoo. The giant panda hasn't been adopted as the emblem of the World Wildlife Federation just for its cuddly features and striking colors – hunting, land-clearance and centuries of deforestation of many areas for fuel have reduced it and many other animal species in China to crisis point.

Industrialization has also taken its toll, and so have the immense pressure for food and the wholesale slaughter of wildlife for ingredients for traditional Chinese medicine; and if you climb Mount Emei in Sichuan, for example, you'll come across a far less illustrious symbol of Chinese conservation – skeletal dried monkey carcasses set up on stalls to advertise herbal and animal medicines.

THE PEOPLE PRESSURE

The most stunning topographical feature of China, however, is its population of slightly over one billion people, a quarter of the human race, packed into 15 percent of its land surface. It has created a stark contrast of its own – teeming eastern and southern cities, with Shanghai and its municipal zone, for instance, crammed with no less than 11 million people, and comparatively deserted wildernesses in parts of the north and in the northwest. It has also created a society whose entire character is governed by one phenomenon – a fuurious competition for all the most basic necessities of life.

It is this unremitting human struggle that is the most challenging, and yet the most fascinating, aspect of a tourist visit to China. If you're not shielded from it on

an official tour you are, in many respects, competing with a billion people for services and amenities. But it is this struggle that makes the Chinese the sort of people they are, and a China tour so unlike most other travel experiences.

Arriving in China you encounter a society that represents the definition of economics taken to its extreme – vastly unlimited demands, severely limited resources. Leaving aside the implications that this has had through 5,000 years of Chinese history, it is more important to consider how this economic nightmare has been tackled over the past 40 years, and how the struggle stands today.

The communist revolution sought, among other things, to slay the economic dragon and rebuild, out of chaos and collapse, a new, prospering, self-governing and self-sufficient China. For all the mistakes, misguided idealism and subsequent chaos that are nowadays being blamed on the Maoist era, some tremendous achievements were made. As an American expatriate I met in Guangzhou succinctly summed up the biggest achievement of all: "They learned to feed a billion people." They also rebuilt an industrial base and an infrastructure – transport, public housing and communications – which lifted the nation out of the hopelessness and grinding poverty of the violent pre-revolutionary years. On top of that, they instituted a crucial form of national effort and discipline, based on a mass campaign, and a code of individual and group responsibility that is still expressed here and there today with the phrase "To be of service to the people." But then, something went wrong. While the people were encouraged to exist in a Utopian mood of cooperation and communal responsibility, power struggles went on in the leadership; and in the most crucial high-level political struggle of all, on the direction in which the development

ABOVE Color emerges from the austere revolutionary character in TOP LEFT shopping crowd in Shanghai, cyclists in Xiamen RIGHT and Spring Festival family gathering in Beijing.

of China should be guided, the embattled Chairman Mao unleashed the Great Proletarian Cultural Revolution. And it got out of hand. The principle of self-sufficiency was taken to an idealistic extreme, the society turned in on itself and the clock of progress stopped while, for almost a decade, another wave of violence and chaos swept the land.

THE BROKEN MAIN SPRING

What is left today, and what any visitor to China should be well aware of – for the

coming few years at least – is the legacy of the broken mainspring, an infrastructure that fell into inadequacy and disrepair and is going to take some time to mend properly. It is what China's new modernization program is all about. It dictates the character of almost everything that is encountered throughout the society.

While there are some very high-class hotels in the big cities, the luxurious Palace

ABOVE Industrialization and intense people pressure has led to the construction of huge public housing projects in the major cities.

Hotel in Beijing, the new Shanghai Hilton International, the Golden Flower and Holiday Inn in Xian and the Garden Hotel in Guangzhou being among the finest examples of them, and while modern new hotels and renovations are being undertaken as swiftly as possible in almost every major center, tourist accommodation elsewhere means old hotels and guesthouses that are still recovering from the stagnation of the Cultural Revolution. Most of them just about manage to offer a reasonably clean and comfortable but comparatively basic standard of service and accommodation in the midst of neglect and disrepair. It's interesting to note the number that have bedside music/clock consoles in their guest rooms, meaning that at some time in the past 30 years travel in China must have been a fairly sophisticated affair. When I was there, none of those consoles worked.

In some hotels, toilets don't work, showers don't work, there's no hot water, the plumbing just about copes, the heating is sporadic, the carpeting threadbare and the beds are sometimes not changed between guests. Blown light bulbs are not replaced, cracked windows are left un-repaired, and the general air of neglect sometimes extends to the hotel staff, who just don't care to notice it let alone do anything about it.

Yet some of this antiquity has a romantic aspect to it, and there are some hotels that should be experienced simply because they are old or rundown but are of an age that means something interesting. The astonishing Renmin (People's) Hotel in Chongqing is a good example – a slightly seedy, grubby, inefficient establishment that nonetheless features neo-imperial architecture that one would swear had been transplanted from the Temple of Heaven in Beijing. The newly-renovated and now French-managed Renmin Hotel in Xi'an is another treat, a monolithic example of Soviet socialist architecture – recalling the grand communist alliance of the 1950s that went badly wrong – with a huge forecourt full of ornamental pools and dancing fountains and pleasantly clean and cozy rooms at rates that are among the best in China.

In Hankou, one of the three old Treaty Port cities that now make up modern Wuhan, the Jianghan Hotel dates back to the days of spats, cabin trunks and tuxedos and features unrenovated suites with latticed veranda rooms and archaic valve radios that you can imagine playing Glenn Miller's latest hits or Abbot and Costello radio shows. On a grander scale, the neon and art deco trappings of the previously gloomy but now renovated Peace Hotel in Shanghai – and, indeed, the entire waterfront stretch, The Bund, on which it stands – lie in such a distant time-warp that the city itself is a living museum, a rare opportunity to see what a Victorian port looked like in the heyday of maritime travel.

Transportation

Transport throughout China is also a confusing clash of neglect and disrepair and the romance of antiquity. There are splendid air and rail networks covering almost the entire country, yet CAAC's jets often do not fly in fog or bad weather and have a terrible record for delays, cancellations and poor passenger service. As for the trains, many of them are obsolete, worn-out, grubby, have "dining cars" that are downright filthy and are staffed by equally grubby attendants who work so hard trying to keep the carriages and compartments in reasonable trim that they have little or no time for passenger service.

The rail system, like the rest of the infrastructure, is also under tremendous people pressure. On any day most railway stations throughout China have up to 2,000 people camped outside them with their baggage waiting for tickets or trains. Others fill the booking halls, struggling and sometimes fighting to get to the ticket windows. The simple process of checking through the ticket gates to get to the trains is invariably a mob scramble, sometimes policed but sometimes uncontrolled, which can leave you breathless, angered and sometimes bruised.

Yet for all this, the trains do run strictly on time, which is more than can be said for the overworked national airline. They are also reasonably comfortable, and they can stir the imagination. As the notes from my travel diary record, all it needs is a subtle shift in thinking to turn the most daunting trip into something of an adventure.

China's strength lies in its people and its railways, I wrote on one journey, both of which somehow cope and manage to keep running in the face of enormous pressures. The people triumph through brute stoicism and improvisation; the rail network is one of the last in the world to keep its huge and proudly archaic steam locomotives in service. Catching sight of one of them, or two in tandem, is a strangely joyful moment. They are beautiful thoroughbred machines, early industrial works of art.

There is little to romance about, however, on the public buses. In most cities they are not only overworked and overcrowded but some are so ramshackle that often they have windows that have fallen out and just haven't been replaced. Their suspensions often droop to one side, their engines need continual running repairs and coaxing and, incongruously, the one piece of equipment that often works perfectly – and at a high-decibel perfection – is a stereo cassette system installed by the driver to blare out Taiwanese pop music along the way.

There are no such things as bus queues or maximum capacities, and a bus ride usually means a fight to get on, a fight for standing room once on them and then a fight to get off. Yet, like almost everything else in China, there's another side to the coin of discomfort. You can often be flattened against the inside wall of a bus, fighting claustrophobia and the urge to burst into anger, and someone will get up and offer you a seat – and insist that you take it, despite your sudden embarrassment and protests – because you are a foreign guest and too important to have to travel this way. These little gestures of comradeship and hospitality happen surprisingly often in China, and they tend to happen at the most crucial moments when the three most vital qualities that every visitor to China must have – patience, understanding and peace of mind – are wearing dangerously thin. They prove, time and time again, the admirable strength of the ordinary Chinese people, their ability to put up with the most grueling, derelict conditions, day after day, and still retain some sense of humor and selflessness. It's merciful that it does happen, because even the most equable Western temperament can reach breaking point in the pitfalls and surprises of this, one of the strangest societies on earth.

THE MILLIONAIRE SYNDROME

China's long period of cultural isolation manifestly affects the way in which the Chinese regard us, the foreigners. To most of them we are millionaires. Certainly, when you compare the standard of living that we exhibit in China with the level at which they live (a university lecturer in Shanghai earns only about ¥90 or $30 a month) we look as though we've got money to burn.

This wide income gap is responsible for the single most nefarious aspect of the China tour – "tourist prices." On trains, airplanes, in hotels, at many cultural attractions, there is one set price for the Chinese and another – often 75 percent or as much as 300 percent higher – for "foreign guests." In between there are other pricing tiers for foreign students, experts and other expatriates who can show a coveted "white card" that entitles them to deal exclusively in Renminbi (RMB), the common Chinese currency.

This "millionaire" syndrome has had other unfortunate consequences along the China trail. There's nothing more irritating, for example, than to be inquiring about details of a trip or tour at a CITS desk and to watch the person you're dealing with fidgeting to get across to you the one thing he's got on his mind: "You pay now." In some of the down-market hotels, desk clerks will try to put you into the most expensive rooms, telling you these are the only rooms available, and you have to be prepared to take a patient stand and try to negotiate them down. If you're backpacking, some hotels will swear they have no such thing as a cheap dormitory. The Datong Guesthouse flatly insisted there was no such thing in their hotel, despite the fact that I'd just been along to room 111 and found six dormitory beds.

At some of the major tourist attractions, particularly the Great Wall at Badaling near Beijing, the terra-cotta army in Xi'an and the Stone Forest in Yunnan province, the hustle for tourist money has become so fierce that you encounter packs of souvenir hawkers more frenzied than any you're likely to see outside, say, Kuta Beach in Bali. At Xi'an they're so persistent that they've had to be confined to fixed areas outside the terra-cotta tomb because visitors were unable to view the soldiers for their sales clamor inside. On the trains, the tourist price of a first-class soft-sleeper berth can be more than the plane fare.

GREAT PEACE OF MIND

These are the major minuses of the China tour that are particularly difficult to feel positive about – but then, there are other tourist destinations that have the same minuses. One thing about China is that any foreign visitor must try to achieve and maintain a certain peace of mind in order to be able to enjoy, not endure, the tour. It helps if you can elevate to a state of patience, understanding and tolerance as well, and try to absorb all the difficulties into the general experience. Make it all part of the trip.

If that itself seems difficult, then try to accept the following fundamental realities about tourism in China: we are richer than them; it's their country; we are being invited in principally to provide much-needed foreign exchange to help bolster their Four Modernizations program. But

BELOW China's national rail network is one of the last in the world to operate steam locomotives alongside modern diesels.

they are offering us the answer to a lot of ambitions and dreams in return.

THE CENTER OF ATTRACTION

What they're offering us does of course have a much more positive and satisfying side to it. China is still a relatively cheap tourist venue – there are not many culturally exciting places left in the world where you can get a reasonably comfortable double room in most hotels for only about $30 a night (that's outside the international business hotels, of course). Also, while we may feel we're having our wallets vacuumed to help put China into the twenty-first century we're also providing another crucial and far more acceptable service in which there is a more obvious exchange or transaction, and one that does make travel in China very worthwhile. We are being studied.

"The new mass campaign is fashion," a genial but orthodox elderly party cadre, clad in a dark gray "Mao" suit and cap, told me on a train trip from Suzhou to Wuxi. "We are being told 'learn from the foreigner.' That's how we'll modernize our society."

We are foreign, modern, wealthy, trendy and every bit as strange to them as they are to us, and they're fascinated by every little aspect of us. Whether it's for good or bad, we're showing them what to wear, how to wear it, what accessories and gadgets to own, when to use them, how the up-to-date human being generally comports in a modern up-to-date world – all very materialistic, but the only practical way aside from television that they have of gaining a little window here and there on a world that has been a mystery to them for decades.

This intense fascination will probably ebb over the coming years as they themselves modernize, but at the moment it means that when you walk the streets you

are under constant public scrutiny. When you are on the trains it sometimes reaches the point where you can hardly bear to move for the attention and excitement that it can generate up and down the carriage. Wherever you go, you become the center of attraction; and while it is generally a nice thing to be, it can also be as tiring as the task of getting there.

But what you get in return is attention. The Chinese not only want to study you, they want to be involved in some way with you. So, if you lose your bearings in the

ABOVE Li River fishermen TOP with tame cormorants - they dive for the fish - near Guilin. Cruise ship takes visitors through river's magnificent karst scenery.

streets someone will inevitably help. If you're at a loss in the railway booking halls, someone will show you where to get your ticket. People will invite you to eat with them, take pictures of them and their children. With what little they have, they'll offer you cigarettes, fruit, sweets, biscuits, sunflower seeds, nuts and other modest but touching gifts aboard the trains and buses. On an individual tour, taking the Middle Way that I've already said so much about, you'll feel at times as though the Chinese people are almost handing you from one to another right across China.

CAN I HELP YOU?

Even in the most fraught situations, when the language barrier threatens to overwhelm you, an angel will usually appear with the greeting, "Hello. Can I help you?" This is the opening gambit of another cultural exchange that foreign visitors are called upon to take part in throughout China. It comes from young students, and there are many thousands of them, who are striving to learn English to "better ourselves" and who have very little opportunity to test their vocabulary and pronunciation.

They must seize upon any foreigner they see, and you have to be completely insensitive to resent it. Most of them are earnest and friendly and, in return for a little conversational practice, will go to great lengths to help with ticketing and other information. If their English is good enough you can also break through the official jargon of China and get some sense of the deeper impulses and attitudes of the society.

One of its paramount impulses for the next 10 to 20 years will be to master English as the key to the technological development that the Chinese are counting on to raise them to true superpower status. So everywhere you go you are likely to be carrying an imaginary sign which says "teacher." I conducted so many impromptu English-language sessions during my tour that by the time I reached Shanghai after nine and a half weeks of it I badly needed a break. Rather than appear rude about it I chose to duck out of each approach for conversational practice with a blank expression and a singular response – "Nein."

I used it very effectively along The Bund, where the students are so persistent they actually operate in teams. I managed to baffle one particular young man so well, answering "nein" to every overture that he made, that the inevitable happened – I ended up getting an English language lesson myself. "This is water. War-terr. That is a boat. Bo-at. We are in Shanghai Harbor. Harr-berr..."

Even as I boarded the ship to leave China for Hong Kong, the English language syndrome followed me. As I passed through immigration, one of the two officers checking my passport said "Ah, *yinguo* (English). We have some questions to ask you. We will come to talk to you on the ship." I spent the next hour holed up in my cabin, trying to recall whether I'd committed an offense against the people somewhere along the trip. When I finally felt it was safe enough, I stepped out to go up on deck, and they were both waiting for me right outside the cabin door. They escorted me from there to the main lounge, where one of them produced a folded and dog-eared piece of paper.

"We are both learning English in our spare time," he said. "We typed this from a magazine article, but there are some points in it that we do not understand. Now, can you explain what is meant by the phrase "He wanted to look his best...?"

THE CHANGING SCENE

Whatever its shocks and drawbacks, Chinese society is modernizing. And in some areas, especially in the tourist industry, it is changing so fast that many of the fundamental physical and social inadequacies will improve or disappear altogether as we head into the 1990s.

Already, tourist accommodation is undergoing a revolution of its own. Brand new hotels are being built everywhere, and at such a pace that there's expected to be a glut in the early 90s which can only bring down tourist and business travel rates. The Beijing-based State Tourism Bureau is predicting no less than 10 million foreign visitors a year by the end of the century, spending something like ¥10 billion ($3 billion) annually. With an incredible target like that in mind, the government is issuing almost weekly orders and exhortations for better staff training in the tourist industry, with a new dedication to service and efficiency.

On the transport side, new up-to-date diesel locomotives and passenger rolling stock are being imported, mainly from the United States and West Germany, or produced in China under license. New rail routes are planned for what is already a very comprehensive national network. For tourists, the most exciting blueprint on the boards in these relatively early days of modernization is a much-needed rail link with Lhasa, the capital of Tibet.

New pilots are being trained for the CAAC air routes, its aging DC-9s and Soviet-built carriers are being replaced with Boeing 727s and other modern short-haul jets, including the McDonnell Douglas MD-82 built in a joint venture enterprise in Shanghai. In fact, the plan is to put 200 new foreign and domestically built airplanes into service by the early 1990s. CAAC has been broken up into hopefully more efficient regional airlines under the new name, Air China, in a bid to modernize and improve the service. Navigation and ground facilities are being upgraded to provide all-weather flying. CAAC is also computerizing its service, and so too are CITS and other national agencies involved in the tourist industry.

English and other Western languages – mainly French and German – are being studied with such a national fervor that the language barrier will crumble as the years go by. The new incentive policy in agriculture is expected to increase or at least diversify the supply of food, and with the rise of a new class of skilled chefs the cuisine will regain something of its traditional splendor. In the meantime, you can get some impression of the improvements to come by visiting any Chinese restaurant in the new international hotels – to be serenaded in some cases with traditional Chinese music, served by friendly, chatty, helpful waitresses in immaculate cheongsams, the traditional high-bodiced costumes with skirts split up to the thighs, and feasted from a remarkably creative menu.

Fashion, personal habits and indeed the whole face of Chinese society will very likely change, in some respects for the better, through the crucial cultural transaction that is going on as more and more foreigners travel the China trail.

OPPOSITE Yangtze River ferries carry commuter crowds between the "three cities" of Wuhan.

THE "LITTLE EMPERORS"

There is a kind of window through which we can perhaps view and anticipate the economic future of China, and it is the same window that opens on to the future of the nation's diminutive but ultra-modern capitalist hand-maiden, Hong Kong. There's a feeling among many observers and analysts of the takeover agreement that the race is on in China to bring the economic level and lifestyle of the mainland millions up as close as possible to that of Hong Kong by the time the colony is returned to Beijing's sovereign bosom in 1997. Whether it can be done with a billion clamoring people remains to be seen. But this immense people pressure and its social implication provides another window on the future – one through which any visitor to China can perhaps anticipate the sort of political society that lies ahead.

Because of China's rigid family planning laws, imposed to try to stop the population from exploding altogether, there are now at least two generations of one-child families in China. More to the point, there is a current vast crop of children, from tiny tots to eight-year-olds, who are growing up with no sibling experience and very little appreciation of the collective responsibility and discipline of the past 40 years.

It is another of China's strange social phenomena, and you can see it wherever you go – the boys, in particular, dressed in little military-style uniforms complete with peaked officer's caps, cute but understandably indulged to high heaven by their doting parents, the apples of everyone's eyes on the one hand but slightly daunting on the other for the demanding, comparatively selfish, cantankerous and even spoilt character that single childhood is giving them. China's leaders of the future.

The Chinese themselves have a special name for them, and one which I think says more than anything else about the future

character of Chinese society. They call them the "Little Emperors."

5,000 YEARS OF HISTORY

THE CULTURAL SAFE-DEPOSIT

Any short visit to China is a fleeting encounter with one of the most complex cultures on earth, touching the tiny tip of an immense and almost limitless cultural iceberg. Any extensive tour is a route-march through the cultural heritage of

4,000 to 5,000 years of recorded Chinese history, and at the end of the march it is still as complex and elusive as ever. You come away feeling that for all you've seen, and all the distance you've traveled, you've really done little more than lightly scratch the surface. In one respect this is all that anyone can really do, for the vast bulk of China's history lies buried in the ground. It's estimated that its current array of temples and monasteries, grottoes and statues, relics and artifacts and great monuments is only about 10 to 20 percent of that which may some day be available to see – the rest of it languishing in a kind of cultural safe-deposit, awaiting the archaeologist's key.

The history that it represents covers such a long and tumultuous span of time and events that no guidebook could ever do it justice, and no visitor other than the lifelong China scholar could really set foot on Chinese soil with anything but the vaguest idea of what it's all about. The best that can be done in any one book, in fact, is to put it into a reasonably understandable perspective. As with its geography, Chinese history must be approached in its simplest form.

THE DISTANT DAWNING

That approach begins with the evidence that proto-human life existed in China at least 600,000 years ago. The most vivid evidence lies in a museum and excavated cave at **Zhoukoudian,** about 50 km (31 miles) southwest of Beijing, where

evidence of this you go to the culturally strategical city of Xi'an where, 40 km (25 miles) to the east, you'll find the **Banpo Museum**, a gloomy, old-fashioned showcase complex in which almost everything has to be peered at through thick glass. Nonetheless, it features bones, pottery, stone tools, a covered excavation of a settlement of that distant Neolithic period and an interesting reconstruction of the circular earthen-walled and mud-roofed dwellings of that age.

Although a lot of China's early history lies in legend, and is attributed to legendary rulers, it's now firmly established that by

two teeth and a skull were discovered in the 1920s and provided the physical profile of one of the most celebrated archaeological finds of all time – the ape-like Peking Man.

As long ago as 5000 BC, Peking Man's more human descendants were farming the rich alluvial valleys and plains of the Yellow River and the Yangtze and other river networks in China's southeast region. And for

ABOVE Contrasting studies of cadre's son LEFT with toy in Shenyang and RIGHT construction worker's infant in Ta'er, Qinghai province.

about 1700 BC the various tribal settlements of eastern China, between what are now Shanghai and Tianjin, had been pulled together under the rule of one monarch to form the state of Shang – China's first dynasty. The first steps were taken toward a sophisticated level of civilization during the subsequent six centuries of Shang rule. The first written records appeared, inscribed on bamboo strips and on oracle bones and tortoise shells used in the first stirrings of institutional religion, including the tradition of divine rule. Also the huge pharmacopoeia of Chinese herbal medicine began to form.

In the later stages of Shang rule the royal capital was based at what is now Anyang in the far north of Henan province, where Shang tombs, ruins and writings have been excavated, and in the now strategic rail junction city of Zhengzhou.

The eventual collapse of the Shang reign around 1027 BC weakened the tradition of centralized rule, and power was spread among independent regional warlords who jostled each other for supremacy but nonetheless owed allegiance to a titular ruler, the duke of Zhou. They were a wealthy, lavishly indulged bunch, as can be appreciated today in the small **Hubei Provincial Museum** in Wuhan where you can view some of the 10,000 treasures and relics unearthed in 1978 from the tomb of one of the prominent nobles of that time, the Marquis Yi of Zeng. The exhibition is evidence not only of wealth and refinement but another important step at that time along the road to civilization – it features a huge bronze musical bell chime, 65 bells in all and each with two different pitches. It is such a sophisticated instrument that its frequencies are close to those of today's modern music.

Inevitably these rival lords fell out with each other and the society stumbled into more than two centuries of almost constant warfare known as the Warring States period. And Chinese civilization came up against its first important crossroad. Wracked by intrigue and bloodshed, it could only hope for a supremely powerful state and an iron-fisted ruler to put it back on the civilized path and save it from continuing barbarism.

THE IRON EMPEROR

The immense power of the strongman who ultimately strode into the breach and saved the society at that crucial time, in 221 BC, can be imagined today when you stand and study one of China's most astonishing historic monuments – the eerie, half-excavated **terra-cotta army of Qinshihuangdi,** the first emperor of Qin, outside Xi'an. This Darth Vader of Chinese history ruthlessly smashed and subjugated his rival warlords and then set about to impose his rule on much of the rest of China.

Although he paid posthumously for his iron reign, his "dynasty" collapsing in a vengeful popular uprising after his death, Emperor Qinshihuangdi established two conventions which have dictated the impetus and attitude of Chinese society ever since: he gave the Chinese race its first real unity, and he began work on a magnificent protective barrier that would shield this unified civilization from outside threat, the Great Wall. He also re-established the Shang dynasty's pyramidal social structure, the peasant masses at the base and the various succeeding levels of merchants, military, scholars and aristocracy reaching upward to the divine authority of one supreme ruler; and this structure not only stayed in place for many dynasties to come but was reaffirmed as recently as in the "reign" of Chairman Mao Zedong.

THE AGE OF THE HAN

After the brief 11-year reign of Qinshihuangdi the first of these great dynasties arose, the Han. During its epic 400-year rule it strengthened the political and social pillars that Emperor Qinshihuangdi had set in place, and so much so that its name has since been synonymous with membership of the Chinese race, the vast bulk of the society referred to as "Han Chinese." It also codified the teachings of a very learned, if ultra-conservative, scholar of a previous age, Confucius (551–487 BC), to provide this society with a set of ethics and responsibilities by which all the different classes of people knew and appreciated their place.

The Han reign is remarkable, though, for its main preoccupation, protecting Chinese unity and civilization. While military expeditions were sent to the south to try to conquer resistant tribal groups and bring them into the Han "family," armies

were also marched north to the harsh deserts of the northwest frontier, beyond the reach of Qinshihuangdi's then-primitive Great Wall, to try to contain and crush the civilization's main enemies, the Xiongnu, or Huns, a fierce confederation of nomadic slave-trading tribes of Central Asia.

One campaign after another was waged against these northern "barbarians," the modern-day descendants of whom can be seen among the strangely alien Turkic-speaking minorities of northern Gansu province and the cities of Hami, Turpan, Urumqi and Kashi (Kashgar) in the Uygur-Xinjiang Autonomous Region. Under Han rule the die of the Chinese imperative was cast – it pitted membership of a select and civilized society against the barbarism that rode the wilds without; and so vital was this imperative that the cost of constant warfare with the Xiongnu eventually exhausted the dynasty and, in the second century AD, brought it to its knees.

ABOVE the legacy of Qinshihuangdi, the ruthless "father" of Chinese unity, his terra-cotta army stands vigil near Xi'an.

Blind Man's Buff

But not before another imperative had been introduced to the Chinese experience – the cultural imperative. The wars against the Xiongnu were waged not only to keep the Han nation intact but also to keep open and free of Xiongnu harassment the society's main link with the outside world – or rather, its link with mysterious lands that lay somewhere far beyond the barbarian domains.

This rather tenuous thread was the fabled Silk Road, the long and often perilous overland trading route that began near what is now the port of Tyre in Lebanon and snaked across northern Persia and Afghanistan, northern India and part of the rugged territory now known as Soviet Central Asia, and entered China at a point near Kashi on the western border of present-day Uygur-Xinjiang. From there the trail split into two to skirt the Taklimakan Desert and Turpan Basin, passed close to Dunhuang and then through the fortified trading city of Yumen Guan (Jade Gate) and continued southeast through Lanzhou to terminate at Xi'an.

With middlemen handling the business in between, two great civilizations, the Roman and the Chinese, traded with each other via the Silk Road like blind men exchanging gifts, each never really setting eyes on the other. Huge camel trains carried Chinese silks, pottery and medicines along the Silk Road to the west, and back the other way came exotic animals and birds, plants, precious metals, precious stones, and products and artifacts of the Roman Empire. And along with them, around the year AD 65, came an invading force that no Great Wall or mighty army could possibly hope to stop – Buddhism, destined to flourish alongside Confucianism and another already established Chinese belief, Daoism, as one of the Three Teachings of Chinese society.

So while the Han dynasty kept faith with the essential conventions of Chinese society – unity, protection of the civilization and the pyramidal social order – it introduced another convention which has dictated Chinese action and attitude ever since. Down through the centuries the Chinese response to foreign ideas or influence has tended to be an alternating pattern of acceptance or invitation followed in many cases by abrupt and even violent rejection when that influence has been deemed troublesome enough to threaten the three pillars of unity, civilization and social order. And this "open closing door" syndrome explains a great deal about the Chinese society that we are dealing with today.

Though Buddhism itself later had its own share of suppression and rejection, it was certainly invited into China in the Han reign. It is said that in AD 64 the Han emperor Ming had a dream in which a golden Buddha materialized before him. He saw this as a spiritual message and sent two emissaries to India to learn more about the religion. Two Indian monks were also invited to visit China, and they traveled in along the Silk Road bringing volumes of sutras, or religious texts, packed on white horses.

The emperor ordered the construction of the White Horse Monastery to commemorate the event, and you can stand and ponder the significance of Buddhism in China at this, the country's oldest Buddhist institution, set into a soaring hillside 13 km (8 miles) north of Luoyang, which at one point became the Han capital.

CHAOS AND THE CANAL

With the collapse of the Han dynasty in the year 220, the pillars of Chinese sovereignty tumbled with it. Confusion and warfare reigned as various triumphant northern tribes fought to take advantage of the power vacuum, and for more than 270 years, from 304 to 580, no fewer than 20 dynasties rose and fell. Most of them were non-Chinese, headed or manipulated by the Xiongnu, the Tibetans and other "barbarian" groups from beyond the northern and western frontiers.

Foreign influence, in the form of Buddhism, rushed to fill the void too, and during the most successful dynasty of that time, headed by the Toba, a nomadic cattle-raising tribe, it was adopted as the official religion and the emperor was declared the reincarnation of Buddha himself.

The Toba court was based first in Datong, slightly northwest of what is now Beijing and close to the present Inner Mongolia border, and later Luoyang, and today we can thank this "barbarian" dynasty and its religious fervor for its three most magnificent artistic contributions to Chinese culture – the huge Buddhist grottoes and their many carved images at Magao near Dunhuang in Uygur-Xinjiang, Yunyang near Datong and Longmen on the banks of the Yi River, 16 km (10 miles) south of Luoyang.

Significantly, it was the continuing barbarian threat from the north that enabled the Han Chinese to regain power for themselves. In the face of attacks by Turkic tribes in the northwest the Chinese and their Toba masters joined forces to defend

the state, and the Chinese were able to take advantage of the pact to eventually drive the weakening Toba dynasty from the throne.

A new Chinese dynasty, the Sui, grasped the reins of power, and although it was very short-lived, lasting only 37 years from 581 to 618, it quickly rebuilt the pillars of Chinese civilization and sovereignty. Unity was restored and even strengthened, the Sui rulers conquering the south and bringing it under Han control and starting work on the single most unifying link between the southern and northern provinces, the Grand Canal.

It's estimated that close to five million peasant laborers were put to work on the canal, which eventually connected four great river systems – the Yangtze, Huang (Yellow), Huai and Qiantang – and made it possible to ship merchandise, men and military supplies from Hangzhou to the Sui court in Luoyang and then north to Xi'an. Extended even further in later reigns, the canal has since been celebrated as the longest man-made waterway on earth, and its importance to Chinese society can be appreciated even today as you stand on the bridges of Suzhou and Wuxi, the most colorful canal cities, and watch flat-hulled cargo boats and long convoys of tethered, loaded barges ply their way along waterways teeming with launches, tugs, sampans and other small vessels.

While the Sui dynasty strengthened and reinvigorated the Han Chinese society it also poured more conscripted labor and costly materials into new work on the Great Wall to keep the society intact. And this protection of the civilization again became the paramount task of the dynastic order that swept the Sui from power in the year 618 and ushered in the "golden age" of the Tang.

ABOVE Terra-cotta altar and joss TOP LEFT at Bamboo Monastery near Kunming. Peeping guardian image TOP RIGHT at Guiyan Temple, Wuhan.

THE GOLDEN TANG

The Tang dynasty (616–907) is noted for its grand cultural contribution to Chinese history. Under its auspices the arts flourished, poetry and literature reached celebrated levels of sophistication and the

all direct contact with the mysterious lands of the West, this time by the rise of Islam in the Middle East. But this was still an era of greatly expanded trade via the Silk Road and by sea, and the "open door" also allowed a growing stream of foreign influences to seep into the society – Nestorian Christianity from Syria and Persia; Manichaeism, also from Persia and driven east by Christian persecutors; Hinduism from India; Zoroastrians and even Jews, along with foreign merchants, mainly Moslem, whose Silk Road caravans were the vehicle of this new cultural invasion.

Buddhism also continued to spread throughout the society and in fact reached its artistic zenith during the early Tang years. Huge monasteries, temples and stupas sprang up along the Silk Road and elsewhere, extravagant Buddhist festivals took their place in the Chinese peasantry's calendar of largely agricultural events and observances. Buddhism and the native "Chinese" Daoism – an older religious philosophy, with many deities, based on the relationship between man and nature – began a kind of cultural exchange in which the gods of one became the incarnates of the other. The Tang emperors themselves added their imperial splendor to the Buddhist grottoes at Dunhuang, Luoyang and Datong, commissioning the taller and more magnificent Buddha statues that make these cliff galleries and caves the tourist draw-card that they are today. The magnificent Grand Buddha of Leshan is another legacy of the Tang reign, along with the dramatic hillside sculptures of Dazu in Sichuan province.

At the same time the Tang rulers had the continuing barbarian threat in the north to contend with. Large military campaigns were fought not only against the persistent Turks of the northwest but the Tibetans to the west too. And then there were increasingly dangerous challenges by the "Golden Horde" Tartars, or Khitans, who rode

development of porcelain, to name but one innovation of that era, thrust the technology of China well ahead of anything else in the world.

But the Tang reign is also significant for the constant dilemma that it faced as regards the world beyond its borders. As in the age of Han rule, it was cut off from

ABOVE Cargo barges snake along in convoy on Suzhou canal.

the same arid steppes and desert basins as the Turkic tribes.

Tang armies were posted on permanent patrol of the frontier regions, operating from fortified garrisons, and at one point they managed to rout the Turkic warriors and bring what is now the Xinjiang autonomous region under Chinese control. In China today you can see all around you one of the most common symbols of the Tang dynasty's frontier wars – ceramic, bronze and iron "Tang horses" which have been popular works of art for centuries. These powerful "heavenly" war-horses

from the wilds of Central Asia were obtained by force of arms in the Han dynasty's punitive expeditions to replace the smaller, weaker steeds that the Chinese cavalries rode up until that time. They proved so successful that Han and Tang sculptors and artists immortalized them, and today some of the original sculptures and block prints can be found in the major museums of China – notably the **Shaanxi Provincial Museum** in Xi'an – and the

ABOVE Patched and battened mainsail powers sampan on the Grand Canal at Suzhou.

National Palace Museum in Taiwan. Elsewhere, cheap mass-produced souvenir copies pack the shelves of the Friendship Stores and arts and crafts centers.

But the constant struggle against the barbarians led to a great deal of damaging intrigue and power-play within the Tang hierarchy, weakening the dynasty. At the same time its authority came under growing challenge and pressure from Buddhism and other influences that had traveled with it down the Silk Road. The three pillars of the Chinese civilization began to shake again, and in 845 the Tang emperor of the day launched a violent reprisal to put things right.

"In the cities, in the mountains, there are nothing but (Buddhist) priests of both sexes," his imperial edict raged. "The number of monasteries grows daily... . A great deal of gold is wasted on embellishing them. People forget their traditional rulers in order to serve under a master priest... . Could anything more pernicious be imagined?"

The "Open Closing Door"

In the ensuing crackdown all foreign religions were banned from China and foreigners were barred from all ports. And in the case of Buddhism, more than 4,500 monasteries were destroyed, a quarter of a million monks and priests thrown back out into open society. Confucianism was restored as the omnipotent national belief. Although trade was allowed to continue along the Silk Road, the Chinese door was firmly closed for some time on all cultural influence from the West, and the pattern of the "open closing dooor" came into being.

Inevitably, the Tang dynasty collapsed into chaos, uprising and constant power struggles that saw no fewer than five northern "dynasties" and 10 southern kingdoms rise and fall between the years 906 and 960. China's social pillars swayed and crumbled, and the power and prosperity of the Silk Road disintegrated with them, beginning an era in which China was almost completely isolated from everything beyond its western borders.

The collapse continued even with the rise to power of another great dynasty, the Song (960–1260). Although the Song rulers fought to buttress the main conventions of the society – the Confucian ethics of natural order and hierarchy were rigidly imposed, for instance, to shore up the society's pyramidal authority – they had considerably less success with the defense of the Han realm. The Khitans finally broke through in the north to establish their own Liao dynasty based at Shenyang, only to be supplanted in turn by another barbarian power, the Jurchens. And an alliance of Turks and Tibetans established another dynastic power-base in the northwest – with the result that the Song dynasty was actually driven south where, for 150 years, it ruled from Hangzhou.

Nonetheless, the Song era is remembered as another great cultural landmark in Chinese history. It was an age of refinement that added new luster to the arts with its particular developments in landscape painting, and it introduced the willowy green-glazed celadon ware to the growing showcase of Chinese ceramic techniques. It was also the age of the poet, one in which these romantic men and women of letters were elevated to the rank of social heroes – and none more so than the renowned Su Shih, better known as Su Dongpo, the product of a talented literary family who was also governor of Hangzhou for two years before it became the Southern Song capital.

You can see impressive statues of Su Dongpo and his father and brother, and study their literary works and stele rubbings of their calligraphy, at the **Temple of the Three Sus** built on the site of their family home at Meishan, 90 km (56 miles) southwest of Chengdu.

THE WRATH OF KHAN

However, preoccupied as it was with the arts and civilized living, and confined

within the southern-central region of China, the Song dynasty was in no shape or position to defend the territory or the integrity of the civilization when, around the year 1206, it faced the most terrible barbarian challenge of all time. In that year a huge confederation of nomadic tribes gathered in the wilderness beyond the northern frontiers and, under the banner of the ruthless warlord whose name has since been a by-word for horrific violence and pillage, Genghis Khan's Mongol hordes thundered down through the boundless grasslands to put China to the sword.

The swift and brutal Mongol cavalries made short work of the Tibetan-Turkic stronghold to the west, and within a short time were ready to crush the Jin dynasty of the Jurchens ruling northern China from present-day Beijing. Only one thing stopped, or rather delayed them, the Great Wall, and it actually took Genghis Khan two years of procrastination beyond the immense barrier to arrive at the conclusion that it could be breached only by massive human-wave attack. He finally hurled the bulk of his armies at it, and despite a courageous stand by its Jin defenders and savage battles that left thousands dead on both sides, his warriors finally smashed their way through and descended upon Beijing in a flood-tide of murder and rapine.

When, after a short siege, the Mongols poured into the Jin capital, they went on an horrific month-long rampage in which almost the entire population was put to death and the city sacked of all its treasures. Then it was razed to the ground. And from there, the Mongols turned their attention to the Song dynastic stronghold to the south.

At this, the most perilous point in Chinese history, it seemed as though the civilization faced complete destruction. The three pillars upon which it stood – unity, protection and social order – lay in ruins. And above the smoke and carnage stood a half-savage bandit chief whose lustful, simplistic outlook on life had been expressed in these bleak terms:

"The greatest joy is to conquer one's enemies, to pursue them, to seize their property, to see their families in tears, to ride their horses, and to possess their daughters and wives."

KHAN THE BUILDER

But then a kind of miracle happened. With the initial conquest achieved, it was left to Genghis Khan's grandson, Kublai, to rule northern China and defeat and subjugate the Southern Song. Kublai Khan happened to have intelligence and a certain vision – he saw himself as the supreme ruler of a vast Eurasian empire, and for that he needed the help of experienced administrators; and, obviously, the only skilled people capable of administering China were the Chinese themselves. So, at the very brink of ruin, the Chinese bureaucracy reassembled and thus survived, and the Chinese civilization set about civilizing its conqueror.

In 1271 Kublai Khan proclaimed himself emperor of China and established a new dynasty, the Yuan. Eight years later he completed the conquest of virtually the entire country and immediately began doing what no nomadic brigand had ever done before – he began to build. First he constructed an entirely new imperial capital from the ruins of the Jin court, now Beijing. From the ashes of mass pillage a new imperial tradition emerged, an empire greater than anything the Chinese had ever seen. And when the intrepid Venetian business explorer, Marco Polo, journeyed along the route of the Silk Road to spend some 20 years in the court of the Great Khan, arriving in the year of Kublai's ascension to the imperial throne, the Chinese civilization was reaching toward the zenith of its power and prestige.

Its pyramidal structure had been restored, the society ascending class upon class to the absolute rule of the Great Khan, the new Son of Heaven. It was well protected, forming the lavish centerpiece of the vast Mongol empire and nothing less

in Chinese eyes than the very "center of the universe." It was also technologically about 900 years ahead of the Western world, as Marco Polo himself recorded, marveling over such inventions as gunpowder, paper, printing, canal lock-gates, the compass and the great four-masted sailing junks that carried him home in 1292.

The Chinese civilization had survived by absorbing and civilizing its conquerors, and after the death of Kublai Khan this process of absorption continued through the reigns of eight succeeding Mongol emperors. It was aided by the fact that, after the Great Khan, the Yuan leadership became inept, the settled Mongol armies became flaccid, the taste for lavish living of the succeeding Sons of Heaven forced increasingly heavy tax burdens on to the peasantry, with traditional consequences.

THE GLORY OF THE MING

With the Mongol authority weakening and the peasantry reaching breaking point, the Chinese rose up in open revolt in 1352 and within four years had wrested back the reins of power and sovereignty, establishing the glorious Ming dynasty. The dissipated remnants of the great Mongol empire were driven back into the wilds beyond China's northern frontier.

Chinese ethnic unity was restored, along with the two other essential social pillars; and, to make sure that they could never be shaken or toppled again, one of the first major tasks that the Ming dynasty undertook was a massive, complete restructuring and strengthening of the Great Wall – a project that took many millions of laborers no less than a whole century to complete.

The strengthening of the Great Wall was more than just a move to keep the retreating Mongols and other barbarians out, it was symbolic of the overriding Ming attitude to the rest of the world. While this era is noted as an age of Chinese exploration, with the eunuch admiral

Zheng He leading large oceanic expeditions to Arabia and Africa, it was also a time in which China again shut the door on contact with the West. The nation's vision of itself as the Middle Kingdom, the center of all things, became more entrenched. The lands beyond Admiral He's junks had nothing that China needed or did not already possess.

The Silk Road, already in decline since its heyday during the Tang dynasty, was completely abandoned, and by the fifteenth century Islam had replaced Buddhism as the driving spiritual force along the old silk routes as far east as the Taklimakan region of Xinjiang, brought there by Arab imperial ventures in the wake of the Mongol collapse. And Islam is as strong as ever in China's northwestern region today, with large Moslem minorities living side-by-side with Han Chinese in an area ranging north from Xi'an and Lanzhou through the Ningxia autonomous province to the Inner Mongolia border and west as far as the boundary of Uygur-Xinjiang.

Behind the Wall

With the rest of the world shut out, the Chinese set about virtually reconstructing their nation during the Ming reign. Beijing, destroyed by Ming forces in the struggle to unseat the last Mongol ruler, was completely rebuilt and firmly established, for its strategic position guarding the north, as the nerve-center of Chinese rule; and much of its present-day historic splendor, such as the Forbidden City and Temple of Heaven, is a legacy of the Ming architects and builders.

The Great Wall was transformed into the monolithic heavily defensive structure which can be viewed today at places like Badaling, 75 km (46 miles) north of Beijing, and at Shanhaiguan at its eastern extremity, overlooking the Bo Sea. Ming engineers built double walls of massive stone blocks and filled the interior with packed earth and rock to form what is, in effect, an elevated roadway with defensive

turrets on either side, along which troops and supplies could be rushed in event of an enemy threat. Some 25,000 fortified watchtowers and garrison towers were built along the huge barrier, linked by a communications system of fires, flags, drums and rockets. The Ming Tombs, another of today's cultural drawcards dotting the plain of Shisanling, 50 km (31 miles) northwest of Beijing, testify to the living power and posthumous glory of the Ming emperors.

In many respects the Ming dynasty recalled the "golden age" of the Tang

reign. It was an era of prosperity, and of population growth, both of which provided a fertile seed-bed for new advances in the arts. Porcelain and ceramics reached their highest level of craftsmanship and creativity; intricate cloisonné, which can be seen in a myriad latter-day forms all over China today, became a celebrated art-form; novelists replaced poets as the society's literary lions. But in the midst of all this social fattening and refinement the Ming court began rotting at the core – and the Forbidden City bears testament to the failure of the dynasty.

While it represents the grandeur of the Ming reign it also symbolizes the hollowness of Ming authority. Within its heavily

ABOVE Decorated doorway opens on to courtyards and palace quarters and the distant vista of Coal Hill in the Forbidden City, Beijing.

guarded walls and courts, beyond which the common people ventured only at pain of immediate death, the later Ming emperors became corrupt pleasure-seeking imperial recluses, isolated completely from the society. Their power was usurped by conniving court eunuchs who virtually ruled the nation behind their backs and amassed huge personal fortunes at the expense of the people. Once again, the three social pillars began to sway.

The moral and political bankruptcy of the waning Ming dynasty was compounded by a famine which spread through the far northern provinces, triggering peasant uprisings. It was ultimately bankrupted altogether by ruthless betrayal – its eunuch overlords treacherously opening the gates of power to a rebel army backed and manipulated by a new invading force from beyond the Great Wall, the Manchus. The glorious age of the Ming finally ended in 1644 in one awful night of madness and murder: the last Ming

emperor, besieged by rebel forces, hacked his closest family to death and then hanged himself on Coal Hill (Jin Shan), an artificial mound built by his more illustrious predecessors from the earth excavated from the moat around the Forbidden City.

ABOVE Wide moat and watchtowers made the Forbidden City both sanctuary and virtual prison of the emperors. Old Silk Road gateway RIGHT near the the Great Wall.

THE LAST DYNASTY

The Manchu Qing dynasty, formed from an alliance of tribes with no real cultural distinction to the north and northeast of the Great Wall, was the last to rule China. Although it remained in power from 1644 to 1911 it presided over the total disintegration of the three vital pillars of society – unity, protection of the civilization and strict pyramidal authority – and when it finally sank into oblivion it left China in the throes of something which, for all its turmoil and upheaval over so many centuriess, it had never experienced before: revolution.

As with the preceding Ming, the early Qing emperors were vigorous builders, and many of China's monasteries, temples and cultural monuments owe their survival to renovations and expansion carried out during their reigns.

These early rulers also wielded enough personal authority to keep the social pyramid intact, and this gave China a new period of stability and prosperity. It also caused another big upswing in the population, but this time the country's food production didn't keep pace with it, so famine and unrest broke out again. But more significantly, China had not kept pace with the rising scientific and technological power of the Western world. Confronted with this power, the later Manchu rulers retreated into hidebound conservatism, clinging to an illusion of Chinese cultural supremacy, and in doing this they slammed the China door shut again behind them. And it was this retreat that destroyed the 4,500-year-old dynastic order.

The Western Challenge

To be fair, the Manchu had inherited a society that the Ming dynasty had already allowed to slip far behind the technological development of the West. Whereas Chinese invention and science had been nearly a thousand years ahead of the West during the Yuan dynasty, by the time of the Manchu rule they were obsolete and virtually helpless in the face of modern Western naval firepower and general maritime strength, military weaponry and the corresponding fierce drive for trade and colonial expansion by the major European powers.

But instead of modernizing to meet the threat, the Manchu response was the imperious dismissal of all that it could have gained from the West; and nothing sums up the Qing dynasty's insular attitude more bluntly than the imperial reply to Britain's demand for a free two-way exchange of trade. "I set no value on strange or ingenious objects," the emperor informed Great Britain's King George III, "and have no use for your country's manufactures."

It was probably the most fateful declaration that any Chinese ruler had ever made, for it set into motion a trade struggle, followed by open armed conflict, that ultimately tore the Chinese sovereignty apart.

The British, following on the heels of the Portuguese and Dutch, had actually been trading with China for years, but their traders were strictly confined to segregated enclaves in Guangzhou (Canton) and Macau. And the trade itself was very much a one-way deal – the British could buy all the teas and silks they wanted but could not interest the Chinese in anything worthwhile in return. The British were forced to pay for all their tea, in particular, with silver bullion, and they bought so much of the stuff – trying to keep pace with a growing national craving for it back home – that at one point the nation's silver reserves sank so low that the Exchequer was almost bankrupted. To try to wrest some of the bullion back, they cast about for anything they could find that would provoke a similar fierce demand in China. And they found the ideal commodity – opium from Bengal.

The Opium Wars

The struggle that followed the wholesale introduction of opium to China can be described in modern-day hindsight as one of the most sordid of history's episodes – two giant addicts standing toe-to-toe with drawn guns. In 1839, when opium smuggling and addiction had reached the point of crisis in China, the Qing administration blockaded the Guangzhou trading depot, confiscated the British traders' opium stocks and burnt it all in front of them. The British retaliated with naval attacks, and in a decisive battle off the southeast coast the advanced guns and rockets of an iron-hulled steam-paddle warship, the *Nemesis,* smashed and sank the Qing navy's main fleet of antique junks. And the pillars of society went down with them.

From that point on, China was at the mercy of the Europeans and the one rival Asian power which was modernizing rapidly to meet the Western challenge, Japan. China became the victim of its own imperial arrogance, ruthless Western expansion and what seems today to be one of history's most bitter ironies – the spectacular Great Wall, costing many thousands of lives to build, standing in permanent vigil against the threat from the north, while the most perilous threat of all came from the south, from the seas and from the "round-eyes" of distant Europe.

In the ensuing Opium Wars, Britain grabbed Hong Kong as a colonial trading post and forced open the China door, establishing Treaty Ports such as Shanghai, Hankou, Amoy (Xiamen) and Nanjing. And from that point on the Europeans, Russians and Japanese rushed to carve the country up into commercial "spheres of interest." In 1870 Japan took Taiwan, then annexed Korea and then, in 1895, secured parts of southern Manchuria. Much of the rest of Manchuria was acquired by Russia as a concession four years later. In 1905 the Japanese defeated the Russians in an historic naval battle, grabbed the Russian Manchurian concession as booty and began what was to become a progressive and bloody campaign to subjugate and colonize all of China. In the south, the French acquired the Indo-China Peninsula – Vietnam, Laos and Cambodia. In the east, the Germans forced their way into Shandong province, establishing Qingdao (Tsingtao) as their own Treaty Port.

The Iron Empress

Apologists for this era of foreign intervention in China often point to the fact that the occupying powers did, after all, build China's first modern infrastructure – factories, roads, railways, telegraph systems. Those who condemn it point to the sole reason why that infrastructure was laid down – to extract the resources that the Europeans were after and distribute the export products from their own countries that they wanted the Chinese to buy.

Whatever, the general picture of that time is certainly not of a backward nation enjoying the white man's benefits. There were dreadful famines and just as dreadful uprisings – including the violent Taiping and Boxer Rebellions, both of them ruthlessly crushed – against the alien rule and the impotence of the Manchu, against corruption, against injustice and against the Western presence.

When it finally became clear that only modernization, by the Chinese for the Chinese, could enable them to resist and possibly drive out the Europeans, another of the bitter ironies of Chinese history came to pass. The stubborn and scheming Empress Dowager Ci Xi, the last effective imperial ruler of China, turned around and fought to restore and strengthen the traditional pillars of autocracy and conservatism that had ruled Chinese society for 4,000 years before her. In doing so she quashed all attempts around her to reform and modernize society and its armed forces – even imprisoning her heir-apparent, Cuongxu, when he came of age and ascended to the throne, for suggesting change.

Her last-ditch stand on behalf of the China of her imperial ancestors was not only imprudent but also all in vain. In the south of China particularly, contact with the foreign communities and the growing practice of many "modern" Chinese families of sending their sons and daughters to study in Britain and Europe had led to an upsurge of modern ideas. The seeds of revolution began sprouting, nurtured and closely watched from exile in Japan and elsewhere by a fervent young reformist from Guangdong province, Sun Yatsen.

As the battle lines of conservatism and reform hardened, so China approached the second most crucial crossroads of its long history. But to give the Empress Ci Xi her due, she held out to the end – even arranging the murder of her politically "wet" emperor son just before she died in 1908.

Of all the evidence that remains of the empress dowager's bizarre but decisive reign, nothing alludes more to its style and character than the extravagant **Summer Palace** she built herself in 1888 about 12 km (7.5 miles) north of Beijing. It cost a fortune, about 24 million taels (42.3 million ounces) of silver – and she appropriated the money from funds set up to modernize the Chinese navy.

The Republican Failure

When the empress dowager died the dynastic tradition died with her. She left another emperor on the throne, (Henry) Pu Yi, but he was eminently unqualified for the job – he was only two years old. A constitutional government, already established in the Iron Empress's fading years, moved swiftly to take the full reins of power. In 1910 China's first National Assembly was held, and a year later Sun Yatsen returned from exile to become president of a provisional government based in Nanjing, where the **Sun Yatsen Tomb** is now one of the main tourist landmarks. For the first time in nearly 5,000 years, China was having its first taste of democracy. And, largely for this reason, the Chinese Republic, the first of the nation's two great modern-day revolutions, was destined from the very beginning to fail.

From today's vantage point it is little wonder that a society structured for such a vast length of time on such a strict autocratic pyramidal rule, and faithful for most of that time to the social order laid down by Confucianism, should find the principles of democracy alien and un-workable. As it was, the period from 1911 right up until the 1930s was one of social and political chaos, with regional warlords vying for power, Sun Yatsen unable to build enough personal authority to institute effective nationall rule, the government in Beijing too weak to run the country properly and the Japanese and the European powers playing one rival faction off against the other to promote their own interests.

Again, there were devastating famines in the north, peasant revolts, trade union strikes and demonstrations that were dealt with violently by the authorities. And out of all this turmoil there emerged the rival, bitterly competing political movements that were to decide the future structure and course of the Chinese society – the Nationalists led by Chiang Kaishek and the Communists under a revolutionary leadership that was eventually dominated by Mao Zedong.

The Revolutionary Struggle

Backed by the European "allies" and the United States, Chiang Kaishek attempted to secure the mandate of the old emperors by establishing himself as the head of a fascist-style military dictatorship. Hardly a government, it nonetheless held power for 20 years, during which time Chiang concentrated his main energies on a campaign to purge the communists from society. He was so obsessed with this that his forces virtually stood by and allowed Japan to expand its occupation of the north.

By 1935 The Japanese had virtually colonized Manchuria and set up the puppet state of Manzhouguo (Manchukuo) with the ousted Qing emperor, Henry Pu Yi, as its king. They had also occupied Hebei province and Inner Mongolia. Two years later, Japanese planes, tanks and infantry smashed their way down through the heart of China, occupying the country as far south as Guangzhou and forcing Chiang Kaishek and his nationalists to retreat to a western enclave in Chongqing.

The communists stayed in the hills and behind the Japanese lines in Shandong province and the northeast, and from there they conducted guerrilla warfare against the occupation army – aided by the local peasant population – that not only helped defeat the Japanese but also shaped the character and outcome of the communist struggle for power after World War II had ended.

To understand the immediate post-war cataclysm in China, it has to be simplified and placed again within the context of the three traditional pillars of Chinese society. In the choice of leadership that the Chinese had before them, there was Chiang Kaishek on the one hand, supported by foreign interests, a proven failure in the defense of the civilization and realm, and self-proclaimed ruler of a pyramid that had most of its essential lower masses looking elsewhere for leadership. On the other hand there were Mao Zedong's communists, comparative heroes for their guerrilla struggle against the Japanese, definitely not bankrolled nor bolstered by foreign governments (not even the Soviet Union at that stage), and, as a result of Maoist political policy and the grassroots nature of their guerrilla operations, intimately linked with the vast bulk of the peasant masses and workers without whose support the abiding structure of Chinese society could not be complete.

The outcome was inevitable: full civil war in which the communist forces drove the nationalist hierarchy further and further south, followed by the communist victory in which Chiang Kaishek and his diehard followers fled to exile in Taiwan, followed in 1949 by the founding of the revolutionary People's Republic of China.

The Three Maoist Pillars
Much has been written about the tumultuous and yet largely misinterpreted 30 years of Maoist communism in China, and much of it has come from over-idealistic observers of the left or hysterical anti-communists of the right. Only an occasional incisive study and coldly objective pen has attempted to place the emotionally charged events and implications of the revolutionary era against the far broader background of Chinese history. Only then have the three pillars of that history been applied to the Maoist experience, and only then has it been considered not so much how Chairman Mao changed the society but what he restored to it.

Mao Zedong restored the traditional ruling principles of the dynastic past to the new Chinese society. And these principles were essential if he was to successfully harness it to the painfully burdensome plow of recovery and reconstruction. He restored unity and national self-respect after many decades of chaos and humiliation. He restored the full vitality of protection and defense, and in ways that may have seemed bewildering to outsiders but were quite demonstrably satisfying to the Chinese.

Foreign presence and influence was removed entirely from Chinese soil. It was also swiftly countered whenever and wherever it threatened – the Chinese response to the American-backed United Nations intervention in neighboring Korea in 1950, and India's military border incursion in 1962, being good examples. Even in its close but short-lived 12-year cultural and technical pact with the Soviet Union, the Maoist government kept faith with the dynastic tradition. When Moscow's influence was seen as a threat (its insistence, for one thing, that revolutionary socialism should be achieved through the industrial proletariat, not Mao's peasant masses), the bond was severed, the Soviets charged with revisionism and their technicians and advisors sent packing. And with that, the Chinese effectively shut the door once again on the outside world.

The basic character of Mao's society was a straight copy of that of imperial times. The pyramid was rearranged and restored, the various classes of Chinese society reaching upward once again from the vast, shifting peasant seas to the authoritative hand of the Great Helmsman. And Mao's authority and popularity rivaled that of the emperors, not by unquestioned divine rule but by the constantly promoted "cult of the personality" that made him, nonetheless, a living god.

Maos's political base amongst the peasantry and his lifelong promotion of the peasant class came not just from his own modest rural beginnings but from an understanding of the lesson that all emperors before him had been forced to learn and heed. "The prince is the boat, the common people are the water," an old Chinese proverb had cautioned them. "The water can support the boat, or it can capsize it."

Mao's policy of industrial and agricultural self-sufficiency, manifested in the controversial Great Leap Forward and its collapse in 1962, echoed the attitudes of the Ming, Yuan and latter Qing rulers toward foreign "manufactures." Mao even resurrected and harnessed the tradition of the mass campaign, only now the huge work brigades dug mammoth canals and constructed hydro-electric dams and power stations instead of imperial palaces, Great Walls and elaborate tombs.

The Red Guards

Mao's most fateful mass campaign, the violent Cultural Revolution beginning in 1966, was launched against the growing power of moderates within the hierarchy whose ideas deviated in one crucial respect from the Maoist dream – they believed, and probably quite rightly so, that China could not modernize and develop behind closed doors, by its own sweat alone. It is tempting, as unlikely as it may seem, to recall the waning days of the Qing dynasty in the subsequent rampage by Mao's Red Guards and the events that took place next – the crackdown on "bourgeois

revisionist" elements who were apparently willing to risk the sovereignty and integrity of China once again with "foreign" modernization and reform.

So fierce was the struggle between the Maoist and "revisionist" factions that the Cultural Revolution almost became an outright cultural civil war, and eventually the Red Guards had to be forcibly reined and disbanded to prevent the conflict tearing the society completely apart. But for more than a decade the struggle continued, with moderate leaders such as Zhou Enlai and Deng Xiaoping attempting to promote

Western-style modernization and Mao's opposing revolutionary line taken to the point of harsh and unacceptable social experiment by the so-called Gang of Four led by Mao's radical wife, the former actress Jiang Qing.

And it was during this long struggle that the clock of progress virtually stopped in China, and society at large, weary of all the in-fighting, suddenly faced the cold and disturbing reality of its position in

ABOVE Mao Zedong, now regarded as "70 percent right and 30 percent wrong."

the global society with the twenty-first century rapidly bearing down upon it: it was technically, scientifically and militarily backward, even with its nuclear and aerospace programs, at a time when the other great powers of the world, the United States, Japan and especially the Soviet Union, were already stepping into an age that was getting far beyond China's reach.

The Four Modernizations

When Mao Zedong died in September 1978, the moderates, now renamed "pragmatists," moved swiftly to prosecute and imprison the Gang of Four. In their place came the Four Modernizations, aimed at repairing and developing the country's infrastructure and sciences and boosting agriculture, industry, national defense and technology to the "front ranks of the world" by the year 2000. Deng Xiaoping emerged as the new Chinese leader, heading the campaign to steer China away from revolutionary socialism and into the economic fast lane of controlled free enterprise, expanded international trade and joint investment with foreign interests. In a moment that delighted the Western world, whatever it may have done to the die-hard socialists backhome, Deng even appeared at a rodeo on a tour of the United States wearing a Texan ten-gallon hat.

The Role of Tourism

Way back in 1978 when the China door first began to open slightly again to foreign visitors, the once-in-a-lifetime China travel experience was a train ride over the Lo Wu border bridge from Hong Kong and two days in and around Guangzhou.

The strictly organized tours included two nights in the huge Dong Fang Hotel and bus visits to the ceramics factories and Ancestral Temple at Foshan, a dried fruit processing commune, Zenhai Tower and the Cultural Park in Guangzhou and, of course, the Friendship Store; and they ended with a banquet and speeches in the renowned Baiyuen Restaurant. And after that you swaggered back across the border sporting your green Mao cap with a revolutionary red star and feeling quite intrepid and privileged, as though the Bamboo Curtain had been lifted an inch just for you.

In the years since Deng Xiaoping took over the helm, the door to China has been opened again – but strictly on Chinese terms. Foreign experts and businessmen – mainly competing Americans and Japanese, but with the Koreans and Taiwanese set to follow behind them – have flooded in to help and take advantage of the immense recovery program. Tourism has become a major industry, providing an immediate source of foreign currency to bankroll the reforms. From history's standpoint, there should be no illusion about tourism's role: we are being invited in to help put China into the twenty-first century.

Nowadays, going to China is like going anywhere else. You can enter the country through any one of eight major or strategically convenient cities, and you can go in by ship, plane, train, luxury bus, hydrofoil, jetfoil, on foot and even by bicycle. You can still pop in just for a couple of days, taking a quick look around Guangzhou, Guilin or Kunming for example, or you can choose a tour with a touch of adventure, nostalgia and romance by following the route of the Silk Road across Asia in the wake of the great camel trains of a thousand years ago. And feel quite safe from Xiongnu attack.

THE CULTURAL LEGACY

THE PERFECT OBSOLESCENCE

The craft and artistry of Chinese culture owes much of its inspiration to animist beliefs and Daoist nature worship that originated in the nation's distant past; and it can thank the divine power and patronage of the various imperial dynasties for the creative heights that it aspired to and achieved over the centuries.

As for the extent to which it has survived, virtually unchanged for almost 5,000 years, that can be marked down to a fairly rigid discipline that has ruled most artistic and technological creation in China from the mists of pre-history. It's a simple discipline, but one that both preserved and, ironically, led to the eventual downfall of the Chinese cultural tradition. In a nutshell, the principle was this: if an art or craft has been brought to perfection, leave it alone. Don't fiddle with it. This explains many mysteries about Chinese art and technology – why ancient architectural styles, especially those of temples and pavilions, have basically survived to this day; why most of the Chinese painting, embroidery, ceramics, sculpture, cloisonné, lacquerware and other artistic products offered in today's Friendship Stores are almost exact modern-day copies of those of the past. It explains why the key principle of traditional painting and calligraphy, for example, is an established and strict discipline of brushwork, hand-motion, colour, light and shade, composition and even mental control, the rule being to achieve excellence or even brilliance within a perfection dictated by the masters of the past – this discipline certainly discouraging experimentation for its own sake.

Perhaps the best illustration of this discipline, and its consequences, is the traditional Chinese sailing craft, the junk. Evolving first from bamboo and inflated-skin river rafts, the development of the junk raced centuries ahead of all nautical technology in the West. It incorporated the principles of the water-tight compartment, battened and easily maneuverable sails and the stern-post rudder and then undertook far-ranging expeditions and trading voyages throughout South-East Asia while Western man was still paddling about in shallow waters in goat-skin coracles.

As ocean-going craft, huge four-masted junks struck out across the vast Indian Ocean on several great expeditions under the flag of the Ming dynasty nautical hero, Admiral Zheng He, reaching the coast of East Africa and, as some historians have claimed perhaps even rounding the Cape of Good Hope. At that time, Western vessels had barely reached the stage where they could confidently venture beyond the sight of land.

Yet while the junk was developed in myriad forms to suit various tasks and conditions on China's lakes, rivers and

coastal waters, its basic principles, once considered perfected, were deemed to be just that – perfect. No further improvement or experimentation was really attempted. And, by the eighteenth and nineteenth centuries, when Western nautical technology had now far outstripped that of the Chinese, the "perfect" junk – rendered even more obsolete by the conservatism of the latter stage of the Manchu Qing dynasty – sailed bravely into the guns and Congreve rockets of the British

ABOVE Deng Xiaoping, once reviled and purged by the Maoists, now China's new helmsman.

iron-clad, paddle-powered warship, the *Nemesis,* and was literally blown out of the water.

What's left of the junk, the tattered sailing barges and fishing boats occasionally sighted on China's major lakes, on some of the rivers and in the fishing grounds off the coast, is a virtual replica, even today, of the craft that ruled the waves a thousand or more years ago. It is also a testament to the fundamental gulf between Chinese and Western cultures – discipline and tradition on the one hand, a constant drive for improvement and its inherent

"planned obsolescence" on the other; and it is a cultural difference that must be considered in any study of the art of the matter in China.

THE ARTISTIC EXPLOSION

Chinese arts, both "art for art's sake" and the applied variety, are said to date back as distantly as around 4500 BC, during the

ABOVE one of above 50,000 Buddha images in the 53 Yungang Grottoes west of Datong, Shanxi province. OPPOSITE Performer dons vibrant make-up and costume for traditional opera in Beijing.

reign of Huangdi, the Yellow Emperor, one of the three mythical fathers of Chinese civilization. It's said that sericulture, or silk-making, originated during his reign, his empress teaching others how to spin it from the silkworm cocoons and weave it into the elegant, diaphanous, fiercely strong material that has ruled fashion tastes all over the globe ever since.

Silk not only fostered a vast and innovative range of fashion and intricate embroidery over the ensuing centuries, it also formed the backdrop to the distinctive and variously acclaimed tradition of Chinese painting. Most early painting was done on silk and, as with many Chinese creative pursuits, what began as a technical expedient was later elevated into the realm of pure art.

During the time of that distant "Camelot" of Chinese history, the first written script was developed, with agricultural records, herbal medicine remedies and spiritual prophesies inscribed on tortoise shell, bones and bamboo strips. A quantum leap took place around 106 with the invention of paper, and from that point on the Chinese visual arts branched into the celebrated tradition of calligraphy – a combination of literature and art. Brushes of pig-bristle and inks of soot and glue were developed. A discipline evolved that ruled the hand, the eye and, indeed, the state of mind that existed, or should exist, for each stroke of the brush. Different calligraphic styles were perfected, some of them branching again into carved stone tablets, or steles, others joining the illustrative arts in the ensuing crucial development of engraving and woodblock printing.

Pottery and decorative firing techniques appeared in Chinese arts and crafts as early as the Neolithic period, but during the Shang dynasty (2100–1600 BC) bronze was discovered and yet another crucial artistic leap forward occurred. Stylized cast bronze tings, or cooking cauldrons, were among the first applications of this new art form, excellent examples of which can be seen in museums all over China.

In architecture, squat mud-brick huts of the Neolithic period gave way to increasingly palatial columned, glazed-roofed buildings and pavilions as the dynastic tradition set in with the reign of the Shang rulers. Almost all early Chinese construction was of wood, and the constant risk and ravages of fire have naturally wiped out almost all trace of ancient architectural styles. However, because of the abiding philosophy of the "perfect obsolescence" – the preservation of a design once it has been perfected – fire-ruined homes, temples and palace buildings were often rebuilt on their original sites and quite close to their original design; so that while most of the present-day architectural monuments in China date back no further than the Ming dynasty, they remain fairly faithful to the styles of the more distant centuries.

Early roofs were thatched, but later clad with ceramic tiles which, in themselves, became an increasingly elaborate form of art. As the weight of all this tiling increased with each new architectural ambition, more and more complicated engineering techniques had to be developed to support it, and a study of any existing palace building or old temple will show the almost incredible system of brackets, columns, beams and levers designed to hold everything up. The distinctive curved or winged roofs are believeed to have been adapted from Indian Buddhist architecture, and became universally popular and increasingly flamboyant from the time of the Song dynasty (960–1279). The Ming and Qing dynasties saw the same flamboyance extended to the ridge ornaments – sculptured animals, people, plants and other motifs – mounted at each end of the roof to repel evil influences.

The arrival of Buddhism in the eighth century gave Chinese arts and crafts considerable new inspiration and impetus, especially in the fields of sculpture and rock carving, wall painting and bas-relief, silk painting and calligraphy and printing. Other than that, the irresistible demands and patronage of the various great dynasties added new artistic drive as they paraded, one after the other, down the annals of Chinese history.

THE DYNASTIC LEGACY

The Han dynasty (206 BC–220 AD) is noted as a major artistic period in which advanced silk weaving was developed, glaze was used on pottery, relief sculpture appeared and the early traditions of Chinese painting and portraiture were laid down. In the later "golden age" of the Tang rulers (618–906), sculpture and rock carving reached their "perfection," painting

achieved almost unparalleled sophistication and porcelain made its debut on the vast artistic stage.

The Song period is regarded as possibly the most accomplished and elegant era of Chinese art, when poets – among them the acclaimed Su Dongpo – were established as literary heroes, when the field of landscape painting flourished with new color and composition. Boosted by the the establishment of an Academy of Art, painters developed new perspectives in their work in which depth and elevation were illustrated with various subtle levels and shades of light and color. It was during the Song reign that the fulll discipline of brush strokes was established. Elsewhere, the Song era became famous for the introduction of the almost translucent celadon ware, and for the simple elegance of all arts ranging from ceramics to carved ivory and lacquer ware.

But it was the Ming reign (1368–1644) that gave China much of the artistic tradition that is still widely evident today. It was a time of hot patriotism – the reins of power returned to Han Chinese control after the short but bloody subjugation under the Mongols – and this was reflected in huge civil engineering feats like the reconstruction of the defensive Great Wall and in the boldness, brilliant color and general exuberance of painting. This burst of color was reflected in other arts – ceramics, sculpture and embroidery – and it also found its way into a new technique of multi-colored wood-block printing. Porcelain became even finer and more elegant in design, and the distinctive blue and white porcelain that we see today originated in the Ming kilns. Cloisonné – strikingly colored enamels fired on to intricate metal designs – developed in Beijing.

If there is a point in the history of Chinese arts where the principle of "perfect obsolescence" is turned up-side down, it is in the ensuing Manchu Qing reign. Ironically, and unfortunately, the elegance and taste that had been achieved up to and during the Ming dynasty in almost all arts and crafts deteriorated into a largely gaudy flamboyance and extravagance from then on – and in any study of existing Chinese traditional art and architecture today, the eyes and instincts search for that almost elusive simplicity of the past in a broad canvas of what can often be described as comparative kitsch.

Lion dancers relax during hotel opening ceremony in Xi'an.

Guangzhou
and the
South

GUANGZHOU AND THE SOUTH

Guangzhou (Canton)

The capital of Guangdong province and the urban centerpiece of China's entire southern region, **Guangzhou** is also the nation's pre-eminent southern gateway and a radial tour center from which you can strike out for major cities and cultural destinations in Guangdong, Fujian, Guangxi, Guizhou and Yunnan provinces, and Hainan Island. Its air and rail links cover virtually all of China.

Guangzhou is also China's most modern and progressive city, its Cantonese-speaking population of five million living with capitalist Hong Kong virtually on their doorstep, only 111 km (69 miles) away, and fed with a constant supply of latest consumer technology by family contacts there. The city and the region have been in close contact with foreigners for around 1,500 years, since Arab merchant seafarers first began trading along the South China Coast. Portuguese Jesuits established a foothold in Macau during the Ming dynasty, and the guns of the British "merchant princes" forced the opening up of Guangzhou itself as a trading port in the seventeenth century.

In the early nineteenth century Guangzhou was the main arena of the fierce test of strength between the British traders and the Qing throne over the alarming rate at which British opium imports were pouring into the society. In the two Opium Wars that followed, British warships and troops broke the back of the obsolete Qing defenses, grabbed Hong Kong as a colonial trading haven and triggered an international carve-up of Chinese territory and sovereignty that eventually caused the complete collapse of the 4 500-year old dynastic order. As that collapse approached at the turn of this century, it was the sons and daughters of Chinese merchants and reformists in Guangzhou and the south – some who'd been educated overseas, some of them influenced by local foreign missionaries, all of them hungry for modernization and reform – who led the first major rebellions against the Manchu rule. Sun Yatsen, the exiled "spiritual" leader of the reformist movement and the first republican president, was born in **Huaxian** to the northwest of Guangzhou. In 1923, Guangzhou was where he formed the nationalist Guomingdang Party, the movement that later formed the military backbone of Chiang Kaishek's brutal campaign to exterminate the Chinese communists.

Nowadays, Guangzhou is a rapidly developing manufacturing and business center, the venue of the major twice-yearly Chinese Export Commodities Fair, and is ahead of every other city in the race to catch up with Hong Kong's wealth and business status.

The City

Guangzhou lies on the delta of the Pearl (Zhujiang) River, a major waterway that brings ocean shipping right in to the city's waterfront from the South China Sea and provides access right across the hinterland as far as Guangxi and Yunnan provinces. It is a flat, sprawling city, crossed from east to west by a main artery, **Zhongshan Lu (Road)** that is all of 15 km (9 miles) in length, and from north to south by two main roads, **Renmin** and **Jiefang.**

If Guangzhou seems at first to be a huge, teeming and difficult city to cope with, these three major thoroughfares help simplify it by linking up the three principal districts that are of interest to tourists – the waterfront and **Shamien,** site of the International Settlement in the treaty port days; the northern commercial and tourist district which includes the **Railway Station, Dong Fang** and **China Hotels, Trade Center** and **Yuexiu Park;** and the cultural district, running to the east along Zhongshan Lu, featuring the main temples and mosques and monuments to Guangzhou's more recent revolutionary history.

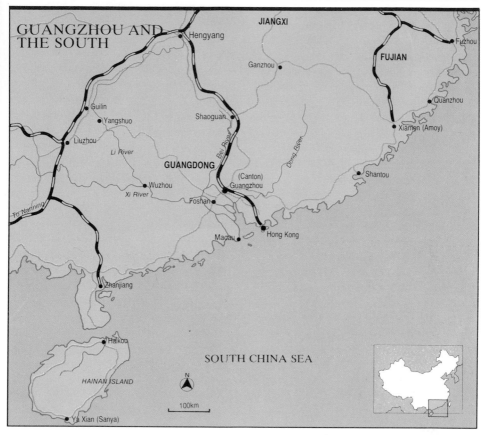

Guangzhou's climate, along with that of most of the southern region, is subtropical, hot and very humid in summer (July and August average 28.7°C or 83.6°F), and in the July-September months the area is prey to heavy monsoon rains and fierce typhoons that boil up out of the Pacific south of the Philippines and dash themselves, virtually one after the other, on the China coast. The most comfortable time to visit is between October and March. This off-season is also the best time for individual travel – you can count on getting a hotel room and a seat on the trains.

Getting around the City

The easiest way to get around Guangzhou is by taxi, taking them to the edge of either of the three main districts and then strolling around from there. You'll find cabs at any of the major hotels and at the main railway station, and you can also hail them in the streets. You can also get a quaint rendering of "Way Down Upon the Swannee River" in Chinese on their stereo systems. Fares are very reasonable, a good guideline being the ¥7 it cost me for trips between the White Swan Hotel on the Shamien and the railway station. The cabs can also be hired on a full-day rate of ¥120 at the major hotels.

Bicycles are available for rent on the street off the rear entrance of the White Swan and from the Dong Fang – China Hotel district. There's also a good trolley-bus service running between the three districts, but like public buses all over China they're overcrowded, slow-moving and distinctly uncomfortable in the Guangzhou humidity and heat. There's a good English-language tourist map which can be found at the Friendship desks of any of the top hotels.

Hotels

Since the **White Swan Hotel** rose up over the riverside on the Shamien, standing like a promise of the modernized China of the future, Guangzhou's character has changed from revolutionary austerity and drabness to a level of development and sophistication almost comparable with parts of Bangkok. In fact, you can lie awake at night in your comfortably furnished, air-conditioned room in the White Swan, listening to the constant growl and burble of cargo boats and tugs on the river, and imagine you're in Bangkok's celebrated Oriental Hotel on the bank of the busy Chao Phrya.

The White Swan is top-class by any standards, and features restaurants which some longtime foreign residents rate as the best in Guangzhou. It is also worth experiencing for its tastefully decorated riverside coffee lounge and vast atrium, which features a traditionally styled pavilion and waterfall and a viewing deck on to which visiting Chinese groups are allowed each day to take photos of each other.

Ranking with the White Swan, the **Dong Fang Hotel,** is a huge 1,500-room Chinese-style establishment surrounded by elaborate gardens in the center of Guangzhou's northern business district near the Railway Station. And the nearby **China Hotel** with its 1,200 rooms, and the equally opulent Garden Hotel, are other testaments to the route that mainstream tourism is taking in China– from its elaborate chandeliered lobby to its bowling alley, swimming pool, roof restaurants, disco, coffee lounge, sun decks, bars, boutiques and beauty salons, the **China Hotel**, particularly, is a place you could spend days in and not have to step outside. It even offers a Hong Kong-style basement **Food Street.** Outside both these palaces, the crowded sidewalks of **Renmin Beilu (North Road)** abound with

souvenir hawkers and black market money changers.

Other huge tourist-rate hotels are the **Baiyuan Hotel** complex to the east of the Dong Fang on Huanshi Lu, the 27-story **Guangzhou Hotel** which is just back from the riverfront to the east of the Shamien, the "continental" **Novotel Guangzhou**, the new **Holiday Inn City Centre** and the **Nanlu,** another luxury "foreign guest" hotel on a lake about half an hour by car from the downtown area. Altogether, 30 new hotel projects were on the drawing board in 1989, meaning possible slashed rates for future visitors.

Among the more middle-range budget hotels, you could try the **Liuhua Hotel** on the edge of Liuhua Lake across from the railway station, the **Guangdong Guesthouse** on Jiefang Lu near the Liurong Temple and pagoda, the **Renmin (People's) Mansion** on the riverfront just east of the Shamien, **Nanfang Mansion,** just east of the Renmin Bridge which crosses the river at the Shamien, and two older hotels on the Shamien itself, the **Shamien Island** and **Shengli (Victory).**

The Shamien Island also caters for the backpack traveler with several guesthouses offering dormitory or three-a-room accommodation. There is also an extended and modern hotel, the **Huaqiao,** just east of the Haizhu Bridge and south of the Guangzhou Hotel that caters exclusively for overseas Chinese visitors.

Restaurants

Being the Cantonese capital, and the center of one of China's richest food-growing regions, Guangzhou offers the very best of the nation's newly re-emerging cuisine. Food is also one of the growth industries of its modernization program – the city is close to the best chefs, the entrepreneurs and the latest culinary trends of Hong Kong. The variety of eating places available ranges from top-class Cantonese restaurants in the newest hotels and in opulent traditional garden settings elsewhere to fast-food snack outlets and the latest

OPPOSITE Poster hails dynamic socialist future at busy intersection in Guangzhou.

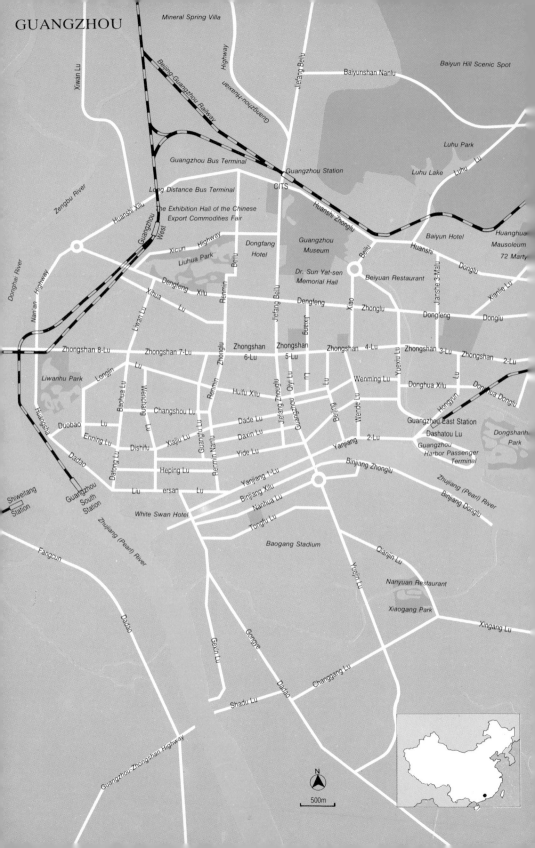

GUANGZHOU

Mineral Spring Villa

Baiyun Hill Scenic Spot

Xiwan Lu

Beijing-Guangzhou Railway

Highway

Guangzhou-Huaxian

Jiefang Beilu

Baiyunshan Nanlu

Luhu Park

Guangzhou Bus Terminal

Luhu Lake

Luhu Lu

Guangzhou Station

Zengbu River

Long Distance Bus Terminal

CITS

Huanshi Xilu

Guangzhou West

The Exhibition Hall of the Chinese
Export Commodities Fair

Huanshi Zhonglu

Baiyun Hotel

Huanghua
Mausoleum
72 Marty

Donghai River

Xicun Highway

Dongfang
Hotel

Guangzhou
Museum

Huanshi

Huanshi

Donglu

Nan'an Highway

Liuhua Park

Dr. Sun Yat-sen
Memorial Hall

Beiyuan Restaurant

Xianlie Lu

Dengfeng

Renmin

Beilu

Jiefang Beilu

Xiao

Zhonglu

Dongfeng

Donglu

Xihua Lu

Dengfeng

Jianshe 3-Malu

Liwan Lu

Renmin Zhonglu

Jiefang Zhonglu

Xiao

Beilu

Zhongshan 8-Lu

Zhongshan 7-Lu

Zhongshan
6-Lu

Zhongshan
5-Lu

Zhongshan 4-Lu

Zhongshan 3-Lu

Zhongshan 2-Lu

Liwanhu Park

Longjin Lu

Baohua Lu

Weichang Lu

Huifu Xilu

Oyi Lu

Yuexiu Lu

Wenming Lu

Donghua Xilu

Hongrun Lu

Donghua Donglu

Duobao Lu

Changshou Lu

Dade Lu

Jiefang Zhonglu

Guangzhou Lu

Beijing Lu

Wende Lu

Guangzhou East Station

Enning Lu

Xiajiu Lu

Guanghu Lu

Daxin Lu

Dashatou Lu

Dongshanh
Park

Dishifu

Datong Lu

Yide Lu

Yanjiang 2-Lu

Guangzhou
Harbor Passenger
Terminal

Heping Lu

Renmin Nanlu

Yanjiang

Binjiang Zhonglu

Shiweitang
Station

Liu ersan Lu

Yanjiang 1-Lu

Binjiang Donglu

Guangzhou
South
Station

Binjiang Xilu

Nanhua Lu

Zhujiang (Pearl) River

White Swan Hotel

Tonghu Lu

Huangsha Dadao

Zhujiang (Pearl) River

Baogang Stadium

Qianjin Lu

Fangcun

Nanyuan Restaurant

Xiaogang Park

Xingang Lu

Dadao

Gexin Lu

Cengye Dadao

Yuejin Lu

Changgang Lu

Shadu Lu

Guangzhou-Zhongshan Highway

N

500m

basement food marts and "gourmet galleries" that have developed out of a hybrid of Cantonese snack cuisine and Japanese retail efficiency in Hong Kong.

There's so much variety that it's difficult to decide exactly where to eat in Guangzhou. There are foreigners who live and work there who swear that the top-class hotels offer the best fare, and they rate the White Swan as possibly the best. It certainly offfers a great deal – Cantonese dim sum, lunch and dinner in two Chinese restaurants and its **International Banquet Hall**, a restaurant featuring northern provincial cuisine, the **Hirat** for Japanese food, a buffet luncheon in **The Palms** buffeteria and excellent Continental cuisine in **The Silk Road** grill.

The China and Dong Fang hotels have a similar range of Chinese, Japanese and Western restaurants, and the China Hotel goes a step further (though which way I'm not sure) with its **Hasty Tasty Fast Food** joint. However, its basement **Food Street**, a joint-venture restaurant, offers the relaxed atmosphere and pick-and-choose dining of the giant Japanese department stores and the street of the same name in Hong Kong's Causeway Bay. And while the prices are definitely in the budget category, the menu is by no means mundane: apart from the standard Cantonese dishes you can choose from a range of exotic treats that include snake broth, fried goby fish, stuffed Canton carp, sliced eel, goose intestines with chili and double boiled papaya with dry almonds. As with all restaurants in China, the Food Street menu warns that "tipping is discouraged by the management." But it adds a 13 percent surcharge to the bill to make up for it.

Outside the major hotels there are enough restaurants to offer a city-wide smorgasbord of treats ranging from roast suckling pig, pigeon and snake to bear's paw, dog and what's touted as the "most popular of Guangdong game dishes" – Fighting Dragons and Tigers, a culinary blend of cat meat and several kinds of snake! There are at least 25 restaurants throughout the city, far too many to cover in a couple of days, but you can let the taste-buds choose from the following select list:

Moslem Restaurant, Zhongshan 6-Lu. ✆ 88414.

Tao Tao Ju (*dim sum*), 288 Xiulu 1-Lu. ✆ 87501.

Caigenxiang (vegetarian), 167 Zhongshan Lu. ✆ 87136.

Guangzhou Restaurant, Wenchang Nanlu. ✆ 87136.

Shecanguan Snake Restaurant, 43 Jianglan Lu. ✆ 22517.

Yeweixiang (Wild Animals) Restaurant, 247 Beijing Lu. ✆ 30997.

But before making any selection, there are two other famous restaurants which, to my mind, should be considered before all others – the **Beiyuan** and **Panxi**. Both have been operating for many years in Guangzhou, both have come through all the revolutionary turmoil with their standards and culinary reputations undamaged and

ABOVE Pagoda and waterfall form showpiece of spectacular atrium in Guangzhou's White Swan Hotel.

both offer exceptionally varied menus in traditional decor and garden settings.

The Beiyuan (North Garden) gets packed early in the evening and has a menu that ranges from its own specialties – fish with pine nuts, roast goose, duck webs in oyster sauce – to the more modest meal that I enjoyed: chicken with bamboo shoots, fried beef in oyster sauce, stir-fried *choisum* with rice and Baiyuan beer. The service is friendly and accommodating and you are no longer hustled upstairs to special "foreign guest" rooms but can eat alongside the citizenry.

The Panxi is Guangzhou's busiest restaurant, and its dining rooms and pavilions are scattered through a quite romantic landscape of gardens, pools and ornamental bridges. Like the Beiyuan its menu is up-market and gourmet – stewed turtle in pottery; swallow's nest and crab-meat soup; white fungus (from stone) and bamboo pith with chicken slices in consommé; fried sea slug with chicken, perch, kidney, shrimp and vegetable. But it also offers fried prawns; fried frog and chicken slices, chicken with spicy sauce and fried noodles and chicken slices in soup, with beer, at quite a reasonable price for a one-night blow-out in a restaurant that, more than any other in contemporary China, recalls the splendor of the dynastic past.

Sightseeing

Guangzhou and most of the entire southern region of China were isolated for many centuries from the imperial seats of power, and therefore are not exactly overloaded with great cultural attractions. However, Guangzhou does have the **Guangxiao Temple,** dating back to the third century BC, and to this it has added the relics of its foreign trading contacts, its monuments to latter-day rebellion and its special present-day social character to offer itself as a city well worth strolling about and touring.

Being as big and spread-out as it is, covering about 60 sq km (23 sq miles),

it's also difficult to get around in the space of a few days unless you approach it from the point of view of its three distinct tourist districts – the Shamien and environs, the northern hotel zone and Yuexiu Park and the complex of temples and monuments spreading to the east off Zhongshan Lu.

The Shamien

The Shamien is a flat, partly reclaimed island, linked by two bridges to the Pearl River waterfront, and is where the "foreign devil" British and French traders and taipans built their warehouses, homes, banks and business headquarters after the British victory in the Opium Wars. The buildings are still there, providing a time-warp of sedate or slightly pompous Victorian architecture and used now as "people's" offices and overcrowded residences, and many of them are showing the scars of years of neglect. There have been unconfirmed reports that the city authorities plan to renovate the Shamien and turn it into an artist's colony and arts-crafts center, but for now it's a little like Shanghai – a place where you can step back into virtually untouched history.

Around the Shamien are two districts in which you can see history in the making – open markets, brought in with the wave of liberalization since 1979, through which you can stroll for hours watching peasants selling their surplus fruit and vegetables and a re-emerging class of street merchants hawking everything from live carp to denim jeans. There's a market area called **Qingping** on Qingping Lu just to the north of the Shamien, and if you go east, cross the bridge to the waterfront, walk along it and turn left into **Renmin Nanlu**, you can turn off into any side street on the right of this main road and find yourself in a large network of open market streets.

It's a raucous, friendly, crowded bazaar in which you wander through living proof of the Cantonese taste for all things bright and beautiful, all creatures great and small

pigeons; caged monkeys, dogs and raccoons; racks hanging with roast dog and a confusing array of butchered furry flesh and offal, all of it bound for the cooking wok. When I went through there just before the Spring Festival (New Year), a man opened a big wicker basket and hauled out a screeching, spitting young ape – but shoved it back again and disappeared when he saw my camera.

The Temple Tour

From the market area you can wander north along Haizhu Zhonglu which runs parallel to Renmin Road, turn right on Huifu Xilu and find the Daoist **Wuxian (Five Immortals) Temple.** This temple was closed for renovation when I was there but should be open again for visitors by now. It's said to be the spot where five rams appeared more than 2,000 years ago, carrying ears of rice in their mouths and ridden by five gods. The gods vanished but the rams stayed and turned to stone, whereupon the local people began planting rice. Since then Guangzhou has also been known as the City of Rams and City of Rice Ears.

The Wuxian Temple has a large rock in its courtyard bearing a hollow that is said to be the footprint of one of the gods. It also sports a huge Ming dynasty bell, three meters (10 ft) high and weighing five tons, which has no clapper and is believed would warn of impending disaster for the city should it ever make a sound.

North of Wuxian Temple on Guangta Lu, the **Huaisheng Mosque** represents the centuries of Islamic culture brought to Guangzhou by Arab traders. Like most Islamic places of worship it's quite severely free of ornamentation and idolatry, but its arched gateways and main hall of prayer are an interesting contrast of Moslem and Chinese architecture. It has a minaret that looms over the sweeping, tiled Chinese-style roofs and looks as though it's been rendered with concrete; but it's said to take its name, Guangta (Smooth Minaret) from this apparently unique surfacing. The

– sugar-cane, fruit and vegetables (watch for succulent lychee fruits in June and pineapples in October); live catfish and carp; eels, snakes and tortoises in netted bowls and big fish tanks sprayed continuously from hoses to keep the water aerated; baskets full of chickens and

ABOVE Religion re-emerges in the post-revolutionary age – joss and towering pagoda TOP and worshiper at Liurong (Six Banyan Trees) Temple, Guangzhou.

mosque dates back to the year 627 in the Tang dynasty and commemorates the Arab missionary Saud Ibn Abu Waggas who was the first to bring the Koran to China.

Further north on the other side of the main east-west artery, Zhongshan Lu, stand the two most interesting temples in Guangzhou, the **Guangxiao (Bright Filial Piety) Temple** and the **Liurong (Six Banyan Trees) Temple** with its towering nine-story **Flower Pagoda.** You can't miss the pagoda, and can reach it by walking north along either Haizhu Beilu or Liurong Lu from Zhongshan Lu.

The Liurong Temple was given its name by the renowned poet Su Dongpo who visited it some seven centuries ago and was captivated by the banyan trees (since gone) in its grounds. Both Liurong and the nearby Guangxiao Temple were built in honor of Hui Neng, the sixth patriarch of Zen Buddhism, and in the grounds of the Guangxiao

complex there's an open pavilion featuring frescoes of Hui Neng preaching to the monks and of the Indian monk, Bodhidharma, who is said to have visited Liurong at one stage.

Both temples attract large crowds of Cantonese sightseers and worshipers, and, as my diary notes recall, they are a pleasant shock – three huge gilded Buddha images in the Liurong Temple and all the incense and other paraphernalia of worship. Religion is coming back in Guangzhou, and none are happier about it than the old grannies who can be seen teaching their grandchildren how to light the joss stick, place it in the incense altars and kowtow to the images.

Part of the Guangxiao Temple is now the **Guangdong Antique Store,** with an interesting exhibition of Tang horses, camels and human figures. It has a **"Sixth Patriarch's Hair-burying Pagoda,"** a **Hall of the Sleeping Buddha** (closed when I was there) and an ancient Bodhi tree with a sign below it declaring: "The age-old Buddha's Tree" (the Sixth Patriarch was given tonsure right underneath it).

The Cultural Park

These two temples are about as far as you can comfortably go in one day's walking, and mark the boundary of my suggested Shamien and environs exploration. At night, there's another treat in the Shamien district which definitely should not be missed – the **Cultural Park.** This large playground off Liu'ersan Lu and Renmin Nanlu just north of Shamien Island is where the Cantonese go at night to have fun. And it's just as much fun watching them enjoying themselves.

In the eerie, ill-lit tropical darkness you come across a fairground and ferris wheel, a roller-skating rink packed with teenagers, an early Buck Rogers rocketship space simulator, a shooting gallery with pneumatic "bazookas" that fire tennis balls, a pool hall and the very latest in modernized leisure in Guangzhou, a video

ABOVE Contrasting simplicity of Isamic architecture at mian entrance to Huaisheng Mosque, Gunagzhou.

arcade. But the most interesting attraction, and one that draws a couple of thousand spectators in the semi-darkness each night, is an open-air Chinese chess tournament in which the competitors play on a floodlit stage and when a move is made it's immediately marked up, to a chorus of gasps or groans, on giant boards on each side of the table and announced over the public address system.

Meanwhile, at an auditorium near the stage, the high-pitched singsong shriek and clash of gongs announces another act in the continuing story of **Cantonese Opera**, with its regal and lavishly-costumed princesses, kings and mandarins gliding and flapping about the stage.

Pet Birds and Pagodas

The Dong Fang-China Hotels district between Renmin Beilu and Jiefang Beilu places you within close strolling proximity of a number of scenic and cultural attractions. To the north, heading toward the railway station, there's **Orchid Garden** where, in a landscaped setting, you can view more than 10, 000 orchids from 100 species, and visit the seventh century **Mohammedan Tomb**, claimed to be the burial place of the same Moslem missionary Waggas to whom the Huaisheng Mosque is dedicated.

The **Youyi (Friendship) Theater** to the west of the tomb, just off Renmin Beilu, is one of several in Guangzhou that present nightly performances of Beijing and Cantonese opera, music, drama, dance and acrobatics.

Liuhua Park, to the west of the Dong Fang Hotel, is a pleasant garden set among artificial lakes, but the much larger **Yuexiu Park** on the eastern side of Jiefang Beilu features at least two places of keen cultural and social interest. The remarkable **Zenhai Tower**, a five-story red wooden and rectangular pagoda, is all that's left of the old city wall of Guangzhou, and from its wide balconies, decorated with fat red traditional lanterns, you can see right over the city.

Recently renovated for the second time in a decade, it houses the **Guangzhou City Museum** and its scrolls, porcelain, ceramic sculptures and other artifacts and relics covering the city's past from the Neolithic age to the 1911 republican revolution and World War II. Close to Zenhai Tower there's a monument to Guangzhou's favorite son, Sun Yatsen, but it's a drab concrete monstrosity and could well be given a miss – except on Sundays, when it's a venue for hundreds of bird-lovers showing off their caged warblers.

The **Sun Yatsen Memorial Hall** to the south of the park is also historically significant but relatively uninteresting. A much more fascinating spot to take a look at is the huge **Sculpture of the Five Rams,** west of Zenhai Tower, a garish stone tableau of the legendary founders of Guangzhou that is nonetheless interesting for the hordes of families that gather there each day to take photographs of each other against it.

You'll not only see amazing bodily contortions as harried camera enthusiasts try to fit their impatient subjects into their upside-down viewfinders, but if you're smart about it you can also catch a good picture or two while all the posing and twisting and laughing and bickering are going on. For more candid photography in which you run little risk of offending anyone's sensibilities, I'd suggest the **Children's Park** about three main blocks to the south of the Sun Yatsen Memorial Hall. You get there by going directly south from the memorial on Jixiang Lu and turning left on Zhongshan Lu.

The Revolutionary Tour

The third main tourist venue of Guangzhou begins roughly at the Children's Park and continues east along Zhongshan Lu. There you'll find the city's contemporary monuments, the **Original Site of the Peasant Movement Institute,** where in 1926 Mao Zedong trained the cadres, including Zhou Enlai, who were to spearhead his communist revolution. Nearby is the **Memorial Garden to the Martyrs of the Guangzhou Uprising,** where, a year later, these same cadres headed a communist takeover of most of Guangzhou, only to be crushed by the ruling Guomingdang forces.

Further to the east along Xianli Nanlu, you can view the **Huanghuagang Mausoleum of the 72 Martyrs,** the monument to a similar, earlier uprising – and similar reprisal – in April 1911 in the last days of the Manchu Qing rule. Beyond that

there's only one major attraction left, **Guangzhou Zoo,** which I suggest could also be passed up unless you're keen on watching pandas and other wildlife in old-fashioned, dank and quite dispirited captivity.

ABOVE Shrine-like setting at Peasant Movement Institute LEFT where Mao Zedong's communist lieutenants were first trained. Another monument of sorts, dramatic Zhenhai Tower RIGHT has now been renovated and turned into a cultural museum.

Foshan

If the thought of all that walking unnerves you, the tour offices in the major hotels run coach tours on certain days to some cultural locations around the city, and their itineraries include ivory carving and other arts and crafts factories. They also operate tours of **Foshan,** the famous ceramics and crafts city 28 km (17 miles) southwest of Guangzhou, where you can watch artists at the **Foshan Folk Art Research Society** making traditional lanterns, paper-cuts and brick carvings, weavers producing

silk in the city's mills and ceramic miniatures being painted in their thousands at the **Shiwan Artistic Pottery and Porcelain Factory**.

The tour also includes a visit to the 900-year-old Song dynasty **Ancestral Temple,** whose remarkable architecture features dozens of ceramic figures and animals lining the crests of its roofs. A warning though: the tour department in the White Swan Hotel quoted me —¥100 for the day-long trip. In fact, it's far cheaper and a lot more interesting to travel there on your own from the Guangzhou-Foshan Bus Terminal which is near the Sishi (Catholic Church) in Guangzhou, just off Daxin Zhonglu to the east of Shamien Island. It's a one-hour ride to Foshan, and you can find budget-price accommodation at the **Foshan Hotel** or the **Pearl River Hotel** if you want to stay overnight. You'll find CITS at 64 Zumiao Lu, just south of the Ancestral Temple.

The Radial Route

You can get out of Guangzhou to just about anywhere in China, and you can do it by air, rail, bus or river craft. **China Southern Airways (CAAC)** have daily flights to Beijing, Shenyang, Nanjing, Shanghai, Xining and Hong Kong and from two to five flights a week to most other major cities. There are daily express trains to Beijing and Shanghai, with both journeys taking about 33 hours. North of Guang-

dong province there are two key junctions that open up the east-west rail routes – at **Hengyang** in Hunan province you change to the daily Shanghai-Kunming express trains for the dog-leg run west to Guilin and Kunming, and at **Zhengzhou** in Henan province you can connect with expresses from Beijing, Qingdao and Shanghai which will take you west to Chengdu, Lanzhou and Xi'an.

Buses leave the **Long Distance Bus Terminal** on the south side of Huanshi Xilu a short distance to the west of the Guangzhou railway station for many up-country destinations in Guangdong province and beyond. You can take a 15-hour bus ride to Shantou on the southeast coast, stay overnight there and carry on the next day to Xiamen (Amoy) in Fujian province. There's also a daily 13-hour bus service to Zhaniang, the southern coastal jumping off point for Haikou on Hainan Island. For

Guilin you can choose a direct bus service or, alternatively, go by bus to Wuzhou and then take a second bus straight to Guilin, or go first to the beautiful Li River township of Yangshao and carry on to Guilin by river ferry.

Ferries and hovercraft to Hong Kong, Macau and Haikou on Hainan Island leave from the **Zhoutouzui Wharf** on the south side of the Pearl River. To get to it you go across the Renmin Bridge and west along the extension of Tongfu Xilu to the waterfront. For the daily river services to Wuzhou you go to the **Guangzhou Harbor Passenger Terminal** on the northern waterfront, east along Yanjiang Zhonglu from Haizhu Square.

There are various places to go to book transport. The tour departments in the major hotels will handle radial bookings, but will also try to pressure you into going by air. The CITS office will book air, rail and boat reservations but will also take a couple of days to get tickets that you yourself would probably be able to take care of in a couple of hours. You'll find the CITS reservations desk at the Railway Station at 179 Huanshi Lu (© 33454), and the CAAC booking office happens to be right next to it. If you want to leave in a hurry you can ask your hotel desk to write out your destination and other requirements in Chinese and go directly to the rail booking office at the Railway Station, to CAAC or to the reservations offices at the ferry terminals.

XIAMEN (AMOY) AND FUJIAN PROVINCE

This southeastern coastal city and its province are famous for their longstanding trading contacts with the outside world, the great Chinese fleets that sailed from here in the Yuan and Ming dynasties to explore and establish trade throughout Southeast Asia, and the waves of Chinese emigration that left these shores for all parts of the world in the last century. Yet for all this, Fujian languishes off the beaten tourist track and has yet to be really explored and opened up by today's waves of foreign visitors.

Compared with western areas of the southern region, Fujian's value as a mainstream tourist destination is debatable. But for the individual traveler looking for a relatively untrodden trail to follow, it offers some quite pleasant physical and cultural surprises.

A rugged mountainous province, it is bounded on the west by the **Wuyi Mountains,** a 250 km (155 mile) range that's been a popular Buddhist retreat since Fujian was taken under the wing of imperial rule in the Tang dynasty. More than 100 monasteries were built among the heavily wooded slopes, and a wealth of surviving architecture and relics awaits the modern-day visitor. The mountains are also renowned for their Dahongpao tea, just one of the many Fujian brands that have made the province one of China's leading producers of the "lusty leaf."

The easiest access to the Wuyi range would be from Yingtan in Jianxi province, the railway junction that links the Guangzhou-Shanghai line with Xiamen. There are three hotels in Yingtan and a long-distance bus station where you should be available to get transport to either Huanggan Shan, one of the major Wuyi peaks, or to Jianning or Nanping, stopping off in the mountains along the way.

Xiamen

Xiamen was established as a major seaport in the Ming reign and returned the compliment by becoming a notorious pirate lair and the launching base for an ill-fated campaign in the seventh century to stem the southward influence of the Manchu Qing dynasty and restore the Ming rule. The campaign was led by one of the pirate chiefs, Dang Sing-gong, better known as Koxinga. He didn't get far in his bid to drive the Manchus from China, but turned around and kicked the Dutch out of what is now the island of Taiwan instead.

Xiamen was also an unofficial trading depot, doing a thriving under-the-counter business in silks with the Portuguese, Spanish and Dutch, until a British naval force stormed ashore after their victory in the first Opium War in 1841 and opened it up as a full Treaty Port. There is evidence today of its roleas an international settlement in the surviving colonial architecture of parts of its skyline. In modern times the city has been in the front-line of a revolutionary confrontation – facing Guomingdang forces from Taiwan based on the nearby islands of Quemoy and Matsu.

The city is actually on an island that is linked with the shoreline by a long causeway. There's another smaller island called **Gulangyu** just off the city's waterfront and linked to it by ferries. There are two older budget-class hotels to choose from, the **Lujiang,** which you'll find near the **Gulangyu Ferry Wharf,** and the **Overseas Chinese Hotel** at 444 Zhongshan Lu. Otherwise, several new business-class hotels have been built as part of a development program aimed at making the city a special economic zone and offer more modern, if more expensive, accommodation.

Xiamen's new International Airport, another result of its special economic status, makes it possible to fly directly there from Guangzhou, Shanghai and Hong Kong. You can also get there from Hong Kong by coastal ferry. There's access by train from either Guangzhou or Shanghai by changing at Yingtan and traveling south on the Xiamen branch line. There are also direct bus services twice a week to Shenzhen which can be booked through CITS in the Overseas Chinese Hotel.

Sightseeing

Xiamen is a good compact walking city and has a fair offering of ancient and modern monuments to its rather intrepid past, including the **Zheng Chenggong (Koxinga) Memorial Hall** commemorating the pirate patriot of the Ming reign, a

features exquisite architecture and an impressive array of Buddhist statuary, including images of the Maitreya, or Future Buddha (also depicted as the rotund Laughing Buddha), several guardian deities, three images of Sakyamuni Buddha, four Bodhisattvas (a kind of novice Being on its way to Buddhahood) and other guardian figures.

Quanzhou is believed to have flourished long before Xiamen came into its own as a trading center, the site of ancient Zaiton, the "great resort of ships and merchandise" that Marco Polo wrote about after his epic travels in Kublai Khan's reign. And an astonishing relic of that grand mercantile era can be seen in the grounds of the Kaiyuan Monastery.

Originally called the Lotus Monastery, it was built in 686 in the Tang reign and renovated during the Ming dynasty, and not only features another impressive collection of Buddha images but also 72 panels of bas-relief carved with figures of lions with human heads that are reminiscent of Egyptian Pharaonic art. But that's just the monastery. Behind it you'll find the **Museum of Overseas Communications History** which, despite its uninspiring name, deserves a good close look inside because in there you'll find a magnificent relic of the power and glory of ancient Zaiton – the excavated hull of a huge ocean-going sailing junk, dating back to the Song dynasty, and maps of the great oceanic expeditions that the eunuch admiral, Zheng He, commanded in the Ming reign to the distant shores of East Africa and Madagascar.

well-stocked **Museum of Anthropology** at the university, and the **Shuzhuang Garden** which features one of the finest landscaped rockeries in southern China. But what really makes Xiamen a place to consider traveling to is its remarkable Tang dynasty **Nanputuo Temple** and its access to the city of **Quanzhou,** three hours up the coast by bus, where there's an even more interesting temple and a surprise in store for anyone interested in the history of Chinese maritime technology and the romantic Chinese sailing junk. The Nanputuo Temple in Xiamen can be reached by bus from the Overseas Chinese Hotel. Although built in the Tang reign it was renovated by the Manchu Qing and

HAINAN

If you were a mandarin, or government official, in the days of dynastic rule in China and you were transferred to the island of Hainan, you would have dragged yourself down there feeling quite thankful that you still had a head on your shoulders. Hainan was, and still is, the far southern limit of the Chinese civilization (if you

---

ABOVE Nanputuo Temple in Xiamen features an impressive array of buddhist statuary and relics, along with a museum containing the hull of a Song dynasty ocean-going junk

count Taiwan as an offshore aberration, that is), and it was a place of exile for any bureaucrat or court official who'd incurred the emperor's displeasure. There's a beach with two big boulders on the island's extreme southern tip that's called **Tianyahaijiao**, or literally "The End of the World," and if you stand there in the sands and gaze out across the seas you can imagine the ghosts of the past standing there with you, still wondering how it all went wrong for them.

Hainan is China's second largest island, covering an area of 32,000 sq km

(12,355 sq miles) much of it clothed in lush tropical forests, rice-fields and fruit growing plantations, low-lying in the north and mountainous in the central region and south. Its tallest hills, the **Limu Ling (Five-Fingered) Mountains**, rise to nearly 1,900 m (6,234 ft) and can clearly be seen from the mainland 18 km (11 miles) away. Aside from forested slopes and balmy beaches, there are fertile valleys where a mixed population of Li and Miao minorities and Han Chinese settlers cultivate rice, rubber, sugarcane, tropical fruits, coffee, tobacco, pepper and cocoa.

The island is another special economic zone set up to attract overseas Chinese entrepreneurs, and in the five years up to 1986 had signed 230 contracts worth

$215 million in foreign investment. It is also strategically important – much of its west coast is a burgeoning naval, air and military base facing Soviet-backed Vietnam. The west also happens to have the main concentration of Li minority villages, and while you can get to them quite freely nowadays you must keep in mind that this is a sensitive militaary zone. On the island's east coast you can find another interesting minority, the Danjia, who operate a fishing and pearling industry.

Access

From the tourist's point of view, Hainan has three immediate destinations, the capital **Haikou** on the north coast, just across the Qiongzhou Strait from mainland Zhanjiang, the port and beach resort of **Sanya** on the south coast and the mountains and colorful mountain folk in between. There's a direct ferry service once a week from Hong Kong to Zhanjiang, and you can also fly there by the twice-weekly service from Hong Kong by Dragonair or get there by boat from Guangzhou. There's also a direct ferry service from Guangzhou to Sanya. From Zhanjiang you can take a daily direct flight to Haikou. CITS in Hong Kong or Guangzhou will handle all air and ferry bookings. Alternatively, you can go by train from Guangzhou to Guilin, then by rail again to Zhanjiang, continue by bus and ferry across to Haikou and then travel right down the island by bus to Sanya. You no longer need a special permit to do this.

Haikou

This port town and commercial center isn't much of a cultural venue and should be regarded chiefly as the jumping off point for the central mountains and southern Sanya. It offers a reasonably luxurious Hong Kong-managed resort hotel, the **Haikou Tower**, along with two budget properties, the **Overseas Chinese Hotel** and the cheaper Seaman's Club. At least eight new hotels were under construction or at the planning

Traditional Chinese style houses in Xiamen.

stage at the time of publication – part of an ambitious campaign to transform Hainan not only into a Special Economic Zone but a major regional tropical resort as well.

The main landmark in Haikou is a traffic circle and obelisk in the center of the town, and from this point you can stroll through a busy and interesting open market district, or you can head north to the waterfront and come across one of the last concentrations of old sailing junks left in China. For travel to Sanya or air and ferry departures to the mainland, you can go to CITS on the ground floor of the Overseas Chinese Hotel or directly to the Long Distance Bus Station.

Ya Xian (Sanya)

This southern port offers marvelous beaches and good seafood along with two comfortable and convenient beach-style hotels. To the east you'll find the **Luhuitou Resort Hotel,** set on a peninsula with guesthouses and beach bungalows. There's also a new tourist hotel called the **Dadong Hai** which charges tourist rates – but which has cheaper dormitory accommodation if you ask for it. To get to the main ethnic attractions of Hainan you go by bus to **Baoting,** about 40 km (25 miles) west of Sanya, which is the center of the Li and Miao autonomous area.

GUILIN AND YANGSHOU

Chinese culture abounds with literary superlatives, paintings, embroidery, murals, sculpture and other artwork that all attempt to express the intrinsic beauty of Guilin and its Li River scenery. Even the very meticulous and businesslike *Official Guide to China* produced by the Imperial Japanese Government Railways in 1915 had to cast about for a little poetic license. "The neighborhood (of Guilin) is rich in picturesque scenery," it observed. "The mountains are singular in that the peaks all rise immediately from the plains, each by itself, so that they have been fitly compared by the poet Fan Shih-hu to young

bamboos sprouting out of the ground, apparently without any connection with each other. On the river banks there are innumeerable grotesque and singular rocks which form objects of interest and attraction to poets."

In fact and in legend, these hill rocks have been littered over the centuries with the wine-flasks of inebriated poets, one of whom, Han Yu, got as far as describing the Li River as "a turquoise gauze belt, the mountains like a jade clasp." Another managed to start a poem but couldn't finish it and promptly turned to stone. And yet another gave up trying to express himself altogether and simply drank himself to death.

What they were struggling to capture in prose was a geological phenomenon called karst – the erosive action of rivers and drainage over many millions of years on a belt of limestone that extends right across the southern provinces, carving away the softer rock to produce abrupt and fanciful hills and extensive underground caves.

Guilin

This sprawling city of 300,000 people has become so famous for its Li River scenery and surrounding necklace of karst hills, and subsequently so crowded with tourists, that its reputation is beginning to work against it these days – you find many of the more worldly individual travelers dismissing it as a tourist trap. I found this a little cynical and unfair. Certainly, Guilin's scenery is beginning to lose its historic splendor in the midst of industrial development, certainly the town is highly industrious in its pursuit of the tourist dollar, but if you put its famed and much-touted rock formations in the background, where they really belong, and concentrate instead on the society it is one of the most interesting and rewarding travel destinations in China.

Its people are friendly, quite proud of their city's reputation and generally anxious that foreigners should leave there quite satisfied that they've had a good time. All you need is a bicycle and street map and a sense of adventure and you'll find there's a lot going on wherever you happen to point your handlebars.

In the three days I spent there I came across children performing acrobatics in the street near the Railway Station, big gatherings of old comrades playing cards in the afternoons on the river front near the Liberation Bridge, street-side open-air beauty parlors, a conjuring show in a tent on the main street, Zhongshan Lu, old floating restaurants being renovated for the new tourist era on the Li River embank-

ment, a café run by China's first long-distance motorcyclist and, on the western edge of the city on the way to Ludi Yan (Reed Flute Cave), a roadside pool game which I was enthusiastically invited to join – hammering away with heavy mahogany cues at balls that were so chipped and sluggish that I was tempted to suggest that we climb up on to the baize and call the game golf.

Access
To get to Guilin you can fly directly from Hong Kong on Dragonair and CAAC, or by CAAC from Guangzhou. Or you can

take a river-ferry from Guangzhou, go by ferry from Hong Kong, go by bus from Guangzhou via Wuzhou, or travel there by train from Guangzhou via the east-west rail junction at Hengyang. The train trip is arduous, but an experience all the same. I traveled hard-seat for 10 hours from Guangzhou to Hengyang, entertained by a carriage full of genial Mongolians on their way back north to Beijing. I found Hengyang to be a grim, uninviting industrial backwater but was saved from a day of boredom and despair by an extremely hospitable Chinese "returnee" from Soho, London. I connected with the Shanghai-Kunming Express that afternoon, managed to get upgraded to soft-sleeper and traveled to Guilin in the company of two companionable party cadres. All in all, the train is the best way to get there: in 24 hours you learn all there is to learn about riding China's rail network.

Getting Around Guilin
When you disembark from the train at Guilin's main railway station at the southern end of the city's north-south artery, Zhongshan Lu, there are taxis which will take you to the major tourist hotels. As in most other cities, it's best to use the taxis for errands between the station and the hotel and cover the city itself by bicycle, and you can rent these anywhere around the Lijiang (Li River) Hotel for between ¥0.60 and ¥1 an hour with no deposit.

Guilin gave me my first real experience of bicycling in China, and I offer the following diary notes as a kind of survival guide:

Bicycling is safe, a lot of fun, easier than trudging by foot and you tend to merge into the masses rather than being a center of attraction on the sidewalks. But a warning: you may find yourself in a slipstream of spit from a careless rider up ahead. Don't try to race – you'll get frustrated in the crush, have a collision and lose a lot of face. You'll also wear yourself out. Save the energy for the uphill sections and don't be too proud to get off and walk the bike up – the Chinese certainly do. Learn to coast and rest on the downhill runs, and on the flats take it at a sedate pace and rhythm and let the weight of the feet rather than muscle power glide you along. You're in no real hurry, and neither is anyone else.

Hotels

At the top of the range in Guilin are the **Lijiang Hotel, Sheraton Guilin, Garden** (formerly Ramada Remaissance) and **Holiday Inn** - among no less than 12 new or renovated hotels which have turned the industry in this tourist center into a hotelier's nightmare. For the tourist, of course, it's a boon. The competition to fill something like 8,000 new hotel rooms is so fierce that reduced rates should prevail for some time yet. Otherwise, there are several budget establishments, among them:

Hidden Hill Hotel, Zhongshan Nan-lu, just up the road from the Railway Station.
Osmanthus Hotel, Zhongshan Lu, just up the road from the Hidden Hill.
Ronghu (Banyan Lake) Hotel, western end of Rhonghu Beilu, facing Banyan Lake.
Guilin Hotel, Zhongshan Lu, just up the road from the Osmanthus.

Restaurants

The north-south Zhongshan Road is so packed with eating places – practically cheek-to-jowl with them – that it would take an entire chapter to list and describe them all. You'll find that they offer mainly Cantonese cuisine with local specialties and variations and appear to have mushroomed in such numbers to cash in on the seasonal droves of visiting Hong Kong Chinese. There are a couple that also offer exotic game dishes – monkey, civet cat, raccoon and the like – which are also aimed at the Hong Kong Chinese palate.

As for hotel food, the **Lijiang** has a reasonably good Chinese dining room that had a staple but unadventurous menu when I was there – fried or shredded pork, beef, chicken, seasonal vegetables, that sort of thing – and I had two main dishes, rice, tea and soup. But with the extent of the renovations that were going on, the restaurant and its culinary fare should be a little more sophisticated by now, and the prices higher too. The **Holiday Inn** offers international-class Chinese and Western restaurants with the added advantage of a Hong Kong management under the leader-

ship of veteran hotelier Han Zaunmayr. For coffee and a quick snack you should try an audacious little eating place on Zhongshan Lu near the edge of Fur Lake, and try it just for the heck of it. It's called **McDonald's.**

At night, Zhongshan Lu transforms into a long strip of alfresco food stalls offering a better range of cuisine than even the hotels. **Xichiang Lu,** off the

OPPOSITE "Downtown" Henhyang, a key junction on the railway route from Guangzhou to Guilin. ABOVE Hengyang infant in bright New Yera's costume.

main drag near the Guilin Hotel, is the best place to head for. It's one big tumultuous open air food mart, lit by hissing gas lamps and doing a roaring trade in fresh meat and vegetable hot pots, noodles and soups. Elsewhere you can find little sidewalk snack stalls – knee-high tables and tiny bamboo stools – which do a delicious and very cheap sweet bean soup with eggs.

Sightseeing

As already pointed out, the best sightseeing in Guilin is the city itself, and the people, and the best way to see it is by bicycle. You can combine a lot of social activity with the main tourist attractions by picking a scenic or cultural spot to ride to and nosing around the streets on the way.

For example, a ride to the **Qixing Gongyuan (Seven Star Park)** on the eastern side of the Li River will take you along the waterfront east of the Lijiang Hotel to the Li River Bridge, passing open markets, an open air wooden bed bazaar, crowded gambling spots, sampan life and a cluster of old floating restaurants along the way. At the park itself, just before the main gate, you can wander off into a riverside market gardening area or pass the time of day with an imperious camel that condescends to be photographed with children on its back but can get quite indignant if you take a picture of it without paying.

The park itself is a well landscaped strolling spot with gardens and traditional hump-backed stone bridges over streams and pools, a precipitous climb that takes you up through viewing pavilions and restaurants to the top of its craggy karst hill, an interesting Ming dynasty bridge called Hua Qiao (Flower Bridge) and six caves with rock formations that have been given evocative names by the Chinese – Monkey Picking Peaches, for instance – but take a lot of imagination to transform themselves from simple stalactites and stalagmites.

The same richly descriptive names have been given to all the karst landmarks in and around Guilin – Duxiu Feng (Solitary Beauty) Hill north of the Lijiang Hotel and Li River Bridge, Decai Shan (Piled Silk Hill) on the city's northern outskirts, Elephant Hill to the south, Old Man Hill to the northwest. And, quite frankly, while they look interesting from a distance they offer little more than a grueling climb and various views of the city when you reach them. But again, there's a great deal of interesting street-life to be seen on the way.

My advice is to pick the formations that have a little more than city views to offer, and at **Fubo Hill** on the river bank west of Duxiu Feng you'll find the **Qianfo Dong (Thousand Buddha Cave)** with many Tang and Song dynasty Buddha images carved into its rock-faces. Further north at Decai Shan you'll find more Buddha

each viewpoint the lighting dies to pitch blackness behind you, so be careful to keep up with the rest of the group.

Guilin's other main tourist attraction is a bespectacled, quiet-spoken and very informative young motorcyclist named "Mr Chen" who runs the **La La Cafe,** a coffee and snack joint on Zhongshan Lu just a few doors up from the railway staion. Chen knows all there is to know about sightseeing, transport and accommodation in Guilin, Yangshuo and Nanning, and has some good stories to tell about the 16 years in which he's been biking around China, begging gasoline and banging on guesthouse doors in some regions, particularly in the north, where the sight of a Chinese traveling his own country just for the love of it, and on a motorbike, has aroused the sort of suspicion that a bunch of Hell's Angels would face in Peoria, Ill.

"People just don't understand why I do it," he says. "They think I'm snooping around or selling something. It's hard to make them understand I'm just doing what the foreign tourists do."

Yangshuo

"The rivers and hills of Guilin are the most beautiful in China," says one of the many historic tributes to this karst region, "and those of Yangshuo's surpass Guilin." In fact, the prime reason for visiting Guilin in the first place is really to take the six-hour, 80 km (50 mile) boat cruise to this small river village, winding down through a fairyland of mounds, towers, cones and craggy pinnacles soaring sharply out of a silken swathe of flat rice land. In the evenings, fleets of lantern-lit bamboo fishing rafts spread down the placid waters, the fishermen using tame cormorants to dive for the fish – their long necks collared to stop them from swallowing the catch.

carvings in its Wind Cave. But the most fascinating cave, by far, is in **Ludi Yan (Reed Flute Hill)** which lies about 15 km (9 miles) to the northwest of the city and can be reached by bicycle if you head out west along Jiefang Lu, cross the railway line and ask directions from there. Another way to get there is by bus No. 13 from Seven Star Park.

Reed Flute Cave is a tour of the underworld as seen through a Disney cartoonist's fantasies – it's an extensive network of beautiful and bizarre natural grottoes, galleries and vast caverns such as the Dragon King's Crystal Palace, which was a local secret for several centuries and used as a place of refuge in times of civil war. Visitors are taken through in groups and the whole attracion is well presented, with imaginative lighting effects adding a touch of magic at each turn of the narrow, winding stone stairways. As you pass through

ABOVE Guilin scenes show ANTICLOCKWISE floating restaurants wintering on Li River, rounded karst hills beyond, audacious foretaste of Guilin "nouvelle cuisine" and Li River city setting.

and drums and dropped rice-cakes to keep the fish away from his corpse.

Nowadays, slim shallow-draft "dragon boats," 40 m (131 ft) long and manned by up to 60 rowers, race up and down the rivers on Dragon Boat Day with gongs and tom-toms beating the rhythm, spectators screaming encouragement and water exploding and cascading everywhere.

Access

There are direct air services between Nanning and Guangzhou, Kunming and Beijing and you can get there by train from

a penthouse restaurant with a good menu and views of the city.

The **Yongzhu Hotel,** at 34 Minzhu Lu, is another tourist-category hotel off to the east of the city center, near the Renmin Park. Also in the budget range is the nearby **Mingyuan** which also has the local CITS office.

Sightseeing

Nanning is a good walking and bicycling city with a lot of activity in its streets, especially in the cool of the evenings when the farmers and open market vendors move

Guilin. There are also special express train links with Beijing, and trains south to Zhanjiang, the mainland access point for Hainan Island.

Hotels

The **Yongjiang Hotel,** situated on a traffic roundabout at the southern end of the city center close to the Yong River, offers tourist-class double rooms, and dormitory accommodation with showers. A special hotel bus meets arriving trains. It also has

into the side-streets with their stalls. Aside from the Nationalities Institute, the main cultural attraction is the **Guangxi Museum**, west of the Yongjiang Hotel, which features, among other relics and artifacts, more than 300 ancient bronze drums, the largest collection of its type in China. Twenty kilometers (12.5 miles) northwest of the city you'll find the **Yiling Cave**, an underground karst formation as interesting as Guilin's Reed Flute Cave with splendid stalactites and stalagmites. It winds for about one kilometer under the ground.

ABOVE Tourist ferry glides through fairyland setting of karst pinnacles and hills along Li River from Guilin. OPPOSITE An chinese artist tries to capture the calm and rural atmostphere of the "Elephant's Trunk" at Guilin.

Kunming
and the
West

KUNMING AND THE WEST

THE "GOLDEN TRIANGLE"

Kunming and Yunnan province can be regarded as another radial tour center interlocking with the southern tour route from Guangzhou and, at the same time, opening up the western tour trail that runs north to Chongqing, Chengdu and the capital of Tibet, Lhasa.

YUNNAN

Yunnan, which translates into "south of the Clouds," is a mountainous sub-tropical province and a kind of Chinese Golden Triangle, bordering Burma, Laos and Vietnam. It shares four main rivers with these neighboring states, including the mighty Mekong, and has a certain cultural intercourse too through its minority hill-tribes. The most prominent of these, the Dai, have their own tribal homeland, the Xishuangbanna Autonomous District to the south of the province, which was opened up in 1986 to foreign travel without special permits. There are also Lisu, Lahu and Yao clans whose tribal domains spread as far as the northern border region of Thailand.

Originally part of a southern kingdom called Nanzhou, Yunnan was conquered by the Yuan Mongols in the thirteenth century

ABOVE Viewing pagoda juts above bizarre natural formations of Stone Forest near Kunming.

and brought under Imperial rule. It was the scene of a violent Moslem rebellion and an equally bloody government reprisal in the nineteenth century and then became a foothold for French incursions into China from their colonial bases in Laos and Vietnam. A legacy of the French presence is a narrow-gauge railway linking Kunming with Haiphong – now unfortunately closed by the current tension between Beijing and Hanoi.

In World War II Kunming became one of the bases of Chiang Kaishek's beleaguered nationalist government and swelled with refugees from the east fleeing the Japanese forces. The British and Americans kept the city alive with vast shipments of supplies from Burma, bringing them in along the famous Burma Road and by airlift from India.

KUNMING

This is a big, wide-open and warm fun city, with a lot of character and much to see and do. If you take my advice you'll spend at least three days there, and if you book train tickets out through CITS you'll be there four days, which is the time they claim it takes to go to the railway station and get them.

Kunming has broad, modern boulevards, narrow older streets lined with traditional prewar "bamboo"-tiled and lattice-windowed homes and shops, a busy street life, grand parks, good hotels and restaurants, open markets and night-time food stalls, several good temples and several more in its Western Hills overlooking the vast freshwater Lake Dian. It is also the access point for bus tours of the Stone Forest and air and bus transport to Dali and the tribal minorities of the Xishuangbanna region.

If you have an English-language tourist map you'll find that the main streets that you have to concern yourself with form a kind of church cross. **Beijing Lu** runs north from the railway station to intersect **Dongfeng Lu,** a major east-west artery that virtually links the city's two most prominent tourist hotels, the **Kunming** and **Green Lake.** A taxi shuttle between these hotels, costing about ¥7, will put you within walking distance of a lot that the city has to offer.

Access

There are five direct flights a week to Kunming from Guangzhou and you can also fly there from Beijing, Shanghai, Xi'an, Chengdu, Chongqing, Guilin and Nanning. Dragonair also flies there from Hong Kong. Daily trains run there from Chongqing and Guilin via the junction of

Guiyang. If you book to go on the normally crowded Shanghai-Kunming Express in Guilin you'll probably only be able to get hard-seat and will have to upgrade once you're aboard.

Again, I ended up in soft-sleeper on this run, paying an extra ¥90, and was put in with a Palestinian and a Yemeni, both medical students from Shanghai. It was a traveling association that was memorable for two things – the very pleasant time we spent together and the acupuncture treatment that the Palestinian, Nasser, administered to cure me of a sudden heavy dose of diarrhea. It involved three needles

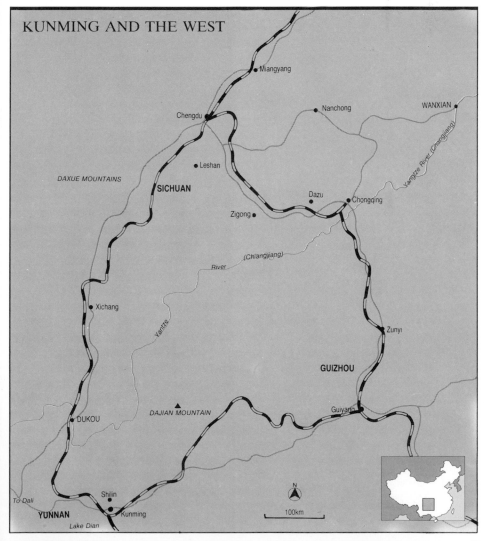

KUNMING AND THE WEST

inserted for half an hour below both knees, and despite the numbing pain I recommend it to anyone. You don't dare have diarrhea after that.

Hotels

There are two main tourist-class hotels in Kunming and two others to choose from if you're traveling on a particularly low budget. The giant **Kunming Hotel**, right in the middle of the central tourist district at the eastern end of Dongfeng Road, has double rooms in the pricier tourist range, and has the advantage of convenience – it's the headquarters of CITS and it's right next door to CAAC for air bookings. It also has a very comfortable dormitory section where you can get beds with shared bathrooms.

Its counterpart at the western end of town, off Dongfeng and right on the edge of the very interesting Green Lake Park, is the **Green Lake Hotel,** offering the same room rates as the Kunming but recently renovated and no longer bothering about dormitory guests. To choose between these hotels is to choose between being centrally located and at the business end of town or close to Green Lake Park, open markets, a great deal of street life and a couple of fine temples.

There's another hotel called the **Kunhu** on Beijing Lu just along from the railway station which is the main venue for low-budget backpackers. The **Yunnan Hotel** on Dongfeng west of the Kunming Department Store is largely for overseas Chinese, but will take "round-eyes" if it has room and offers room rates that fall between the two top hotels and the Kunhu.

If you want to stay outside Kunming on Lake Dian, there's a tour-group hotel with individual rates and dormitory accommodation called the **Xiyuan (West Garden).** It's on the western edge of the lake close to the Tiahua Temple.

Six faces CLOCKWISE of Kunming – young couple sport new fashion trends, Kunming acrobats perform heart-stopping feat, abbot of Bamboo Monastery poses while Kunming sugar sculptor creates, "Texas" Wong rides again and little belle says hello.

Restaurants

Both the Kunming and Green Lake Hotels have excellent Chinese restaurants and quite reasonable prices – and when I was there they were also both offering good breakfast of eggs, toast and coffee for ¥4. Elsewhere, there's a wide range of restaurants and cuisine to choose from. The **Yinjianglou Moslem Restaurant** at 360 Changchun Lu serves good Hui minority cuisine, mainly mutton and beef dishes. It's also in a teeming old-style district in which you can stroll at night and gaze upon lanterns glowing softly through the distinctive latticework of the tenement buildings. But get there early. I was there at seven o'clock one evening, asked for a table and a waiter borrowed my pen and wrote something on the palm of his hand. He held it up before me. It said OFF. I don't know to this day whether it meant the food was off, or that I should buzz off.

Just down from the Kunming Hotel on Dongfeng is a restaurant with the unfortunate name the **Cooking School,** which offers good Cantonese traveler's fare, and beyond that there's a place called the **Olympic Bar** where two American travelers were given a message as cryptic as mine – a card on their table saying NO, IT'S NOT.

You can take your pick of any number of restaurants and snack bars along Dongfeng Lu itself, among them the **Shang Dao Sweetmeats** and **Cold Drink Cafe** and the **Shanghai Restaurant** which is virtually right across the road. Further along to the west, around the Yunnan Hotel, you can find the **Beijing Restaurant** at 77 Xiangyun Jie, and the Sichuan-style **Chuanwei** on the same street.

There's one particular place where you can be assured of good food, a friendly atmosphere and efficient service and a pair of complimentary chopsticks thrown in. And that's **Tong's Coffee Shop** which is not a coffee shop at night but a full-scale, packed eating house at 81 Ching Wan Street, north of the Green Lake Hotel. Mr Tong himself is a lively, wiry old Burmese-Chinese gentleman with a wispy gray beard who

knows exactly what budget tourists want and is on to a good thing with it.

In the daytime there's a clean, friendly eating place below Tong's restaurant where you can watch the chef cooking your meal on an open charcoal brazier and dine on basic but well-prepared Cantonese dishes. In the evenings the action is all upstairs, where Mr Tong holds court for a continuing stream of local cadres, businessmen, foreigners and jade dealers from Hong Kong. It's best to get there by 6:30 pm. By seven you won't find room to stand. It's not an easy place to find, but the desk at the Green Lake Hotel will gladly direct you there.

Sightseeing

The bicycle is the best vehicle for sightseeing in Kunming, and you can rent one at the Kunming Hotel for ¥1 an hour. CITS, at the hotel's front desk, will show you how to get around to the main attractions, but otherwise will only help individual travelers with train and plane bookings out of town. The Green Lake Hotel has a tour desk linked with CITS and manned by a very efficient and helpful lady, Chen Xinhua, who will point you to the right buses for the major cultural spots.

Green Lake Park, opposite the hotel, is the immediate attraction, a landscaped cultural park and leisure area with quite beautiful gardens and traditional halls and pavilions set around ornamental pools. It's a good place to meet the local citizenry and watch them rowing on the lake, roller-skating and photographing each other.

ABOVE Lanterns and pavilions at eventide in Green Lake Park. Traditional lion head door-knocker on old Kunming store BOTTOM. Winged roof OPPOSITE hangs over Kunming watchtower and canal bridge.

There are often arts and crafts exhibitions in the grounds and outside, and at weekends the adjacent street is full of market stalls, ice cream vendors, "sugar sculptors" who fashion elaborate filigrees of dragons, butterflies and other subjects out of thin strands of hot toffee, shooting galleries, paper silhouette artists and even old fairground "Test Your Strength" machines.

South of the park at the main traffic circus at **Dongfeng Lu, Daguan Jie** and **Renmin Xilu,** you can watch minority tribespeople arriving in town to sell their produce; and at night, alongside the Yunnan Arts and Crafts Store, the street turns into one of the most colorful and clamorous open air eating places that I encountered anywhere in China.

East of the Green Lake Hotel, on Yuantong Jie, you'll find the **Yuantong (Enlightenment) Monastery,** constructed in the Yuan dynasty between 1301 and 1320 and featuring a huge ornately sculptured gateway, an elegant triple-arched stone bridge, an eight-sided pavilion and spectacular Buddha images in the main hall. It's another excellent place at which to study the religious liberalization that's occurring now in China – the brisk back-to-business reverence with which the older matrons plant their joss sticks and kowtow to the images and altars. Another easily accessible cultural attraction is the Jindian (Golden Temple) which lies about seven kilometers (four miles) northeast of Kunming and can be reached by bicycle or a No. 10 bus. It was built in the Ming dynasty and became the summer residence of a Manchu military turncoat, General Wu Sangui, who was sent south in 1659 to put down a rebellion and set himself up as a rebel warlord instead.

The Bamboo Temple

The most fascinating temple by far is the **Qiongzhu (Bamboo Monastery)** 12 km (7.5 miles) northwest of Kunming. It's recognized as the first Zen monastery to be built in Yunnan province, but the original Tang dynasty buildings burned down and were replaced in the fifteenth century. During another face-lift between 1883 and 1889 the Sichuan sculptor Li Guang was commissioned to decorate one of the halls with images of the 500 arhats, or immortal personages commanded to remain on earth and protect the laws of Buddhism.

Li and five assistants produced a lifelike but bizarre and even Boschian human tableau, filling the walls of the hall, that was later condemned as a sick caricature of some of the important personalities of the time. Thankfully, no-one doubted the artistry enough to have it destroyed, and today it is among the cultural relics of China that must be seen.

To get to the Bamboo Monastery you take a bus from outside the Yunnan Hotel on Dongfeng Lu. It'll cost you ¥0.50 and put you down right outside the temple steps.

Lake Dian

For a rewarding full day's excursion from Kunming, and one that combines physical exercise, fresh air and cultural interest, take a No. 6 bus from the Xiaoximen bus depot near the traffic circus just down from the Green Lake Hotel and head out to the

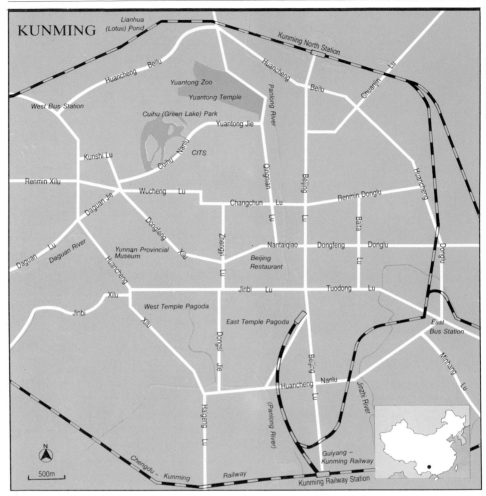

KUNMING

Lianhua (Lotus) Pond

Kunming North Station

Huancheng Beilu

Huancheng Beilu

West Bus Station

Chuanjin Lu

Yuantong Zoo

Yuantong Temple

Cuihu (Green Lake) Park

Parlong River

Yuantong Jie

Kunshi Lu

Cuihu Nanlu

CITS

Renmin Xilu

Qinghian

Beijing

Renmin Donglu

Huancheng

Wucheng Lu

Daguan Jie

Changchun Lu

Lu

Lu

Baita Lu

Dongfeng Xilu

Zhengyi Lu

Nantaiqiao

Dongfeng

Donglu

Daguan Lu

Yunnan Provincial Museum

Huancheng

Beijing Restaurant

Daguan River

Xilu

Jinbi Lu

Tuodong Lu

Xilu

West Temple Pagoda

Jinbi

East Temple Pagoda

East Bus Station

Dongsi Jie

Beijing Nanlu

Minhang Lu

Haigeng Lu

Huancheng Nanlu

Jinzhi River

(Parlong River)

N

Guiyang – Kunming Railway

500m

Chengdu – Kunming Railway

Kunming Railway Station

Western Hills and Lake Dian. You can also take bus No. 4 from the Yuantong Temple to **Daguan Park** at the lake's northernmost point and from there take a boat cruise, departing at 8 am, to **Haikou,** passing under the sharply rising hillsides which are called Sleeping Beauty because their contours are said to resemble a maiden at rest.

From the No. 6 bus terminal the road winds upward through forested slopes to provide panoramic views of Lake Dian – the second largest freshwater lake in China – with its spreading thickets of fish-traps and elegant square-sailed cargo junks that flutter lazily like white moths down its main channel. As the road winds higher and higher there are several interesting temples and grottoes along the way – the

eleventh century **Huating Temple,** the biggest around Kunming, the Ming dynasty **Taihua Temple** with its magnificently grotesque door gods, and the **Sanqingge Temple,** a former country villa built in the Yuan dynasty and later turned into a Daoist place of worship.

At the top of the climb you'll find the **Longmen (Dragon Gate)** complex of grottoes and pavilions set high in a cliff-face and commanding another panoramic view of the lake. Dragon Gate was built some two centuries ago in the reign of the Qing emperor Qianlong. The paths and caves took 72 years to hack out of the rock, and then a sculptor named Zhu Jiage spent another eight years fashioning the various images that adorn the main cave, including a large statue of the god of literature. One day, so the story goes, Zhu was shaping a pen-brush in the statue's hand when it snapped off. He was so mortified that he hurled himself from the precipice to his death.

You can round off your Western Hills tour by climbing down to the lake itself. Below Dragon Gate there's a steep pathway that switch-backs down to a sleepy fishing village right at the water's edge. From there you can stroll out along a causeway to a narrow channel and sit a while watching the sailing junks pass through. There's a sampan ferry there that packs with day-trippers and their bicycles and is poled across the narrow neck of water. On the other side you can walk about a kilometer to Haigeng Beach and board a No. 24 bus back to Kunming.

The Stone Forest

Everyone who goes to Kunming goes to the **Stone Forest (Shilin),** a bizarre mushroom patch of fungus-shaped gray rocks that are believed to have been formed and sculpted by two natural forces – the earth's crust pushing upward and the wind and rain eroding the bared limestone outcrops. They are quite a remarkable spectacle, and what is also remarkable about a visit there is the tenacity with which hordes of colorfully-costumed souvenir hawkers, mostly women and girls of the Sany Zhu, a clan of the Yi minority tribe, will try to sell you ornately embroidered "hill tribe" bags, purses and other items.

Although the Stone Forest is interesting, there's a much more fascinating attraction around the small lake at the forest's entrance – the **Five Tree Village** with rustic old mud-brick homes featuring "horned" roofs and traditional doorways, wandering pigs, goats, donkeys and other livestock and, in the autumn and winter, huge bunches of corn hanging high in the trees above the homes to dry.

There are various ways to get to the Stone Forest, but the easiest and cheapest means is to book aboard a No. 6 tour bus at the Kunming Bus Service Company directly across Dongfeng Lu from the Kunming Department Store. The trip costs ¥12, departs between 7 am and 8 am, takes three hours with a toilet stop on the way and allows you a good four hours at the forest. You can book tickets that will allow you to stay overnight there, and there's a good hotel on the edge of the rock formations called the **Shilin** – but quite frankly, a day trip is quite enough.

DALI

This developing tourist town lies northwest of Kunming, about eight to 13 hours away by bus, and was the capital of a

kingdom ruled by the Bai minority tribe until conquered by the Yuan Mongols in the thirteenth century and absorbed into the empire. In many respects, the town still lies somewhere in the Middle Ages, a time-warp of traditional wing-roofed and neatly whitewashed homes, an encompassing wall and old town gates that are still the main access for a daily parade of farmers from the surrounding countryside with their horses and carts. Bird cages hang in the narrow streets and alleys, householders can actually be seen scrubbing the outsides of their homes, and Dali should be visited as quickly as possible before all this charm begins to get businesslike.

The best time to go there is in April when Bai tribespeople from all over the region flock there for the Third Moon Street Fair. However, in June, the town stages a

ABOVE Buses and cars take the fast lanes on Kunming boulevard, separated from bicycle traffic.

spectacular Dragon Boat Festival, too. At other times the Bai pour into Dali every Saturday for the open markets, and another market is held every Monday at Xatin, just two kilometers (one and a quarter miles) away.

The Bai are a devoutly Buddhist minority, and artistic, and the architecture of Dali and its neighboring smaller towns reflects the depth of their culture. They're responsible for the Shizhong Mountain Caves in the southeast of Jianchuan county, a series of 16 grottoes filled with Buddha images and carvings depicting the court life of their pre-imperial reign. It's also fascinating to see what they've done with the Dali Catholic Church.

Hotels

Dali has a guesthouse with double rooms and beds in four-berth dormitories, but it's a fairly primitive establishment with squat toilets and "public" baths. It's best to commute from **Xaguan,** which is right next door to Dali and has two far cleaner and more comfortable establishments, the **Erhan** (named after the nearby lake) and the **Windy City,** both offering double rooms at reasonable rates.

There's plenty to eat, and the main place to go is the **Garden Restaurant** in Dali, where you can dine outside in the sunshine or rising moon. The **Peace Cafe** is another recommended spot. In Xaguan there's a friendly and well recommended **Sichuanese Restaurant** which you can't possibly miss – it has four bear's paws displayed in the window.

XISHUANGBANNA

This special autonomous region in the south of Yunnan province is the heartland of the Dai minority. Like the Bai, they are fervent Buddhists of the lamaist school and are famous for their elaborate Burmese-style temples and their homes, which are built on stilts, leaving room underneath for boats and livestock, and their traditional dress – the women wearing an exotic combination of colorful turbans, silver bracelets and necklaces and long slim ankle-length sarongs.

The Dai are also renowned for their spectacular rites and festivals, and there's hardly a tourism documentary on Chinese TV that doesn't promote their tribal dances, with their blaze of strange animist costumes and headdresses – particularly their ceremonial Peacock Dance. The best time to see this ritual performed is in April, at the time of the Dai New Year, when it's presented along with Dragon Boat races and the Water Festival. In this day-long Mardis Gras – also a feature of the festive calendar in northeast Thailand – the revelers drench each other with water in a very enjoyable "wringing in" of the New Year.

Xishuangbanna was opened up to travel without special permits in early 1986. To get there you still had to fly from Kunming to Simao, stay overnight in one of the three guesthouses that are available there and then take an eight-hour bus trip to the Xishuangbanna capital of **Jinghong**. However, a new airport was under construction at Jinghong and it is now possible to fly there directly from Kunming.

Jinghong has a guesthouse with comfortable double rooms in the 30-50 range, and with the region obviously under development as a major tourist attraction it would be advisable to check with CITS in Kunming on any new hotels that may have sprung up there. The town is surrounded by small, picturesque Dai hamlets and jungle temples, so there's plenty to see and do. One intrepid traveler saw a huge temple with a "soaring white stupa" about 18 km (11 miles) south, close to the Vietnam border, but wasn't able to get to it. It awaits those who dare.

CHONGQING

Chongqing is a grimy, hilly industrial city at the confluence of the Jialing and

OPPOSITE Remarkable Stone Forest (Shilin) was formed by massive upheaval and erosion of limestone.

Yangtze Rivers that is smog-bound for more than 100 days of the year and in the summer is so fiercely hot that it's known as one of the three Furnaces of the Yangtze. But having said all that, there are three good reasons why it must be included in any western travel itinerary.

First, it has one of the most architecturally stunning hotels in China, the **Renmin Hotel** with its magnificent triple-eaved "Temple of Heaven" domed auditorium and huge columns along its two residential wings. Secondly, the city is the western starting point for the Yangtze River ferry

services that cut right across the heart of China, linking the west with Shanghai. Thirdly, you go to Chongqing to get to Dazu, one of the four most famous centers of Buddhist cave sculpture in China.

Although it has a long past, Chongqing's contemporary history is much more relevant to its appeal today. It was the headquarters of Chiang Kaishek and his Guomingdang forces during Japan's relentless drive to occupy all of China in the 1930s and suffered devastating Japanese bombing as a result. A legacy of that violent period is a network of tunnels and shelters cut into its many

hillsides, some of which have since been turned into small factories. At one point the city was a command post for both nationalist and communist forces in their brief military pact against the Japanese. The communists based their command at **Red Crag Village** on the Jialing River 10 km (6 miles) from Chongqing, and Zhou Enlai and his wife lived in house No. 13 and also at 50 Zeng-jiayan in the city itself.

Access

Being a junction city, Chongqing is accessible directly by air from Beijing, Guang-

zhou, Chengdu, Guilin, Kunming, Nanjing, Shanghai, Wuhan and Xi'an. There are direct trains to Beijing and Chengdu, and if you're approaching on the clockwise route from the south you travel directly on a dog-leg route via Guiyang.

Yangtze River Ferries

Ferries travel both ways on the Yangtze River, so that you can book east to Wuhan and Shanghai or travel west to Chongqing from either of these destinations. Ferry tickets can be purchased through CITS on the ground floor at theSouth Wing of the Renmin Hotel.

A new luxury river ship called the *Great Wall,* with 200 beds, a swimming pool,

OPPOSITE Traditional dance at Stone Forest, Kunming. ABOVE Mechanical dragon breathes "fire" at Chongqing New Year's fair close to "Temple of Heaven" dome of the Yangtze city's most prominent architectural landmark RIGHT, the Renmin Hotel.

dance hall, bar, gymnasium and solarium, has gone into service between Chongqing and Shanghai, but it costs a lot more than the ordinary ferries. Aside from the access to the east, the Yangtze River trip features the reasonably thrilling experience of a cruise through the Yangtze Gorges – Qutang, Wuxia and Xiling – which are reached on the second day near the ancient town of Fenjie. But from that point on the Yangtze is really just a wide dun-colored sweep of river with an occasional passing cargo boat or string of barges and relatively non-descript river cities until you reach Wuhan.

Hotels

There are several hotels and guesthouses in Chongqing, but only two really worth staying in. The remarkable **Renmin Hotel** offers clean and cozy double rooms (but you pay in advance for the number of nights you plan on staying there) and it also has cheap dormitory accommodation with shared showers and toilets. Its staff are young English-language students, all uniformed in identical redwindbreakers that make them look a little like an Oriental version of the old Mickey Mouse Club – The hotel also has a good, reasonably priced Chinese dining room in its North Wing. But for real comfort, **Holiday Inn** have moved in with a new hotel, established mainly to catch the city's burgoening business traffic.

Sightseeing

The Sichuanese like to compare themselves with their cuisine, regarding themselves as the fiery "Latins" of China. The people of Chongqing are not exactly fiery, but they are quite bold and forthcoming in the streets. One chirpy kid greeted me one morning with a hearty "Good morning, teacher!"

Being hilly, Chongqing isn't the sort of city you want to bicycle around. The buses are also particularly overcrowded. But the hills also confine the city center enough for it to be covered quite easily on foot, and there are a number of interesting places to visit. A stroll along the southern

bank of the **Jialing River,** past the main bridge, will take you over clusters of European-style rooftops and homes that date back to Chongqing's days as a Treaty Port. If you head down Minzu Lu toward Chaotianmen Dock at the eastern end of the urban wedge, you'll find the **Liberation Monument,** which is a huge clock tower, and, close to there, an interesting old temple called **Luohan** which features an imposing seated golden Buddha and was being renovated at the time I was there. Liberation Monument is also the center of the city's main commercial and

tourist district, and around it you'll find the Friendship Store, arts and crafts shops, several restaurants and the Xinhua Bookstore where you can buy a good English-language city map.

By taking Zourong Lu south toward the Yangtze River, you climb steps toward one of the city's urban ridges and, right on the other side, you'll find a small recreational area where the city's old-timers gather to gamble in the afternoons and show off their caged birds. Below the park there's a big roller-skating rink where you can watch the younger folk enjoying themselves. Another interesting strolling venue is a bustling open market that kind of tumbles down a steep "ladder street" toward the railway station, and which you can reach by going south on

ABOVE Boy carries earth LEFT past sheltered Song dynasty images of Buddha at Dazu Grottoes. Huge Sleeping Buddha RIGHT dominates remarkable cave sculptures at nearby Baoding.

Zhongshan Lu from the Renmin Hotel and crossing over to it from the giant Shancheng Cinema. On the way down Zhongshan Lu I called into the **Working People's Cultural Palace,** set in a big park, and found a trade and cultural fair going on – the grounds decorated with lanterns and huge red balloons, elaborate sideshows and exhibits, and a big mechanical dragon that swung its head about and actually breathed smoke over the crowds. Admittedly, it was close to the Spring Festival (New Year), but the cultural park seems to be the central fun place in Chongqing.

Dazu Buddhist Caves

From the tourist's point of view, Dazu is really what Chongqing is all about. The town itself lies 160 km (100 miles) northwest of the city, and you get there by tour bus from the KFL Bus Company depot on Renhe Jie, which is about five minutes up the hill to the east of the Renmin Hotel. The one-way fare was ¥9.70 when I was there, and the bus leaves each day at 8 am, depositing you at around midday at the **Dazu Guesthouse** after an interesting ride through the rice terraces and farming villages of southern Sichuan.

The hotel is very basic but acceptable for a one-night stay, and you can get a double room for around ¥50. **Dazu** itself is quite quaint and rustic and has two restaurants in its main street, heading back from the bus depot in the main square, where you can eat pork and green peppers, vegetable soup and rice for two for about ¥2.40. To get to the

Dazu Grottoes you continue up off the main street and out of the town, climbing toward **Bei Shan (North Hill)** which has a pagoda set dramatically on top of it. If you climb right up to the pagoda you'll find something of immediate interest – three beautiful Song dynasty Buddha images sitting side-by-side in the courtyard of a farmhouse. The cave sculptures themselves – among some 50,000 of them dating back to the Tang and Song reigns and found at 45 sites scattered throughout this region – are back down the hill from the pagoda; but while they're interesting, and while Bei Shan offers stunning aerial views of the surrounding rice-lands, this is really not what you've come to Dazu to see.

Baoding Shan (Treasure Peak Mountain) is what you've come here for. It lies 15 km (9 miles) northeast of Dazu and you can get a bus there from the town's main square. Baoding is a huge horseshoe-shaped grotto, something like an amphitheater, lined with more than 15,000 statues, engravings and bas-relief images. They were started during the Southern Song reign and took from 1133 to 1162 to complete. Most of the sculptures refer to epic Buddhist stories, and many depict animals and rural life and the stages of childhood, but they are dominated by two magnificent examples of Buddhist art – the ornate **Thousand-Hands-Thousand-Eyes Buddha** which you'll find in one of the pavilions, and a huge 31 m (102 ft) recumbent **Sakyamuni Buddha (The Sleeping Buddha)** which fills one entire wall of the grotto. Just this one dramatic and inspiring sculpture explains why Baoding is rated with Dunhuang, Luoyang and Datong in the immense legacy of Buddhist art, and why you came to Chongqing.

CHENGDU

Chengdu, the Sichuan provincial capital, has had many names in the past. During the Han dynasty it was called the City of Brocade for the beautiful silks that it produced. In the Song era of the tenth century it was the City of Hibiscus for the flowers planted along its main wall. Nowadays its name translates into Perfect Metropolis and it is an important industrial city that has somehow managed to retain an atmosphere of clean, well-ordered and expansive leisure, with wide boulevards, interesting monuments and temples and fine parks.

It is also another vital access city for tourists, the most convenient departure point for the exciting new frontier of travel in China, Lhasa and Tibet, and the gateway to one of the nation's most extraordinary

Buddhist relics, the Grand Buddha at Leshan.

The city itself features another remarkable but more contemporary relic, a towering, centrally located statue of the Great Helmsman of the Chinese Revolution, Mao Zedong. Chengdu also has a somewhat important link with the post-Maoist society as well: its province is the birthplace of the new Chinese leader, Deng Xiaoping.

ABOVE Pretty balloon vendor poses on eve of New Year (Spring Festival) celebration in Chengdu.

Access

You can reach Chengdu from all directions by air, with direct flights from Beijing, Guangzhou, Chongqing, Kunming, Guilin, Nanjing, Shanghai, Wuhan, Xi'an and Lhasa. You can get there directly by train from Xi'an, Lanzhou and Beijing, and from Chongqing if you're following the clockwise tour.

Getting Around Chengdu

Chengdu is flat, spaciously laid out and thus another good bicycling town, and you can rent bicycles at a number of places including a shop set into the wall around the main tourist hotel, the Jinjiang. There are taxis operating from the railway station and the Jinjiang, and outside the hotel gates you can hop into a pedal rickshaw for a sedate return ride to just about anywhere in the inner city area for a flat ¥10, or ¥7, or ¥5, depending on how hard you're willing to bargain. CAAC have a brand new reservations office right across Renmin Nanlu from the Jinjiang.

Hotels

The **Jinjiang Hotel** is the main tourist venue. It's a big comfortable hotel with a remarkable dining room that throws you back to the days of art deco and ballroom dancing, but I found the bank, Friendship desk and postal staff sullen and difficult to deal with. I also trapped a rat in my room after it had made three valiant attempts to drag a half-pound of Shanghai milk chocolate down to a hole in the wall left by an uninstalled power point. On each floor there's a secure left-luggage room, which is important if you want to go to Lhasa but don't want to collapse with high-altitude sickness because you're lugging too many bags.

Across Renmin Nanlu from the Jinjiang you'll find a brand new 23-story hotel called the **Minshan,** with room rates starting where the Jinjiang's leave off. Down-market a little, the **Chengdu Hotel** on Dongfeng Lu near a monument and traffic circle offers three-a-room dormitory accommodation with clean linen and showers, and is a good source of travel information for backpackers and trekkers heading to Tibet.

Restaurants

There are a number of reasonably good restaurants around Chengdu at which you can enjoy the fiery, peppery character of the Sichuan cuisine. But no visit is really complete without a meal in the **Jinjiang Hotel's second floor dining room.** The menu there isn't very adventurous, though the meals are well cooked and reasonably priced. But it's the chandeliered decor, the theatrical colored lighting, the stage at one end covered entirely with a huge and dramatic Chinese-style painting of a waterfall, that make it something of a dining out, or in, experience.

All that, and a stereo system that plays Chopin one minute and that infernal "Auld Lang Syne" in Chinese the next. Expatriates from the US Consulate next door to the hotel had an arrangement when I was there whereby they could come over late in the evening and play their cassettes on the system – attracting a fairly sizable audience of people fed up to the teeth with "Auld Lang Syne."

Elsewhere, the new **Minshen Hotel** should by now be adding a range of more modern restaurants to the culinary scene, while the **Chengdu Restaurant** at 642 Shengli Zhonglu is the most popular dining spot for foreigners outside the hotels.

Aside from its spicy cuisine, Sichuan has a celebrated culinary specialty which should not be passed up – Sichuan duck, which in many respects is more sophisticated than its Beijing counterpart. The Sichuanese chefs have developed dozens of ways of presenting duck without the fat and grease of the Beijing variety, a famous recipe being Zhangzhou tea duck, the masterpiece of a Qing dynasty chef, in which Zhangzhou tea, camphor leaves and cypress twigs are used to flavor the skin and flesh. Another popular recipe is roast duck with *moyu,* a jelly made from the root of a taro grown in Sichuan. Yet another is savory and crisp duck in which the bird is first soaked in salt water, then smoked, steamed and fried and seasoned with prickly ash.

Former United States president Richard Nixon is said to have stunned and delighted his Chinese hosts with his reaction to Sichuan duck during his historic visit to China in 1972. When asked by Premier Zhou Enlai what he thought of the Sichuan fork-roast duck at a state banquet in Beijing, Nixon let out a loud and appreciative "Quack!"

Sightseeing

First stop on any sightseeing around Chengdu is the five-story **Exhibition Hall,** a giant department store, and the towering statue of Mao Zedong that looms over the city's busiest traffic circus at the junction of Renmin Nanlu and Renmin Xilu north of the Jinjiang Hotel. From there you can bicycle to the **Wuhou Temple,** which is in the southern suburb of Nanjiao across the Nanhe River to the south of the hotel. Built in honor of Zhu Geliang, a brilliant military strategist and advisor to Emperor Liu Bei of the Three Kingdoms Period (220-265), the temple features the tombs of both men, several shrine halls built in the much more recent Qing dynasty and a nearby lake and parkland with pavilions and a very pleasant tea -house.

Another pleasant temple park is **Wanjiang Lou (River Viewing Pavilion)** which is dedicated to the Tang dynasty poetess Xue Tao and lies to the southeast near Sichuan University. And, five kilometers (three miles) to the west of the city center, following the road from Xinximen, you can reach the famed **Thatched Cottage of Du Fu,** where one of the most illustrious poets of the Tang reign retired after serving in various official posts and wrote some 240 melancholic works that summed up his most vivid impression of all those years of official duties – the suffering of the people.

If you go beyond Chengdu's western gate, heading northeast along Honggung Donglu, cross a creek and then turn left into the back-streets, you'll find the **Temple of Wang Jian,** a Tang dynasty general who proclaimed himself emperor of Shu in the tenth century. The central coffin chamber has interesting wall carvings of female musicians, dancers and musical instruments of that era, along with jade tablets, imperial seals and a carved stone portrait of Wang Jian himself.

Another popular venue is the **Wengshu (God of Wisdom) Monastery** which was built in the Tang reign and reconstructed in the seventeenth century and features a striking Tibetan Buddha image. Wengshu is worth a visit not only for its own architecture and relics but also for a busy tea-house within the grounds and the religious street life that goes on around its gates, with stalls loaded with devotional joss sticks, candles and fireworks.

If you have time to make a day of it, you could also bicycle about 18 km (11 miles) to the northeast of the city, out along Jiefang Beilu to the **Baoguangsi (Temple of Divine Light).** It's a big monastery, founded in the ninth century and featuring a Qing dynasty Arhat Hall housing 500 clay sculptures of Buddhist immortals, including the Qing emperors Kangxi and Qianlong. Among the other treasures and relics there you'll find a Burmese white jade Buddha, paintings and calligraphy from the Ming and Qing reigns and a stone tablet engraved with hundreds of Buddha images.

Most of these cultural attractions – and others such as the ancient **Qin Dynasty Dujiangyan Irrigation System** 50 km (31miles) northwest of Chengdu – are included in one- and two-day organized tours offered by CITS at the Jinjiang Hotel. Their tours also cover three popular venues outside Chengdu, the **Su Dongpo Mansion** in Meishan, the "sacred" Buddhist hill-range, **Mount Emei,** and the one spectacle that I personally regard as the main reason for any visit to Chengdu

– the monolithic **Grand Buddha at Leshan**.

The Grand Buddha

Leshan is a colorful, architecturally pretty town dating back to the Tang reign and set alongside sweeping river flats at the confluence of the Min, Qingyi and Dadu rivers about 165 km (102 miles) from Chengdu. In the eighth century it was decided that something had to be done to control the dangerous torrents at this river meeting place and a monk named Haitong suggested that only a monumental spiritual force could possibly

tame the waters. The result is the awesome 71 m (233 ft) sitting Buddha carved into the face of Mount Lingyun, right across the waters from Leshan.

The Dafu (Grand Buddha) is so immense that 100 people can congregate on its head. You could fit a couple of football teams on its toes. When it was built it was painted and gilded with gold leaf and a 13-story pavilion, or "Buddha House," protected it from the elements. That shelter was destroyed in the Ming reign, and since then the monolith has been totally exposed – but saved from serious erosion by an ingenious internal drainage system. You can climb all over the statue, view it from the Grand Buddha Temple alongside its head, or take a ferry trip from the Leshan Pier which will give you astonishing perspectives of its size from the river.

CITS offer a two-day package tour that allows you an hour and a half at the Grand Buddha and then rushes on to the Su Mansion at Meishan and an overnight stop and a lot of hiking at Mount Emei. The cost: ¥109 all-in. Having tested this tour I can quite honestly recommend that while the other two destinations are reasonably interesting, the overnight stop should be at Leshan. The town has a very accommodating and comfortable hotel, the Jiazhou, right on the river front, with double rooms at budget rates, and aside from the Grand Buddha there's a lot to see and do around the district.

In fact, I would suggest ignoring the CITS tour and concentrating instead on a couple of relaxed, unorganized days of sightseeing in Leshan. You can get there by train in four hours from Chengdu, or by bus from the Xinanmen bus station near the Jinjiang Hotel. You can study one of the world's greatest religious monuments from all angles, in your own good time and at your own convenience, and you can take it from me that there's nothing else within striking distance of Chengdu that is in any way comparable to it.

The astounding 71-meter Grand Buddha stands guard over the Min River at Leshan – so gigantic that visitors flock over its toes.

Lhasa and Tibet

LHASA AND TIBET

To visit Tibet is to step through a portal from the materialism of the modern age to a society which is still, to a large extent, ruled by deep medieval spiritual impulses. Tibet is transcendental – even the main route to Lhasa by air from Chengdu is a journey toward the heavens, soaring upward over the vast and awesome snow-tipped ranges of the Tibet-Qinghai Plateau to touch down in a dusty valley two miles above sea level.

Tibet is also vivid technicolor compared with the far more mundane revolutionary character of the Chinese "lowlands" – a sudden blaze of tribal costume, coral and turquoise beadwork, gilded temple roofs, garish gods and demons, fluttering prayer-flags, spinning prayer-drums, silver and brass and rich golden yak butter, priests in flowing crimson robes, lamas in deep maroon, saffron and yellow – and through the seemingly incessant whirl of color, the mournful squeal and rumbling bellow of temple pipes and horns.

For centuries, all this was isolated, almost inaccessible, a forbidden citadel hidden in the eaves of the very roof of the world. Today it is the most coveted of all the tourist drawing cards in China, the place where just about every China traveler wants to go.

THE LAND AND THE PEOPLE

There is a striking incongruity about Tibet – how it can be so socially warm and welcoming and yet so physically inhospitable. It covers an area of close to 750,000 sq km (290, 000 sq miles) bordered by China, India, Nepal, Burma, Sikkim and Bhutan, and it is mostly mountainous, very sparsely inhabited, has few serviceable roads and no railway. And it has a climate in which the temperature can fall to freezing point on mountainsides even at the height of summer and plunge to minus 40°C (minus 104°F) in winter, bringing heavy snowfalls that block the mountain passes and make many areas more isolated than ever.

Its main travel artery is a road that runs west from Lhasa to Xigaze and then cuts south to the border with Nepal. Another key mountain road carries on from Xigaze and skirts the Himalayas, following the western border right around through Burang and Yecheng to continue north to Kashi in the Xinkiang-Uygur Autonomous Region. Lhasa is also linked with the "lowland" by a road that runs to Golmud in Qinghai province.

The Tibetan people are believed to be a mixed Mongoloid-Turkic breed and were very much a cultural mystery until they embraced Buddhism in the seventh century and developed a written language. Living mainly in small hamlets dotted about the hilly wilderness, they raise yaks, cows, horses, sheep and goats and trade yak butter, skins, meat, beads and religious artifacts in the main markets. Their social structure was a religious feudalism, a society based on the sweat of the farmers and herdsmen and the divine and absolute authority of their living god, the Dalai Lama, until the revolutionary Chinese occupied the country in 1959.

The Chinese military rule closed many of the country's 4,000 monasteries, disbanded the monkhood and caused the Dalai Lama to flee into exile in India. Nowadays, the Beijing government would like to see him return, and have in fact renovated his private apartments in the Potala Palace in Lhasa, but there appears to be little chance of this former religious monarch regaining any real measure of power.

For two decades after the Chinese takeover, Tibetan religion was virtually driven underground. But in the current liberalization it is beginning to flourish again, and since early 1986 regular "summonses" of the various sects and temple festivals have been restored in Lhasa and throughout the mountain domain. There is still strife between the occupying Chinese and Tibetan independence groups, though, as the riots in 1988 violently proved, and travellers are warned that this tension could close the province to visitors at various times.

Buddhism and Bon

Tibetan Buddhism, or Lamaism, was bonded on to a form of animism called Bon, which ruled Tibetan spiritual life in ancient times. Some of its imagery and ritual have been absorbed quite comfortably into the Buddhist practices – spirit and demon worship, prayer-flags and offerings to the guardian spirits of mountain passes, for instance – adding the color, reverence and mystique that distinguish its ceremony and monastic life, and death rites, from all other Buddhist schools of thought.

Access

At the moment, Lhasa is directly accessible by air from Chengdu and Xi'an, but with the country opening up and becoming a major tourist venue it's almost certain that direct flights will be started from Beijing, Shanghai and Guangzhou. There's no railway link with the "lowlands," but a plan is on the drawing boards for an extension to Lhasa of the railway line from Xining to

Three faces of Tibetan culture - beaded market woman LEFT, masked Butter Festival dancers CENTER and tribeswoman ABOVE prays at Lhasa temple.

Golmud in Qinghai province. Golmud is the starting point for the main access to Lhasa by road, and the other main overland entry is through Nepal.

LHASA

After arriving by air from Chengdu there's a two-hour bus ride between the Gonggar airstrip and Lhasa. Whether the airport is so far from the capital to keep it out of Tibetan hands, or because distance doesn't mean much in the rarefied Tibetan psyche, is a question you can ponder as you bounce along.

The route follows the wide flat valley beds of the Yarlong Tsangpo River and Kyichu River, winding alongside rearing mountain peaks. As it approaches Lhasa the barren terrain is broken by Tibetan farming compounds – white-walled, flat-roofed stone buildings with carved door-ways and window frames and prayer-flags rippling from stripped saplings on the roofs. These in turn give way to a

ABOVE Tribesman carries dried mutton for sale in Lhasa bazaar while three Tibetan pilgrim women OPPOSITE sport "spring" bonnets and ornate silver-decorated costumes.

dusty, unattractive suburban sprawl of Chinese military compounds, admini-strative buildings, work unit barracks and tin-roofed warehouses, the "new" Lhasa that has sprung up since the 1959 occupation.

As the bus reaches the city itself, that most photographed, alluring and ren-owned symbol of the spiritualism and cul-ture of "forbidden" Tibet rises up over the tarmac road and more picturesque huddles of traditional Tibetan homes and stores – the soaring white, gold and ocher ram-parts, towers and apartments of the huge Potala Palace.

The bus pulls into the city's main depot right underneath the Potala's eastern walls. CAAC is right next door. The central post office is just down the street on one of the city's major intersections. One of the great comforts of Lhasa is al-ready quite apparent – it is one of the easiest cities in China to get around.

You'll find that the street map of Lhasa is dominated by two main arteries. **Xingfu Lun** runs east-west right through the heart of the new and old sections of the city, link-ing the Potala with the newer tourist hotels and, five kilometers (three miles) to the west of the city, the famed Drepung Monastery. To the east it links the post of-fice with the main bazaar and pilgrim's path, the Barkhor, the holiest of all Tibet's temples, the Jokhang, and, beyond them, the most popular low-priced Tibetan guesthouses and restaurants.

To the north, starting from the rear of the bus station, **Jiefang Beilu** runs into dusty wastelands beyond the Sports Com-plex toward another huge religious cen-ter, the Sera Monastery. South of the city, the Lhasa River trickles and bubbles east to west over wide, flat pebbled beds and sand banks. Beyond the river, further south, the city is guarded by a high, sharp-ly sculptured mountain range which acts as a kind of natural clock, or regulator of the rhythm of tourist life. In winter, for example, when the night air is ab-solutely frigid, only the brave or most

brazen visitor stirs and moves from the bed covers before the dot of 9 am, when the sun blasts over the range and begins softening the bitter chill.

Getting Around Lhasa

Unless you're staying in one of the high-priced tourist hotels east of the Potala, there's really only one readily available form of transport in Lhasa – the bicycle. But the city is flat and its social atmosphere so dreamy and laid-back that any other means of perambulation would be tantamount to reckless haste.

Health

Attractive and challenging as it is, any plan to visit Lhasa must take health into account. Because of the high altitude it is definitely no place for anyone with a heart condition, anemia or any other form of chronic ill-health. Elderly people, particularly, should think twice about risking it. Even young, healthy visitors are affected by the 4,000 m (13,100 ft) altitude, the most immediate symptoms being a slight shortage of breath, an initial sense of lightheadedness and a gradually consuming lethargy. On a long bicycle ride or a trudge up the endless stone stairways leading into the Potala, all these symptoms come together in panting exhaustion and headaches if frequent rest-stops are not made along the way.

Some people, young or old, suffer a more severe form of altitude sickness, with chronic nausea and headaches, caused by an insufficient supply of oxygen to the brain. Altitude sickness strikes at random, and whether you come down with it or not will depend on your own metabolism. It can often be eased with aspirin and a period of complete rest, but if it persists and is extremely debilitating there's only one cure – get a plane back down to the "lowlands."

Otherwise, the simplest way to cope with it is to always take things easy, attempt only one major excursion or errand a day, drink plenty of tea, and if you wake up gasping for breath in the middle of the night don't panic – it's just your brain changing your pattern of breathing to suit the high-level conditions. Just go back to sleep and await the sun's nine o'clock alarm call.

Hotels

There are two comfortable and modern group tour hotels in Lhasa, the **Holiday Inn Lhasa** west of the Potala on Xingfu Xilu and the new **Tibet Guesthouse** which is close by. Both offer Western-style rooms and suites with bathrooms, along with restaurants and bars. And both are in the higher price range. Their disadvantage is their distance from the city center. Another hotel called the **No. 3 Guesthouse,** operated by CITS, is even more isolated – lying 10 km (6 miles) northwest of the city.

The **No. 2 Municipal Guesthouse** is likewise a considerable distance from the city center – and remember, distance is important at this altitude. It offers an all-in room rate, including meals, but is on the city's southeastern fringe near the Tibet University.

If you're reasonably young, healthy, regard Tibet as both a cultural dream and a challenge and are willing to rough it a little, there are really only three places to stay, and all within easy walking distance of the bus station – the **Hotel Banak Shol, No. 1 Regional Guesthouse** and the **Snowland Hotel.** All three are traditional Tibetan guesthouses, beautifully rustic and antique, friendly, informal and offer the company and companionship of dedicated travelers. They are, in fact, an integral part of the Tibetan experience.

The Snowland is on Xiao Hua Zi Lu, south of Xingfu Xilu, and is conveniently close to the Jokhang Temple and the Barkhor. You can get a double room there at a "backpack" budget rate. It also rents bicycles.

The Banak Shol is a more intimate guesthouse fronting on to Xingfu Xilu, which its signboard proclaims as "Happiness Street." Life is certainly happy in the Banak Shol. It has a rough, dark earthen-floored "lobby" and rustic wooden stairways that are more like step-ladders leading up to its guest floors, and when you first walk in your immediate

impression is that you've stumbled into that bizarre Central Asian scene in *Raiders of the Lost Ark*. The third floor is reserved for foreigners and features a long south-facing, sun-blasted balcony and patio called The Beach, a solar cooker for boiling eggs and heating stews. Hot water is provided three times a day for tea and washing. The lifestyle when I was staying there lay somewhere between the heady years of the sixties and the last puff of liberalism in the late seventies, transplanted from Kathmandu and flourishing in its new environment.

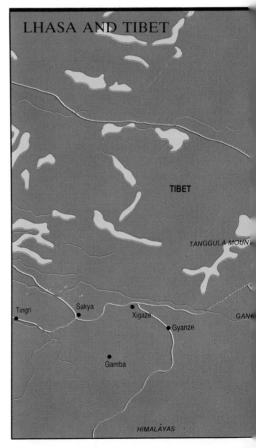

LHASA AND TIBET

TIBET

TANGGULA MOUN

Tingri   Sakya   Xigaze   GAN

Gyanze

Gamba

HIMALAYAS

The Banak Shol is where I awoke one morning to the sound of lusty male voices singing, of all things, the "Eton Boating Song" – "Row, row, row your boat / Gently down the stream / Merrily, merrily ..." etc. I lay there for a while wondering if the altitude, the fierce sun, yak butter tea and various herbal tonics hadn't finally got to me. After a while I investigated and found that it was coming from a Tibetan English-language class being conducted by an American volunteer in a room down the balcony.

Restaurants

Not only is there not much of a cuisine in Tibet, there's not that much to eat either. The Tibetans themselves subsist on salted tea mixed with yak butter and *tsampa,* a barley flour, dried yak meat and mutton, cheese and yogurt. The Chinese have

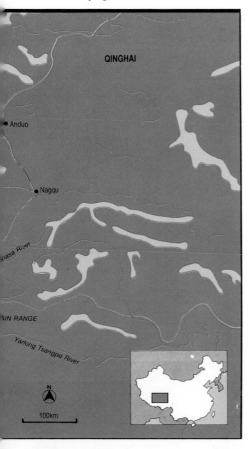

introduced rice, fruit, vegetables and fish. Other than that, it's a place where you pick off stalls and nibble in the daytime and try to get a full, reasonably nourishing meal at night.

The two top hotels, the **Holiday Inn Lhasa** and the **Tibet,** both have reasonably

good Chinese dining rooms and Western breakfasts, at tourist rates, and can be counted on if you feel as though you're fading away with hunger. The Banak Shol and Snowland have more informal eating places where you can get cheap, nourishing breakfasts, soups, noodles and stir-fried dishes. Across Xingfu Xilu from the Banak Shol there's the **Meiweixian (Tasty) Restaurant** where you can choose stir-fry ingredients in an open kitchen and have them cook up good soup-noodle dishes to suit your taste.

Just west of the Banak Shol on Xingfu Xilu you'll find the **Halal Moslem Restaurant,** another rough-and-ready venue for cheap noodle and mutton stew dishes, steamed bread and Tibetan-style green tea brewed in covered cups with dried lychee nuts and big lumps of raw sugar. There are other Moslem restaurants near the main mosque to the north of Yanhe Donglu and in the Barkhor bazaar.

For a real night out, Lhasa does boast one private tourist-style restaurant, the **Dharkoy** on Linkuo Lu, two blocks from the Banak Shol and serving substantial breakfasts and Sichuan fish and vegetarian dishes. Other than that, much of the daily life in Lhasa is spent foraging for supplementary supplies. Stalls along Xingfu Xilu and around the bus station sell canned peaches, lychees and other fruits, canned juices, biscuits, chocolate and nuts. If you get to the Barkhor early enough in the morning you can feast on delicious yogurt sprinkled with raw sugar. Elsewhere there are fruit and vegetable stalls, and the department stores are well stocked with canned meats and fish and other munchies. You certainly will not starve.

Sightseeing

Lhasa's main cultural attractions are involved in one way or another with its religious life, so much of the time there is spent checking around for "events" at the local temples and monasteries. Because of the long suppression of religious activity, the full religious calendar is only now

being slowly restored, and "events" can often be announced only days before they are about to happen. But if a temple is opening up for a day of worship by pilgrims, or if new lamas are being chosen or inducted, or if a new *thangka* or sacred tapestry is being unveiled, word buzzes around the tourist community pretty fast.

First, though, any new arrival needs an immediate immersion course in the Tibetan social and cultural character, and the place to get this is in the Barkhor, where you find the main bazaar and a bustling and picturesque rabbit warren of streets

that form a sacred pilgrim's path around the Jokhang Temple. The bazaar is a crowded, kaleidoscopic whirl of friendly faces, the stunned expressions of out-of-towners, "Honest Joe" bead and artifact traders and colorfully costumed tribespeople from all over the country – their mahogany faces so hauntingly reminiscent of another time and another culture that the entire pageant looks like a massive gathering of the North American Indian nations.

The Jokhang

As for the Jokhang Temple, it is the sacred spot around which everything

else revolves. Built in the seventh century by King Songsten Gampo, a fierce military campaigner and the founding father of Buddhism in Tibet, it is the nation's holiest shrine and contains its most revered religious relic, a gilded and bejeweled original image of Sakyamuni Buddha. The Jokhang is beautiful and fascinating, its roof laden with gilded bells, birds, beasts, dragons and two deer holding the Buddhist Wheel of Dharma, its forecourt usually packed with worshipers either prostrating before the doors or lighting fragrant juniper in a tall juniper hearth to please the gods, and inside, among its shrine halls and relics, a vast gallery of brass prayer-drums spinning in unison as the lines of faithful file through.

The area in front of the Jokhang was once part of the walled precincts of the Old City. Now it's been cleared and turned into a wide pedestrian square, flanked by arts and crafts and provisions stores, and is the city's main social hub. At the far end of the square there's an interesting tea-house set on a first-floor patio where you sit for hours sipping sweetened green tea, eating noodles and studying the activity below. It also has a hi-fi system that blares out a continuous stream of Nepalese and Chinesse pop and a peculiar little Pakistani offering called "Krishna Rock."

The Potala

The Potala Palace dominates all cultural sightseeing in Lhasa. It's such a magnificent structure that it takes days just to study it from all angles and in all weather and lighting before actually going inside. In the morning it blazes with gold in the first rays of the sun, and then, as the sun climbs higher, it settles back into white and ocher. If there's an early morning mist or dust-storm about, it seems to float on a bed of clouds.

The Potala was built by the Great Fifth Dalai Lama, another military and religious strongman who ruled from 1617 to 1682. He brought the Tibetans together as one

---

ABOVE Rooftop apartments of the Potala Palace, the stronghold of the Dalai Lamas, now a vast museum OPPOSITE of .palace treasures, chapels and shrines, libraries and tombs of eight supreme rulers. PREVIOUS PAGE The magnificent Potala Palace.

sovereign people, established the ruling supremacy of the Yellow Hats – one of the three main Buddhist sects in Tibet – and provided the Potala as the seat of Tibetan government and both palace and tomb of the Dalai Lamas for centuries to come. The section that the Great Fifth built is known as the White Palace, the administrative and residential section, entered from the soaring eastern stairways and huge doors above the village of Sho at the foot of the temple-fort.

The western half of the Potala is the Red Palace, the religious center, and is packed

at all, and often it's closed from 12:30 pm to 2:30 pm for the lunch-time siesta. It is always advisable to check with other visitors whether it's actually open before attempting the long climb to its main entrances. It's an exhausting approach in the thin air, and should not be rushed.

Behind the Potala you'll find a small park with a pavilion set in the middle of it. This was a trysting spot built by one of the black sheep of the dynasty, the Sixth Dalai Lama (1683-1706) who became so debauched that he was kidnapped and murdered by his subjects.

with chapels and shrines, golden stupas, the tombs of eight Dalai Lamas and vast libraries full of Buddhist scriptures. The entrance to this section is a massive ornate gateway at the western end of the Potala with heavy medieval wooden doors decorated with knotted yak hair left as devotional offerings by pilgrims.

The Potala is supposed to be open to the public from 9 am to 4 pm every day except Sundays. Sometimes it just doesn't open

The Summer Palace

Three kilometers (two miles) to the west of the Potala, near the Lhasa Hotel, you'll find **Norbulingka (Jewel Park)** the Summer Palace of the rulers. It was laid out by the Seventh Dalai Lama (1708-1757) who ascended to the throne with the backing of China's Qing dynasty and whose reign brought Tibet for the first time under Chinese control.

The park features woods and gardens, pavilions, a small zoo and palace buildings erected by several rulers, including a new palace constructed by the present Dalai Lama before he fled Tibet. The whole complex is worth a full day's visit, and is less exhausting than the Potala. One interesting section that should not be missed is the **Kasang Temple** where you can study some 70 magnificent hanging *thangkas* depicting Buddhist stories and mandalas. These fantastic weavings, some of them so big that they're draped right down the central facade of the Potala Palace during special religious events, are so deeply treasured and revered that they're often unveiled only once every 20, 30 or even 50 years.

Drepung

Drepung (Rice Heap) Monastery, about five kilometers (three miles) west of Lhasa city, or an hour's sedate travel by bicycle, was where the powerful Great Fifth Dalai Lama resided and ruled while the Potala Palace was being built. It's a huge monastery – in its heyday it had rich estates, held sway over about 700 subsidiary

monasteries and was staffed by no fewer than 10,000 monks. Most of its high lamas fled to India with the Dalai Lama in the Chinese military crackdown.

Nowadays only a few hundred monks and novices are left there, and part of the northwestern section, the Gwoma, is in ruins. A striking aspect of any visit is the vehemence with which some of the lamas will sometimes speak of the Chinese – the monastery fared badly in the Cultural Revolution. Wandering through Drepung is like stepping through a medieval town, with narrow stone alleyways rising and

winding between the monastery's main temples, colleges and chanting halls. It is rich in relics, religious and historical, and as you move from one building to another you can find huge *thangkas* and murals, gold stupas, the tombs of three Dalai Lamas, yak butter sculptures, ancient weapons and armor, garish oracle dolls and the monastery's holiest treasure, a huge gilded Buddha.

In the hills to the west of the monastery you may stumble across young lamas practicing the temple pipes and long bronze trumpets that are sounded in religious rites. One of the hills, Mount Gyengbu-wudze, is a sacred spot where, on certain occasions in the summer, pilgrims flock to spend the night chanting and dancing. Again, you need to keep an ear to the ground to learn when these devotional singsongs are to take place.

Sera Monastery

North of Lhasa, **Sera (Merciful Hail) Monastery** is a less formidable distance to ride. It takes about half an hour to get there along Jiefang Beilu, turning off to the right before you reach the Regional Military Hospital. Founded in the fifteenth century, Sera has had something of a reputation for rebellious behavior, and in 1947 its high lamas actually plotted to overthrow the Dalai Lama and put their own man in the Potala.

The monastery features three interesting chanting halls and a wealth of religious artwork including an image of Ayaguriba, a horse-headed demon that typifies the blending of animist Bon and Buddhist beliefs, a huge image of the Maitreya Buddha, rock paintings, a magnificent array of murals in its Drezame chanting hall and its holiest relic, an image of the many-handed, many-eyed Bodhisattva Chenrezi – Tibet's version of the Avalokitesvara of India and China's goddess of mercy, Guan Yin.

In the hills to the west of Sera the maps pinpoint a spot called the **Sky Burial Site.** It's a place which you'll find is fiercely debated among the traveling community in Lhasa – it's where the traditional Tibetan funerals take place, the bodies broken up and cast among vultures and other scavengers to be picked clean. This practice, gruesome as it may seem to outsiders, is necessary because the frozen ground won't allow normal burial and fuel is too scarce for elaborate cremations. It has taken on a spiritual significance over the centuries, representing a fundamental principle of the Tibeetan death ceremonies – that the spirit is sacrosanct and the earthly body means nothing.

Where the debate comes in is whether it should be regarded as a tourist attraction. If the answer's not immediately obvious,

---

ABOVE Sacred wheel and deer sculptures OPPOSITE LEFT atop Jokhang Temple, bizarre Sky Burial Site RIGHT and Jokhang Temple prayer wheels BOTTOM AND ABOVE.

the *domdens,* or body breakers, settle the matter quite effectively: they will not tolerate any foreign visitors, and when I was in Lhasa a Japanese girl was chased and beaten for intruding. The most sensible and understanding policy is to stay right away from it.

Street Sights

Aside from the color and splendor of its monasteries, Lhasa offers a few cultural sideshows that should not be missed – the **Moslem Mosque** in the heart of the Islamic Old Quarter south of the Banak Shol, for instance, and the **Lhasa Carpet Factory,** the biggest rug weaving center in Tibet, to the southeast of the city near the University of Tibet. In the west, opposite

the Tibet Guesthouse, there's a **Tibetan Performing Arts School** where, on certain days, you may be lucky enough to catch a rehearsal of local song and dance or one of the Tibetan opera companies.

If you're interested in medicine, go along to the **Tibetan Traditional Hospital,** on Renmin Lu just west of the Jokhang Temple, which practices the complex folk-science of Tibetan medicine based on herbal treatments, astrology, acupuncture, moxibustion and even the Buddhist sutras. One interesting fact is that it forbids surgery: it was banned "forever" in the ninth century when the mother of the ruler of that time died during what must have been a primitive and agonizing operation.

THE TIBETAN TRAIL

Beyond Lhasa, one of the world's most forbidding and yet exciting landscapes awaits the more intrepid visitor to Tibet. The hinterland offers rugged adventure, breathtaking views of the Himalayas and Mount Everest and a gem-string of relatively undisturbed Buddhist wonders. Travel is arduous, accommodation and general living conditions are primitive,

but the rewards are well worth the struggle.

Until the tour trails in Tibet become a little more sophisticated, the easiest route for organized groups and individual travelers is the Lhasa-Nepal route via Xigaze and Zhangmu (Kasa) on the Nepalese border. It's still the only route that foreigners are officially allowed to follow, but while only "tour" groups are being admitted from the Nepalese side of the border an increasing number of individual travelers are managing to go right through the other way by public bus and hitchhiking. And while visitors no longer need a special permit to enter Tibet, a Public Security Bureau stamp is still needed for any travel outside Lhasa, along with an exit visa to cross into Nepal.

There are currently two choices of official travel in Tibet, by organized mountaineering and trekking tours offered by agencies outside the country, or by organized trips offered by CITS and a number of other travel agencies in Lhasa. CITS operate a large fleet of four-wheel drive vehicles and tour buses that can be chartered by groups of around 10 or more, but the cost is quite high. Cheaper excursions can be negotiated with free-lance drivers at the Snowland and

Banak Shol Hotels, or at the following transport agencies:

Lhasa Travel Service Company, No. 2 Municipal Guesthouse, Yanhu Donglu.
"Taxi Company", Xingfu Donglu opposite the Barkhor.
Lhasa City Transport Unit, No.1 Regional Guesthouse, Renmin Lu.

One in a Billion

Unofficially, there are public buses servicing most parts of the country at a fraction of the organized excursion rates, though it must be appreciated beforehand that most coaches in Tibet are ramshackle and usually overcrowded with travelers and baggage, and rarely follow a timetable. By the same token, the innate friendliness of the Tibetans can make the most grueling journey a memorable experience; and if you have the necessary stamina and sense of adventure, this is really the only way to see Tibet.

On the **Lhasa-Nepal** route you can get a bus from the New Bus Station

---

ABOVE Faces of Lhasa – OPPOSITE traditional guesthouse entrance, Halal Moslem restaurant and rug seller. Sidewalk stalls ABOVE offers watch repairs LEFT and colorful handmade garments RIGHT.

near the Lhasa Hotel for the eight-hour run to **Gyanze**, a rustic truckstop with a magnificent stupa temple, the **Kumbum**. It also features the equally striking **Palkhor Monastery**, which has an interesting array of Buddha images and a bizarre "chamber of hell" in which the skeletons, figures and murals depicting Sky Burials are covered up because they are considered too grotesque for public display. There's another room with walls papered with sheets of the *Illustrated Indian Weekly* of 1946 featuring high society Punjab weddings, Swedish temperance clinics and advertisements exhorting readers to "Lose Weight Fast with Bile Beans!"

Gyanze has two guesthouses, both of them cheap but rough truck-stop establishments, and an eating place called **The Restaurant** which dishes up potatoes, yak meat and vegetables. But the conditions are tolerable enough for a couple of nights before taking the next step of the journey either by bus or by hitching a lift for ¥10 a time on the Tibetan trucks to Xigaze, 95 km (59 miles) or about three hours to the northwest.

Xigaze

Xigaze is Tibet's second largest city and the junction for the route south to the Nepalese border. It's also the traditional seat of power of the Panchen Lamas, the divine "prime ministers" of the Tibetan Buddhist hierarchy, appointed from the abbots of the city's huge **Tashilhunpo Monastery**.

One of the four greatest Buddhist monasteries in Tibet, Tashilhunpo was founded in the fifteenth century, sacked and looted by an invading army of Nepalese Gurkhas in 1791, stormed and closed down by the People's Liberation Army in 1960, yet survives today as one of the most splendid of all Tibet's religious centers. It is famed for its immense nine-story *thangka* wall from which huge Buddhist tapestries are displayed during festivals, its 26 m (85ft) high Maitreya Buddha, and the Panchen

Lama's Palace, the main treasure of which is a priceless gold and silver stupa studded with precious gems. It also has its own exhibition of grotesque demons to recall the psychic horrors of Bon animism.

There are two other interesting Buddhist monasteries close to Xigaze, both built in the Mongolian style. **Shalu Monastery,** 22 km (13.6 miles) south of the city, was a center for psychic training in which lamas are said to have developed incredible paranormal powers, and some of the feats that they allegedly performed are depicted in a series of murals. **Narthang (Ladang) Monastery,** 15 km (9.3 miles) west of Xigaze, built in the twelveth century, was a leading theological center and printing house. It was almost completely destroyed by the Red Guards in the 1960s.

One other interesting center of culture is still flourishing in Xigaze, the **Silver Crafts Factory** where visitors can watch craftsmen and their young apprentices fashion traditional cups, bowls and yak butter lamps from gold, silver and copper, working over charcoal furnaces and yak-skin bellows.

Xigaze has begun to develop its tourist potential with the new **Xigaze Hotel,** opened in early 1986. The rooms are absolutely luxurious by Tibetan standards

and the room rate matches the decor. CITS has its office there.

There are two other old Tibetan hangouts, the **Xigaze No. 1 Guesthouse,** opposite the Tashilhunpo Monastery, a friendly but rather basic trucker's hotel, and the **No. 2 Guesthouse** which features a reasonably good Chinese restaurant and offers reasonably cheap dormitary beds and expensive double rooms. Both establishments have one thing going for them – they are where you can negotiate a lift by truck for the third stage of the journey to the Nepal border.

Himalayan Grandeur

The 530 km (329 miles) stretch to the border town of Zhangmu crosses three high passes, the third of which, Lalung Leh (5,214 m or 17,106 ft), beyond the town of New Tinggri, offers the grand physical and spiritual spectacle that draws almost every foreign pilgrim to Tibet – a panoramic view of the majestic snow-capped peaks of the Himalayas. On the way there are other splendid sights, the monolithic Sakya Monastery, a Mongolian temple-fortress 26 km (16 miles) off the main highway from the Sakya River Bridge which itself is 128 km (79 miles) from Xigaze; also the Rongbuk, a 5,000 m (16,404 ft) peak near New Tinggri which

not only offers a clear view of Mount Everest but is only six kilometers (3.7 miles) below the Everest Base Camp. As for Tinggri, it has a reasonably comfortable guesthouse with three-a-room beds and a restaurant.

Beyond New Tinggri the road climbs through the high Lalung Leh Pass and breaks through the Himalayan barrier – and from there it plunges 3,000 m (9,842 ft) over a mere 90 km (56 miles) down to the Zhangmu border crossing and the warm, lush "lowlands" of Nepal. On the Nepalese side, truck rides can be negotiated from the village of Tatopani to Barahbise, an hour's drive south, where buses leave four times a day for Kathmandu.

Sunrise on the Lhasa River LEFT on the city's southern boundary. Animism of Bon and refinement of Buddhism RIGHT in Potala Palace wall painting.

Xi'an and the Northwest

XI'AN AND THE NORTHWEST

XI'AN

Xi'an is one of China's oldest and most illustrious cities – the capital of Shaanxi province, cultural hub of north-central China and the principal gateway to the remarkable oasis towns and cities, Islamic minorities and Buddhist treasures of the arid northeast. It is really the north-central crossroads of China, providing access by train between east and west and linking the northern and southern provinces.

The city has played a strategic role in Chinese history for more than 3,000 years. Known as Chang'an, it served as the capital of 11 dynasties covering a period of 1,100 years up to the reign of the Tang (618–907). It was also the eastern terminus of the Silk Road and, lying in the path of the main Central Asian conduit into the heart of China, was a heavily fortified frontier post for several centuries.

In 1374, engineers of the Ming rule, already strengthening the Great Wall, bolstered Xi'an's defenses by tearing down and reconstructing the wall that had encircled the city since ancient times. The massive structure, 12 m (39 ft) high and 14 to 18 m (46 to 59 ft) thick and running for about 12 km (7.4 miles) around the city, still stands today and is the first vivid impression of Xi'an's historic importance that visitors get as they arrive by train.

All this historic prominence has endowed modern Xi'an with one of the greatest treasure troves of ancient culture to be found anywhere in China, and it's given the city a new strategic role as the nation's number one tourist mecca. In the high summer season it is packed with tour groups and, unfortunately, it is also a clamoring bee-hive of frantically persistent souvenir hawkers, especially at the most renowned and astonishing of all its cultural attractions – the life-size terracotta "army" of the iron man of Chinese history, Qinshihuangdi.

Access

Xi'an can be reached by air from most parts of the country, with direct flights from Beijing, Guangzhou, Shanghai, Chengdu, Golmud, Urumqi, Lanzhou, Kunming and Nanjing. There are also direct trains from Beijing, Shanghai, Chengdu, Qingdao and Wuhan and di-rect rail services in turn to Xining and Urumqi, opening up the "wild west" of Qinghai and Xinjiang, and the route of the old Silk

Road. You can also fly directly between Xi'an and Lhasa.

Hotels

There are several tourist-class hotels in Xi'an, with room rates to match – the **Golden Flower Hotel** at 8 Changle Xilu, west of the city wall, catering to the business travelers and high-priced package tour groups, along with the Holiday Inn Xi'an, the renovated and Holiday Inn-managed Bell Tower Hotel in the city's downtown atrea, the Xi'an Hotel, New World Dynasty (not to be confused with the locally-owned New World) and at least six other major international-class establishments which have guaranteed somewhat cut-throat room rates for some time to come. For a central location with comfort and easy access to the city's main cultural attractions, the Bell Tower would rate the best, with the Holiday Inn, Golden Flower and New World Dynasty also offering the service and cuisine that comes with international management. The huge Soviet-style **Renmin Hotel** on Dongxin Jie to the northeast of the Bell Tower, has been renovated and put under French management, but still features its grand forecourt with ornamental pools and fountains.

Restaurants

The four leading hotels all offer a range of excellent to middling Chinese restaurants and Western-style coffee shops. Beyond that, the huge **Xi'an Restaurant** at 298 Dong Dajie, a short walk east of the Bell Tower, offers cuisine ranging from Beijing duck to steak and fries in its 14 dining rooms containing 300 tables and capable of seating a total 1,800 diners.

The **Wuyi Restaurant** at 351 Dong Dajie between the Bell Tower and the Xi'an Friendship Store serves Yangzhou cuisine and Western food and proclaims itself famous for its "assorted cold dishes in the shape of flowers, birds, scenery and animals" and its "squirrel fish" – a fish fried in a thick sweet-sour sauce that curls up and is said to look like a squirrel when it's ready to serve.

Another giant eating place is the **Dongya (East Asia) Restaurant** at 46 Luoma Shi, just south of the Bell Tower, and there's also a good **Sichuan Cuisine Restaurant** on Jiefang Lu, east of the Renmin Hotel. The **Minsheng,** right next to it, is another popular venue.

Sightseeing

There are two main aspects to sightseeing in Xi'an, the city itself and the cultural attractions that lie within its ancient walls

and the Qinshihuangdi Mausoleum and a host of surrounding attractions on a wide plain to the northeast. In Xi'an itself, the **City Wall** is worth more than a casual inspection, especially at its four main gates to the north, south, east and west over which the Ming engineers built small multi-story forts with firing points from which teams of archers and sappers could shower hostile forces with arrows, gunpowder bombs and blazing oil and naptha.

As for the **Bell Tower,** transplanted at the hub of the city from an earlier fourteenth century site during the Qing dynasty, it's such a central landmark and so

festooned with trolley-bus cables that you can't help but notice it every day. Before the 1949 revolution it was used as a garrison and prison by the Guomingdang nationalists. There's a smaller and more interesting **Drum Tower** just slightly to the west of it, and beyond that a far more fascinating place to inspect – the **Qingzhen Si (Grand Mosque),** one of the biggest Islamic places of worship in China.

The **Provincial Museum,** lying close to the old city's South Gate, is part of an old Confucian temple with exhibition halls rebuilt in the 1960s to the Ming and Qing architectural styles. Its three main halls are packed with relics covering the period from prehistory to the Tang

ABOVE Tranquillity of Grand Mosque in Xi'an
OPPOSITE Contrasts with boisterous color of souvenir hawkers at tomb of terra-cotta soldiers.

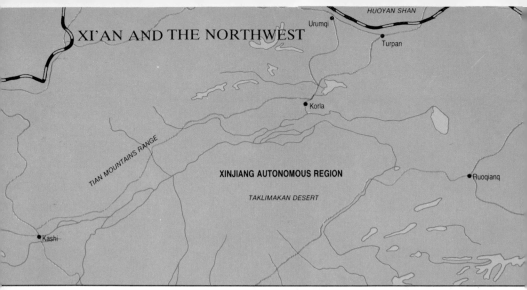

HUOYAN SHAN

Urumqi

Turpan

Korla

TIAN MOUNTAINS RANGE

XINJIANG AUTONOMOUS REGION

Ruoqianq

TAKLIMAKAN DESERT

Kashi

dynasty, and they include terra-cotta horses from the Qin reign, gilded Sui dynasty Buddha images, carvings from the Warring States period and Tang pottery, figures, horses and camels.

The museum's most prized exhibit is the extraordinary Forest of Steles – 2,300 large stone tablets engraved with imperial edicts, commentaries on the classics, celebrated styles of calligraphy and other records of the ages back to Han times. One stele dated 781 records the appearance of the Syrian Christian school of thought, Nestorianism, which found its way to ancient Chang'an via the Silk Road.

South of the city wall there are two Tang dynasty pagodas, **Dayan (Big Wild Goose)** and **Xiaoyan (Small Wild Goose),** the larger one built to honor the Buddhist monk Xuon Zang who first brought the Buddhist scriptures from India to China and to house the 1,335 volumes of translations that he spent virtually the rest of his life producing.

Geming (Revolutionary) Park and the nearby **Memorial Museum of the Eighth Route Army,** north of the city near the railway station, commemorate the communist revolutionary drive against the nationalists and the Japanese in the 1930s. It's a place of special interest to Canadians, because Norman Bethune, the Montreal medic who joined Mao's forces and became one of the most beloved foreign

heroes of the communist cause, lived and worked here with Zhou Enlai and Deng Xiaoping at one stage of the campaign.

ABOVE Faces of Xi'an – majesty of Big Goose Pagoda LEFT, timelessness of terra-cotta soldiers RIGHT and ornate architecture of old imperial playgroung, the Xi'an Hot Spings.

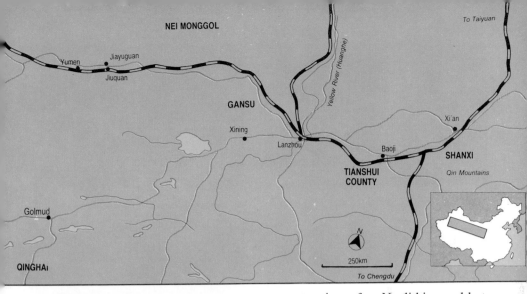

reconstruction of a Neolithic mud-hut hamlet and relics of that distant age – including clay jars in which children were buried – and the **Huaqing Hot Springs resort,** a complex of baths, temples and halls in which the Qin, Han and Tang rulers languished and bathed.

The tour calls into the **Tomb of Qin-shihuangdi** for about an hour and a half, and as I've mentioned before, visitors have such a hassle with the hordes of souvenir hawkers there that any longer could mean getting very peeved and irritated. The exhibition is, however, awe-inspiring – the packed ranks of some 6,000 life-size fully armed and armored warriors, each of them bearing the distinctive features of the men they were modeled on, standing with their horses under the sweeping roof of a protective exhibition hall. The aspect that I found particularly interesting is a section to the rear of the main vault where there are ranks of figures that are only partly excavated – the heads and torsos emerging from the earth as though from the depths of history itself.

Of all the historic landmarks of the great China pilgrimage, this is perhaps the place of deepest sanctity. It exudes a reverence and power, and it can also be quite amusing: although photography inside the hall is strictly forbidden, everyone who visits it has one desperate aim in mind, to get their own picture of the spectacle.

The Terra-cotta Soldiers

Outside Xi'an there's a whole plain dotted with tombs, pagodas and temples, but there's really only one great attraction to make every effort to see – the **Qinshi-huangdi Mausoleum** and its terra-cotta army. Most tours take in the **Banpo Museum,** where you can view an interesting

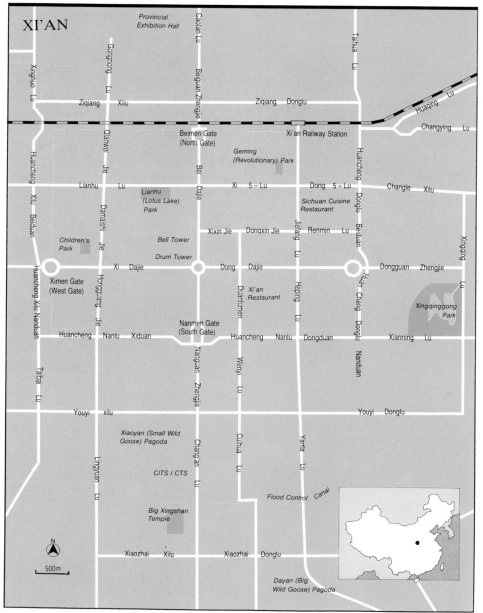

XI'AN

Provincial Exhibition Hall

Caolan Lu

Taihua Lu

Gongnong

Beiguan Zhengjie

Xinghuo Lu

Huaqing Lu

Ziqiang Xilu

Ziqiang Donglu

Changying Lu

Qianwei Jie

Beimen Gate (North Gate)

Xi'an Railway Station

Huancheng Xilu Beiduan

Geming (Revolutionary) Park

Bei Dajie

Huancheng

Lianhu Lu

Xi 5 - Lu

Dong 5 - Lu

Changle Xilu

Damaishi Jie

Lianhu (Lotus Lake) Park

Sichuan Cuisine Restaurant

Dongju Beiduan

Children's Park

Xixin Jie

Dongxin Jie

Renmin Lu

Jiefang Lu

Xingqing Lu

Bell Tower

Xi Dajie

Dong Dajie

Dongguan Zhengjie

Hongguang Jie

Drum Tower

Ximen Gate (West Gate)

Duanlumen

Xi'an Restaurant

Heping Lu

Huan Cheng Donglu

Xingqinggong Park

Nanmen Gate (South Gate)

Huancheng Nanlu Xiduan

Huancheng Nanlu

Dongduan

Xianning Lu

Taibai Lu

Nanguan Zhengjie

Wenyi Lu

Nanduan

Youyi xilu

Youyi Donglu

Xiaoyan (Small Wild Goose) Pagoda

Chang'an Lu

Cuihua Lu

Yanta Lu

Lingyuan Lu

CITS / CTS

Flood Control Canal

Big Xingshan Temple

N

500m

Xiaozhai Xilu

Xiaozhai Donglu

Dayan (Big Wild Goose) Pagoda

And, to do them justice, everyone has a trick or two up their sleeve to try to thwart the harassed and rather unfortunate attendants whose job it is to jump and bark at the first sound of a shutter release.

You see innocent, engrossed "students" of Qin history wandering around with their cameras hanging loosely at their waists, clicking from the hip like spent revolvers as they sidle along the barriers. You see others cringing behind the columns, frantically trying to focus up and adjust their apertures before one of the guards pounces on them. It becomes a sport, the shutter-bugs and the guards playing cat-and-mouse all over the catwalks. I found that the best way to get a shot was to simply raise the camera, casually line everything up and shoot a half-dozen frames, and when the bristling features appear and the voice barks "No photo!" grovel with apologies and promise never to do it again. And be content with what you've managed to get.

ABOVE Faces of Moslem China – textile merchant displays wares in Qinghai provincial bazaar OPPOSITE LEFT, master swordsman drills in Lanzhou ABOVE, young Spring Festival dancers with masks RIGHT.

LANZHOU

If Xi'an is the crossroads of central China, Lanzhou is its radial right arm. From this former Han dynasty garrison and frontier post there is access by rail to the heart of Qinghai province, and from there by road to Tibet. Another rail route runs directly to the old Silk Road oasis towns of the northwest, and yet another sweeps across the northern reaches of China, across the vast grasslands of Inner Mongolia, toward Beijing.

Although it's now a key industrial city, Lanzhou is modern, well laid out with wide streets and boulevards, and has good hotels and department stores. It also sports a huge Beijing-style central city square, about 10 minutes' walk west of the Lanzhou Hotel, where thousands of people meet every day to fly kites and balloons and climb a very strange and novel sightseeing tower which looks like a Moslem minaret with a children's slide winding around it.

The city's Moslem community is quite large, and it is really the first major center heading into the northwest where you can recognize the distinctive, surprisingly Middle Eastern features of the region's Turkic-speaking Hui minority. It also has a number of historic and cultural attractions, including an interesting set of Buddhist cave sculptures dating from the Tang dynasty.

Access

There are direct air services to Lanzhou from Beijing, Guangzhou, Nanjing, Xi'an,

Hotel is another monument to Soviet socialist architecture with comfortable double rooms and a dormitory. I found the relatively new **Jincheng Hotel,** one block north of the Lanzhou, to be an excellent place to stay at budget rates for a clean and almost luxurious room, a good restaurant and lobby coffee shop and all the facilities and amenities that any traveler needs.

There's another hotel, the **Shenli,** to the west of the inner city near the railway line, too far from the railway station to be considered a convenient place to stay. However, it's the main access point for public transport to the Buddhist caves.

Sightseeing

Lanzhou lies on the south bank of the Yellow River and has a mountain park-land called **Baita Shan (White Pagoda Hill)** just across on the northern bank featuring Ming and Qing dynasty pavilions and a Buddhist pagoda. Elsewhere, there's the **Temple of the Town Gods** that can be reached on foot east of the central traffic circle at the Lanzhou Hotel, and another recently renovated temple near the bridge that crosses the river to White Pagoda Park.

The Provincial Museum, opposite the Friendship Hotel, has the skeleton of a prehistoric mammoth dug up in 1973 and an interesting array of Neolithic and Han era pottery, murals, clay and bronze figures and the revered "Flying horses" that gave the Han and Tang cavalries the speed, mobility and endurance they needed to fight the nomadic Huns.

You'll find CITS in the strangest of places, a bus depot between the Lanzhou and Jincheng Hotels. They're on the second floor of an office building on the right towards the end of the yard. They're a friendly, accommodating bunch who will handle all radial train and air bookings out of Lanzhou, and also get you a bus tour, if there are enough people available, to the city's prime attraction, the **Bingling Monastery Grottoes of Dasi Gully** about two hours away. First dug about 1,500

and Shanghai, and, coming from the northwest, Urumqi and Dunhuang. There are two alternative train routes linking the city with Beijing, one sweeping over Inner Mongolia via Baotou, Hohhot and Datong, and the other cutting across the center of China via Xi'an and Zhengzhou. Direct trains to and from Shanghai also take the Xi'an-Zhengzhou route.

Hotels

The **Lanzhou Hotel** is probably the best in town, if you can get into it. More often than not, it's booked out by business conventions and tour groups, and its rates reflect its popularity. The **Friendship**

ABOVE Tibetan family TOP proudly show off cassette recorder at Ta'er Monastery near Xining while lamas (monks) examine newly printed sutras in monastery's school.

years ago, one of the grottoes has an inscription that is recognized as the oldest example of cave writing in China.

In the year 420, Buddhist monks extended the grottoes and began work on an impressive parade of carved Buddhas and other devotional art. More were added over the centuries until there were 195 caves crammed with art and relics by the time of the thirteenth century Mongol rule. Only 34 of them now remain, but they contain nearly 700 Buddha images, including a 27 m (88.5 ft) high Maitreya sculpture, more than 80 clay figures and a big display of Qin and Tang dynasty murals. **Bingling Monastery** itself is almost as old as the grottoes, parts of it built as early as the sixth century, and its name is a Chinese translation of the Tibetan "Hundred Thousand Buddhas."

Aside from CITS, the Friendship Hotel also organizes bus tours to the caves, or you can hire a taxi for a round trip. Alternatively, you can take a public bus there from the Shenli Hotel.

Maiji Shan

Another possibly more impressive cultural site to inquire about as the tourist industry develops in Gansu province is a series of Tang dynasty grottoes and Buddhist sculptures at **Maiji Shan,** one of the hills at the western edge of the Qin Range in the southeast of Tianshui County. In the years 384–417, hundreds of grottoes were cut into the cliff, but in 734 a violent earthquake buried many of the caves and the treasures within them.

In 1952 a team of Chinese archeologists carried out a survey of the collapsed hill but found it was too dangerous to excavate. However, some 194 grottoes survived the quake and more than 7,000 remarkable clay and stone Buddhist sculptures are said to have been found in them, some more than 15 m (49 ft) tall, along with an elaborate mural of a horse pulling a carriage which appears to change the direction of its walk as the viewer changes position around it.

The Radial Route

From Lanzhou you can travel by train and bus all the way to Lhasa, crossing one of the most rugged, least explored tourist areas of China, Qinghai province.

There are daily trains to Xining, the capital of Qinghai, and the trip is short enough to take a first class soft-seat or even venture into the hard-seat section and roll along through a green-swathed terraced loess landscape in summer – the ancient sculpture of the Yellow River – or, in midwinter, the bleaker and perhaps even more dramatic scenery that I recall here from my diary:

Through a milky, misty sunrise, the same bleak dun-colored terraced mounds and hills, over frozen rivers and streams – a shock of pure white against the parched earth. Loess landscape, loess fields, mudbricked walled compounds and villages, some of them with old decrepit traditional main gates with huge doors and flying eaves. An occasional donkey kicking its heels in the morning sun and dust, following its master out into the neat flat farming plots.

At one point the train follows a river, sliding with it through a narrow flat-floored valley, the waters patchworked with ice-floes and frozen sheets spreading from both banks. Here and there, big fat cocoons of plastic – warm-houses for winter vegetables and seedlings – look like snow-drifts or mounds of ice. My God, Qinghai is cold!

XINING

Xining itself was another military garrison and trading center from about the sixteenth century, and a place where Chinese were sent, sometimes exiled, and definitely not where anyone particularly begged to go. Today it's a fairly modern industrial city with a population that provides an interesting contrast of Han Chinese and Moslem Hui groups. Its eastern inner-city district is where you'll find the **Moslem Quarter,** a crowded market enclave around the picturesque fourteenth century **Dongguan (East City Gate) Mosque.**

The city is remarkable for its huge well-stocked department stores, probably a reflection of its continuing frontier role as a supply and provisions depot for the vast and largely inhospitable Tibet-Qinghai Plateau which sweeps away to the west and right to the foothills of the Himalayas. The city also has a big central post office, a Friendship Store, some reasonable restaurants – notably the **He Pyng Zhong Xi Restaurant** and the interestingly ambitious **Siwan Chinese and Western Dining Room** – and one tourist-class hotel, the **Xining Guesthouse,** where I was charged ¥54 a night for a double room that turned out to be a comfortably furnished suite. It's probably double that now. It also has dormitory beds, five to a room. You'll find CITS there, and a surprisingly good dining room which offers a six-course set menu at mealtimes.

Sightseeing

Although it doesn't have much to offer tourists except its crowded Moslem Quarter, I have a soft spot in my heart for Xining because it was the first place in China where I ran into a spectacular Spring Festival parade – a gigantic procession of prancing lions and dragons, masked dancers and clowns, teams of marching girls, cymbal and tom-tom bands and extravagantly colorful floats that featured an armed forces exhibit with a model of a jet warplane blasting off the back of the truck.

Otherwise, Xining is the access point for **Ta'Er,** about 25 km (15.5 miles) to the southeast, where you'll find the magnificent Tibetan-style **Ta'Er Monastery,** originally one of the six greatest lamaseries of the Yellow Hat Sect. It was built in 1560 in memory of the founder of the sect, Tsongkapa and is famous for its ornate yak butter sculptures of human figures, animals and landscapes.

To get to Ta'Er you take a bus from the Long Distance Bus Station, about one kilometer west of the post office in Xining,

and the 40-minute ride costs ¥0.70. To be honest, I did not make it to the monastery. I reached Ta'Er, decided to check the town out and ran into another even more spectacular Spring Festival parade – this one featuring young men in opera make-up and costumes and robes performing Gaoqiao, marching and dancing on four meter (13 ft) high wooden stilts, looking for all the world like exotic long-legged birds doing an elaborate mating ritual. I spent so much time deliriously photographing them that my fingers, ears and jaw froze in the bitter conditions and I had to get back to Xining in a hurry to thaw out.

To Lhasa

There are two trains a day from Xining to Golmud in the center of Qinghai province, and from there you can either fly to Lhasa or go there by bus. The bus trip is a rugged one, 31 hours non-stop and much of it along precipitous mountain roads, but it's also cheap – only ¥60 one way. When the new railway line is built to Lhasa it'll probably be an extension of the Xining-Golmud route. There is also a bus service from Golmud to **Dunhuang,** home of the **Magao Buddhist Grottoes,** the most famous surviving treasures of the old Silk Road.

The New Silk Road

From Lanzhou, a northwest rail route opens the door to the great garrisons, oasis towns and cities and Buddhist relics that were among the wonders of the Silk Road and have survived the ravages of time since its death. **Jiayuguan** is the first convenient radial point on the Lanzhou-Urumqi railway, providing access by bus to Jiuquan, a similar outpost that was prominent in the Han dynasty's expeditions against the

OPPOSITE Faces of China's west - CLOCKWISE Tibetan worshiper at Ta'er Monastery near Xining, simple beauty of city's Dongguan Mosque, Tibetan opera performer steps out, and crowd watches Ta'er Butter Festival, one of the main spiritual observances of lamaism.

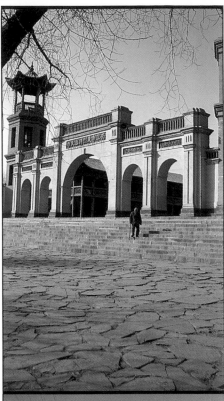

Xiongnu, and **Dunhuang** and the fabulous **Magao Caves**.

Jiayuguan was also an important Han military outpost, but it was not until the Ming dynasty that its strategic position, guarding the Jaiyu Pass, was considered critical to the defense of the northwest frontier. The Ming emperor Hongwu bolstered the garrison by building the Tianxia Xiongguan (World's Greatest Fortress), a huge stronghold which, from that point on, served as the western extremity of the Great Wall. The Ming engineers were so meticulous, and their specifications so exact, that when this "Impregnable Defile Under the Sun" was completed only a single brick was left over. It is now proudly displayed in one of the fort's halls.

The town has a new tourist-class hotel, the **Jiayuguan Guesthouse** with a range of accommodation, a post office and bank right across the street and buses outside that leave four times a day for the 15-minute hop to the fort. There's a six-way traffic circle about 15 minutes west of the hotel from which buses leave at 7 am each day for the more arduous but nonetheless interesting desert journey to Dunhuang.

DUNHUANG

At this hot and dusty oasis town you can check into the **Dunhuang Hotel**, which offers double rooms and cheaper dormitory accommodation, and be rested and ready the next morning for the bus ride at 8 am from the Long Distance Bus Station to the Magao Grottoes 25 km (15.5 miles) to the southeast.

There are 492 of these Thousand Buddha Caves left out of more than 1,000 that were originally excavated and filled with carvings, murals, clay sculptures and other artwork over several centuries dating from the year 366. But even those that have survived are crammed with treasures, murals covering a total 4.5 hectares (11.12 acres), 3,400 bas-relief and three-dimensional wall sculptures, several thousand pillars with the lotus motif and floral floor tiles,

and five ornate Tang era wooden shrines. At the turn of this century a Daoist priest broke through to a sealed grotto and came upon another 50,000 relics dating from the Jin to Song period.

The grottoes were started by the Turkic-speaking Toba rulers of the Northern Wei dynasty (386-594) and added to in the ensuing Sui, Tang, Five Dynasties and Song reigns – each dynasty stamping its own artistic style on this amazing exhibition. The aesthetic high point was reached in the Tang reign, and the sculptures and murals of that time reflect the dynasty's three thumb-rules to acceptable art – richness, exuberance and opulence. The Buddha images are made of clay and painted, and range in height from a few centimeters to a towering 33 m (108 ft). Among them is a huge sculpture of the Maitreya Buddha executed by Ma Sizhong between the years 713 and 741.

The Chinese are very sensitive about the Magao Grottoes, and photography is strictly no-go. They have a fairly good

Donkey carts venture across the Turpan Depression with sun-baked slopes of Flaming Mountains behind.

XI'AN AND THE NORTHWEST

young dark-haired olive-skinned man with Caucasian features who was looking for a "money change" deal. I was so sure he was an expatriate Middle Eastern student that I immediately responded in Arabic. He turned out to be a Uygur from Urumqi, the capital of Xinjiang – a member of the biggest and most prominent of some 13 Moslem Turkic-speaking or Mongol minorities that inhabit this harsh, sun-baked region. Alongside the Uygurs there are ethnic Russians, Tartars, Uzbeks, Tajiks, Xibes, Dours, Khalkhas, Kazakhs (Cossacks), Talmuks and Hui in this huge melting pot of previously fierce nomadic tribal groups of Central Asia. The region itself has had a variety of names over the centuries, including High Tartary, Chinese Turkestan, Kashgaria and Serinder (the Silk Route).

Divided by the Tian Mountains into two vast desert basins, Xinjiang is one of the most physically hostile places on earth. In the south lies the dreaded Taklimakan, an 800,000 sq km (308,880 sq mile) hell on earth with 100 m (67 ft) high shifting dunes and fierce sandstorms, which in the Turkic tongue is known as the place where travelers "go in (and) don't come out." To the north lies the Gobi, which stretches up into Mongolia and, to the southwest, is another waterless sea of dunes known as the Land of Death. In the central west the desert sinks more than 150 m (492 ft) below sea-level to form the pitilessly hot Turpan Depression.

reason to feel that way. Over a period of years from the late 1800s to the 1930s, several Western scholar-adventurers, notably the Swede Sven Hedin, the German Albert von Le Coq, the Frenchman Paul Pelliot and Great Britain's Aurel Stein, infiltrated the paths of the Silk Road from the west and virtually ransacked its "lost" and barely surviving oasis centers, including Dunhuang, of some of the most splendid Buddhist artwork and relics – an act for which the Chinese have never really forgiven the West.

Access

To get back on to the main Lanzhou-Urumqi railway line, there are buses from Dunhuang to the station at Liuyuan, about three and a half hours away. From there, the path is open to the second great frontier of modern travel in China – the barren, boiling but fascinating "wild west" of Xinjiang-Uygur.

XINJIANG

When I was in Beijing I was approached in the street outside the Beijing Hotel by a

TURPAN

Situated right in the middle of the furnace, Turpan is the first major tourist destination on the northwest trail. The oasis town was an important link in the Silk Road, and a jewel in the Buddhist crown, until the eighth century when Islam spread from the West, its forces destroying much of the region's Buddhist statuary as they went. The town now presents an interesting contrast of the two religious influences, a key center of the Moslem Uygur culture and an access point for some of the surviving Silk Road Buddhist relics.

Turpan has the **Turpan Guesthouse** with cheap rooms, a new tourist wing, friendly and accommodating CITS clerks and vine-covered verandas where you can sit in the cool of the evening dining and enjoying the town's most famous product, grapes, and wondering if you'll ever feel the sweet chill of winter again. There's also a **Turpan Restaurant** in the center of town which offers a some-what pleasing change from Chinese cuisine to the mutton and beef shishkebab and flat unleavened bread of the Moslem world.

Sightseeing

As in most of the oasis centers, transport around town is mainly by foot or donkey-cart, though there are taxis and mini-buses operating from the guesthouse. Turpan's cultural attractions start with Uygur cultural shows at the guesthouse, featuring song and dance and local costume. East of the guesthouse there's an eighteenth century Afghan-style mosque, the **Imin Pagoda.** Outside Turpan there are two ruined Silk Road cities, **Gaochang,** about 14 km (9 miles) to the east, which was the capital of the Ouigour state established by the Uygurs when they migrated into Xinjiang from Mongolia in the ninth century, and **Jiaohe,** 20 km (12.4 miles) east, which was a Tang dynasty garrison in the wars against the Turkic tribes.

Both towns are derelict but give a clear impression of the mud-brick and rammed earth architecture of that age, and the thoroughfares and lanes, official halls, monasteries and pagodas, homes and courtyards, corridors and underground passages and thick earthen walls of what were, in fact, relatively sophisticated settlements. Underground chambers were dug below each dwelling to give shelter from the fierce daytime heat. At Gaochang you'll find the remains of a monastery with some parts of it still reasonably intact. To the northwest of Gaochang there's an ancient burial complex, the **Atsana Tombs,** with murals of some of the dead.

North of Turpan, right in the central pan of the Turpan Depression, the **Huoyan Shan** (Flaming Mountains) offer a vivid experience of the intense heat of the region. The daytime temperature on the slopes often reaches 70°C (158°F) and you can literally fry an egg on the rocks. The rock and red soil flare into shimmering "fire" when the sun strikes, hence the name. There's a Ming dynasty novel which describes how the monk Tripitaka and his disciples were caught in the raging "fires" on the range and were saved by the Monkey King, Sun Wukong, who put out the flames with a fan so that they could continue on their way.

Beziklik Grottoes

Turpan's most famous attraction, how-ever, is the **Beziklik Grottoes** about 50 km (31 miles) northwest of the town, believed to have been cut into the western slope of Huoyan Shan in the Northern Wei period just before the rise of the Tang dynasty. The 64 grottoes, excavated or built of mud-brick, feature Buddhist shrines and chambers – most of them in poor condition, but others have withstood looting and the ravages of time – adorned with murals of standing Buddhas, Bodhisattvas, musicians, religious stories and one particularly dilapidated wall-painting which is said

to be the only one in China depicting Judgment and Hell. In one cave there's a Buddha image with paintings of musical instruments on its back.

Much of the finest artwork of Beziklik was swiped by the German Silk Road explorer, Albert von Le Coq. The murals were shipped to the Berlin Museum, where they were destroyed by Allied bombing in World War II.

URUMQI

This, the Xinjiang capital and the next stop along the northwest railway line, is a disappointingly drab city but it has a very ornate mosque and the two most interesting museums in the region. The **Museum of National Minorities** has exhibitions of Daur, Kazakh, Tajik and Mongolian culture, including a furnished yurt and Daur fur hats fashioned from animal heads, and the **History Museum** features some of the clay figures and other relics of the Silk

Road that managed to escape the attention of Albert von Le Coq.

For a closer look at the minorities and their lifestyles there's a pastureland called **Baiyanggou (White Poplar Gully),** about 60 km (37 miles) south of Urumqi and accessible by bus or taxi, which is a traditional gathering place for the Kazakh (Cossack) herders. Visitors can watch them tending their sheep, horses and cattle and, for a fee, can spend the night in their yurts feasting on mutton and rice and being entertained with Kazakh song and dance.

But the most splendid attraction lies 50 km east of Urumqi – **Sky Lake,** sometimes called Heavenly Lake, set into the slope of Mount Bogda, the 5,445 m (17,860 ft) high principal peak of the Tian Mountains. This towering range rises in central Xinjiang and marches 2,500 km (1,550 miles) into the heart of Central Asia, presenting a stunning contrast of soaring snow-capped peaks set amidst the fiery flat desert wastes. The marauding Xiongnu regarded the Tian range as their heaven. It has an incredible number of glaciers – 6,896 of them – forming an enormous reservoir of ice which, as it melts, feeds six big rivers in Xinjiang and the region's vital subterranean cisterns.

ABOVE Ornate Islamic decoration OPPOSITE on new Turpan mosque, ruins of ancient Jiaohe TOP and classic lines of Islamic architecture in Turpan.

Sky Lake, in the words of one recent visitor, is "as close to any temple as you can get" – a beautiful and quite spiritual blend of snow-tipped mountain scenery, heavily wooded slopes full of medicinal herbs and a number of surrounding mosques and Tibetan-style monasteries, including **Fushou Monastery,** also called Iron Tiled Monastery for its blue brick-work and the metallic glaze of its tiles. You can take a bus out to the lake for a day or stay overnight or longer at the **Heavenly Lake Hotel,** which has double rooms and dormitory beds. There's a stable where you can hire horses and ride up into the hills, picking snow lotuses on the way.

Urumqi itself has three places to stay. Top of the range is the new tourist-class **Yanan Hotel** which charges tourist rates for a double room. The **Kunlun Guest-house** charges about the same but also offers cheaper dormitory-style three-a-room accommodation. The **Overseas Chinese Hotel** has clean rooms with baths and dormitory beds and a high-season arrangement where you can flop down in a sleeping bag for a few bucks a night.

Access

From Urumqi there are only two ways to get to the border oasis of Kashi (Kashgar), by air or by bus. There are daily flights which take about five hours with a passenger pickup at Aksu. The bus trip takes a little longer – three and a half days – and while the grueling journey offers a first-hand experience of the sun-blasted desolation and wind-sculptured dunes of the Taklamakan, it is obviously only for the very fit or extremely determined traveler.

KASHI

Kashi is where every determined China traveler nowadays wants to go, but in many respects it is a challenge rather than a cultural attraction. For one thing, it's said to be further from the sea than any other town on earth. In the heyday of the Silk Road it was a vital watering hole, trading

post and supply center for merchant camel caravans, Buddhist pilgrims and the occasional explorer like Marco Polo – and it was a prime target of nomad attack.

In the nineteenth century it was a great bazaar in which Indian, Afghan and Russian traders jostled and rubbed elbows with Moslem and Mongolian tribesmen, Chinese settlers and exiles, bandits, brigands, corsairs, tomb and temple robbers and some of the scurviest, most dangerous human flotsam of Central Asia. Aside from that, it was rather nice. It had its spies too – agents of a Russian intrigue centered on Afghanistan that the British took so seriously that they established a consulate and dispatched the redoubtable George and Lady McCartney there for 28 years to keep an eye on things. From their official residence, a fine colonial mansion called China-bagh, they kept tabs on the Russian consul and offered hospitality to archeologists like Hedin and Stein as they trekked through to ransack the crumbling ruins of the Silk Road. Both China-bagh and the Russian consulate are now hotels.

Since May 1986, Kashi has leapt into tourist prominence through the opening of the border for travel to and from Pakistan via the Friendship Highway, which runs to the southwest and crosses the Karakoram Mountains.

Hotels

The tourist-class hotel in Kashi is the **Kashgar Guesthouse** which has comfortable double rooms with bathrooms, much cheaper dormitory beds and hot water all day. However, it's out on the western edge of the town. Right in the center there's the **Renmin Hotel** which is somewhat cheaper, and to the east the **Tuen Park Hotel,** which is cheaper still and has no baths or showers, only taps in the courtyard. The **China-bagh Hotel,** the old McCartney residence and consulate, is

ABOVE Unleavened bread TOP LEFT on Urumpi market stall - Islamic influence blending with Mongolian yurts TOP RIGHT, BOTTOM on shores of Sky Lake.

also a cold tap establishment, favored by Pakistani traders but well situated near the central market. The **Seman Hotel** has reasonable rooms and is supposed to have hot showers too, but they rarely work.

Convenience is important because Kashi has no buses and the main form of transport is by donkey-cart or bicycle – or jeep, if you can afford it and can hire one from the Kashgar Guesthouse.

Sightseeing
Kashi is a good ethnic microcosm of the northwest, with its population made up

mainly of Kazakhs, Mongols and Uygurs. Its central bazaar and nearby **Id Kah Mosque** and main square are where all the daily trading and pageantry take place. The mosque is designed in the typical Moslem, rather than Chinese style, with a huge arched main entrance and doors, elegantly tiled minarets and a domed prayer hall, and there are others in the backstreets around it including a large one that has fallen into quite colourful ruin.

But the main attraction of Kashi is the stunning Moslem architecture of the **Abakh Hoja Tomb** on the eastern outskirts of the town, a seventeenth century family mausoleum that grew in the ensuing centuries into a major burial spot for

the Moslem aristocracy of the region. Today it presents a contrast of both the severe simplicity and ornate architecture of Islam – it is surrounded by cone-shaped graves the color of baked clay, and out of the center of them rises the principal grave chamber with its splendid domed roof, decorated with green and amber tiles, and minaret-style towers at its four corners.

This main tomb contains 72 burial places, most of them decorated with mosaic tiles and draped with colorfully patterned shrouds. It's said that the tomb became a popular spot for wealthy Moslems because they wanted to lie in rest beside the central sarcophagus which, as legend has it, contains the costumes of Xiangfai (Fragrant Concubine), a renowned beauty of the region who was kidnaped by a Qing dynasty ruler and taken to the Forbidden City in Beijing.

Kashi's other big attraction is, of course, its access via the Friendship Highway and forbidding Karakoram Range to Pakistan. CITS are the people to go to for information about exit visas and buses for the cross-border journey. Other buses leave daily from the Long Distance Bus Station for Urumqi – a three-and-a-half-day desert odyssey via the oases of Aksu, Korla and Toksun. Another three-day bus trip will take you right to Turpan. Or you can return to Urumqi by air.

ABOVE Silversmith shapes inscriptions on plate in Ta'er workshop. Young Kazekhs (Cossacks) OPPOSITE on horseback in their traditional costume.

Across
the
North

ACROSS THE NORTH

If you're entering China along the Friendship Highway, Urumqi is the railhead for the swing right across the north of the country, through the boundless grasslands of Inner Mongolia to Beijing. If you've cut up into the northwest from Lanzhou there's no alternative, other than an expensive plane flight (Urumqi-Kashi ¥226), to retracing your route by rail back to this key junction for access across the north.

There are, in fact, two rail routes to the north from Lanzhou, and care must be taken when booking tickets not to be stuck aboard the wrong one. One direct service heads to Beijing via Baotou and Hohhot in Inner Mongolia, then Datong, the third of the three greatest centers of Buddhist cave art in China. The other cuts back southwest to Xi'an, then across the heartland of China through Luoyang, the site of the Longmen Grottoes, and Zengzhou, the access point for the Shaolin Monastery, after which it heads north to Beijing through Shijiazhuang in Hebei province.

Luoyang and Zhengzhou can be approached just as easily from the east, from Beijing, Shanghai and Guangzhou, leaving the trip across the northern plateau the most exciting route from Lanzhou.

THE GRASSLANDS

This route takes you through the panoramic flat green seas of Gobi scrubland and lusher pastureland that stretch from horizon to horizon across Nei Monggol, broken only by occasional settlements of yurts, the pudding-shaped animal skin tents of the nomadic sheep and cattle herders. Until the railway line was pushed across the plains, the Dahingan Range, a thickly wooded stretch of hills running northeast to southwest across the plateau, effectively isolated the Mongolian tribes, or "banners," from the rest of

the world, and for the most part kept the rest of the world out of Mongolia too.

As for the Mongolians themselves, they were a warring, fragmented and greatly feared "barbarian" race ruled by khans or tribal chiefs until one man turned their solitary, idyllic existence upside down for them – Genghis Khan. In one of the most incredible, explosive events of history these sheep and cattle herders – brilliant horsemen and cavalry tacticians, to be sure – suddenly banded together under this savage warlord's command and thundered out of the wilderness to conquer China and carve an empire that stretched beyond the western borders of Russia and Persia. And, just as swiftly as they pillaged and subjugated much of the vast Eurasian land-mass, so their terrible adventure ended: within less than a century they had been crushed in China by the Mings, pushed back out of the territories to the west and were straggling and limping back into the grassy wilds far beyond the Great Wall.

From that time of retreat and withdrawal, the Mongolian "nation" was divided between the tribes of the north and the remnants of the China "expedition" in the south – a division that the Manchu Qing dynasty was happy to maintain for its own sake when it brought the entire region under Chinese control in the seventeenth century. By the turn of this century the Russians were competing for control of the region, and in 1924 the Soviet Red Army moved in and promoted the establishment of the autonomous People's Republic of (Outer) Mongolia in the north, leaving the southern Nei Monggol to Beijing. The region is now heavily settled with Han Chinese, who vastly outnumber the estimated two million Mongols, many of whom have returned to their greener but far less ambitious pastures with little to show for their historic glory but two spiritual legacies – Tibetan-style Buddhism and Islam.

BAOTOU

The first major stop on the journey to the east is Baotou, the autonomous region's largest city and a rather ugly industrial center supported by iron and

coal mining. However, it is also the site of one of the main centers of lamaist Buddhism in China, the magnificent **Wudang (Willow Tree) Monastery** which lies on a hillside 70 km (43 miles) northwest of the city.

It's not only one of the finest surviving lamaseries in Nei Monggol, but its size alone testifies to its importance – it contains more than 2,500 living units, classrooms, temples and prayer halls. Its origins are similarly illustrious. It was built in 1749 by the reigning Dalai Lama himself and has since been a temporary residence for at least seven Tibetan rulers. Its architecture is flat, whitewashed and Tibetan on the outside with blazes of color inside in its temples and schools. Ornately woven pillar rugs, beautiful Tibetan carpeting and huge murals decorate the main hall, Suguqindu, where the lamas pray and chant the scriptures. Other halls are filled with images of Sakyamuni Buddha, including one bronze statue that's 10 m (33 ft) tall.

Decorated wooden door and colorful interior hangings grace Kazakh herdsman's yurt near Urumqi.

Hоннот

Hohhot, the capital of Nei Monggol, has a lot more of the Buddhist legacy to offer, including the once-magnificent **Xilitu Temple,** set into the old wall of Huhehaote, as the city was known in pre-Pinyin times. Built in the Ming dynasty, Xilitu has an architecture that is mainly Han Chinese with a main shrine hall and sutra hall in the Tibetan style and features an eight-sided pavilion inscribed with details in Chinese, Manchu, Mongolian and Tibetan of the Qing emperor Kangxi's victorious military expeditions against unruly tribes in the northwest.

The great sutra hall, or Dajingtang, has walls inlaid with peacock-blue tiles with silver decorations. The roof of the building is strictly Tibetan, mounted with an ornate gilded vase, prayer-wheel, flying dragon and a deer, all cast in copper.

Near the People's Park you'll find the **Jingangzuo (Sheli) Pagoda,** a series of five square brick and stone towers faced with glazed tiles and richly carved with Buddhas, Bodhisattvas and Bodhi trees, images of lions, elephants and birds, mandalas, and a total 1,119 small Buddha niches. These towers, mounted on a stone base, are all that survives of a much grander Cideng (Five Tower) Monastery which was built there in the eighteenth century.

The **Huayan Sutra Pagoda** in the eastern section of Hohhot is also known as the Ten Thousand Volumes of Avatamasake Sutra Pagoda, but you can call it simply the White Tower, which most of the citizenry do. It's a lofty 45 m (147 ft) tall eight-sided tower of wood and brick, probably built between 983 and 1031 when Buddhism flourished again in the wake of the late Tang dynasty crackdown, and stands on the site of what was once a monastery called Daxuanjiao. It features an interesting display of ancient graffiti – inscriptions carved by visitors as far back as the twelfth century and written not only in Chinese but also Mongolian, Nuzhen, ancient Syrian and Persian.

For one of the city's most prized Buddhist relics you have to visit the **Dazhao Monastery** in Hohhot's southern district. The Chinese call it the Silver Buddha Monastery in honor of its most treasured possession, an image of the Sakyamuni Buddha cast entirely in silver. Again, the monastery's design is half Chinese and half Tibetan, built in 1580 and extended during the reign of the Qing warrior emperor Kangxi.

Nine kilometers (6 miles) south of Hohhot on the south bank of the Dahei (Great Black) River there's a tall loess mound, 33 m (108 ft) high, which isn't much of a sightseeing attraction – just a huge bump in the terrain – but is worth a picnic while you sit and ponder over the legend and superstition that goes with it. It's the **Tomb of Wang Zhaojun,** who is said to have been a concubine of the Han dynasty ruler Emperor Yuan. When a prince named Huhanye of the dreaded Xiongnu came to the court and asked to marry Wang Zhaojun, the emperor naturally saw the union as a god-given

opportunity for some peace and quiet on the northern border.

Despite the harsh conditions that she had to endure beyond the Great Wall and the fringe of the Han civilization, Wang Zhaojun is said to have been a dutiful consort and ambassadress, her stoicism and dignity keeping the barbarians under reasonable control. Since her death, her tomb has been endowed with the power to cure infertility in women, and childless visitors take a pinch of soil from the mound and pray there in the hope that it will help make them pregnant.

Yonder Yurts

Hohhot is also the main center of the Mongolian culture, present and past, and its **Museum of Inner Mongolia** features an interesting display of costume, weapons, cavalry trappings and a traditional yurt – along with another huge skeleton of a mammoth that was excavated from a coal mine. The present-day yurts and their inhabitants are found in Mongolian communes north of the city, and group excursions lasting two days or more are organized by CITS, which is based in the city's main tourist-class hotel, the **Hohhot Guesthouse** between Xinhua Lu and the Beijing-Baotou railway line. There's also a bicycle rental shop right across from the hotel.

Access from Hohhot is by bus to Datong or Baotou, or by train to Baotou and Lanzhou or Datong and Beijing. There are also direct flights to Beijing.

ABOVE Three faces of Mongolian grasslands in mother and child and sweeping double-eaved roof of Qing dynasty tomb.

ACROSS THE NORTH

Beijing
and the
Northeast

BEIJING AND THE NORTHEAST

THE CAPITAL

Beijing, the capital of China, is a city of broad ceremonial thoroughfares and monumental architecture in which the scale of mere humanity is reduced to solitary awe and obeisance. It is a place of eminence and imperial might in which you can stand on the edge of the vast Tiananmen Square, in the sweeping courtyards of the Forbidden City, or before the majestic blue-tiled Ming roofs of the once-sacred Temple of Heaven and sense, even in this sacrilegious age of clamoring traffic, bicycles and tourist crowds, the power and unquestioned authority of the 24 emperors who ruled from here, and the fear that struck at the heart from the traditional exhortation that ended each of their imperial edicts: "Tremble and obey!"

In another sense it is China's Washington DC, another grand architecture of the ego, a repository of pomp, sentiment and grandiose pride, the tomb of all the mortal fantasies and follies that history endows with immortal greatness and nobility. It is where the triumphant Jurchens of the Jin dynasty quaked and cowered and awaited horrific mass murder and destruction as Genghis Khan's cavalries smashed their way through the Great Wall to the north; where the boulevards and squares of the new capital that Kublai Khan built here were designed for immense length and breadth so that the Mongol cavalrymen could get a good unhindered run along them on their horses; where the illustrious rulers of the Ming dynasty bathed and caroused in the treacherous care of their eunuch courts, unable to see or hear the rage swelling beyond the walls; where the long and harsh Qing reign of the Manchus committted virtual suicide, encircled by its own angry masses and the armed might of the Europeans; where, amid billowing revolutionary flags, the biggest mass rallies the world has ever seen chanted and waved little red books in homage to their new and perhaps last imperial figure, Chairman Mao Zedong. It is where, in April 1976, the same masses turned in rage on the same revolution – prevented by the Gang of Four from paying homage to the newly dead Premier Zhou Enlai – and the course of Chinese history swerved dramatically once again.

The Northern Vigil

One thing that strikes any visitor to Beijing is the contrast between its monu-

mental and more mundane character. If you took the imperial landmarks away, much of the remaining city would be a flat, drab honeycomb of secretive walled homes clustered in their thousands off narrow backstreets and alleys, called *hutongs*. This characterless, almost inhospitable aspect of the city could be taken as a reflection of the contrasts of its past - a fairly insignificant border outpost, pitted with the sweeping dust-storms that blow regularly from the Gobi Desert, slumbering in the shadow of the Great Wall, then, because of the strategic nature of its location, suddenly robed and decorated with imperial splendor and regarded as the great prize of the nation's north.

The barbarians beyond the wall were the first to take its location seriously. The Khitan Tartars of the Liao dynasty made it their southern capital, calling it Yanjing or Swallow City, and in 1125 their triumphant rivals, the Jin, established it as Zhongdu, their capital. In both cases the city appealed to them because it was close to their tribal domains on the Mongolian Plateau to the north.

Genghis Khan ravished, depopulated and looted the place and burned it to the ground,

and his grandson Kublai, the Great Khan, rebuilt it completely and established it as the Yuan capital Dadu, the most splendid of all the cities of the Mongol Empire. Marco Polo stood amidst its vast halls, palaces, temples, walls and squares as awed and open-mouthed as any visitor who contemplates the grandeur of the city today.

Much of Beijing's present historic character and architecture is the legacy of the Ming rulers, who, after crushing the Yuan and razing their magnificent Dadu to the ground, rebuilt it as their capital, Beiping, or "Northern Peace." It was the Ming emperors who gave it its real

strategic value – for them it was a powerful garrison, listening post and command center from which they could maintain a vigil on the dangerous tribal lands beyond the Great Wall. When the Manchus grabbed the imperial throne in 1644, Beiping was a convenient center of power for them because of that same close proximity to their own homelands.

Nowadays the opulent hallmarks of the imperial ages stand like antique precious gems in a sprawling industrial setting that is as contrastingly drab as the surviving

mazes of *hutongs*. The city is modernising, to be sure, with mushrooming high-rise office blocks and new international hotels giving it a more cosmopolitan air. And right in the middle the hallmark of the most recent imperial age has already set fast into the gem-string of Chinese history – Tiananmen Square and the famous portrait of Chairman Mao, a memory now, on the Gate of Heavenly Peace.

The City

Beijing's main boulevards and backstreets follow a neat and very convenient "chessboard" grid that was established in the Yuan reign and restored in the Ming reconstruction. The entire metropolis centers on the **Forbidden City,** also called the

ABOVE Faces of Beijing – silk veil protects strolling shopper OPPOSITE from dust, ABOVE old woman and grandchild, and "bunnies" at Spring Festival gaterhing.

Gugong (Palace Museum). The main entrance of the walled complex, the Gate of Heavenly Peace, fronts on to Tiananmen Square and the wide never-ending boulevard, Chang'an Avenue, which runs east-west for about 40 km (25 miles) and has carried much of the city's modern industrial, commercial and residential development with it.

Tiananmen Square and the modern revolutionary monuments of Beijing – the Great Hall of the People, Monument to the People's Heroes and the Chairman Mao Memorial Hall – lie to the south of Chang'an Avenue. To its east and west, radiating from the square, lie the main tourist centers – the central Beijing Hotel, Beijing railway station, the Friendship Store, International Club, Long Distance Telegraph Office and the major department stores, restaurants and bookshops.

The central north-south rectangle of the Forbidden City has an outer ring around it formed by the Circle Line of the Beijing Subway, an underground railway with 18 stations, most of which are within convenient strolling distance of the main cultural attractions. To the north of the Forbidden City lie the **China Art Gallery** and **Beihai Park** with its distinctive White Pagoda; to its northwest you'll find the **Beijing Exhibition Center, Beijing Zoo, Five Pagoda Temple** and the **Shoudu Gymnasium.** To its south, toward the Tonghui River canal which marks the inner city boundary, stands the **Natural History Museum** and beautiful **Temple of Heaven.**

Transport

Outside this central core around the Forbidden City, Beijing is so spread out that it'll wear you down and send your shoe repair bills soaring if you try to walk it. As with Guangzhou and the other major cities, the best way to get around is either by bicycle, choosing a particular cultural site or section of the city each day, or by taking a taxi to each area of interest and strolling about from there.

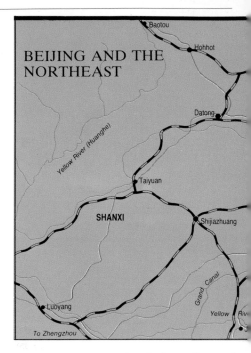

BEIJING AND THE NORTHEAST

Beijing has a lot of taxis, huge fleets of them operating from all the main hotels, and they are surprisingly cheap and reasonably honest (though don't take that as gospel). Most of them have meters, and most of the drivers use them.

Other than that, there's the subway running right around the core of the city and west along Chang'an which has a flat fare of ¥0.10 for any distance. But it is also extremely crowded, especially at peak commuting times when the vast bureaucracy of Beijing pours in or out of its offices.

Hotels

Since the China door opened again, Beijing has been something of a nightmare for foreign visitors, expatriates and business people – the political, economic and cultural hub of China with nowhere near enough hotel or residential accommodation to cope with its own importance. That, and hotel rates that have been frighteningly high. But things are now improving radically as more and more hotels are built and rushed into operation, and while the rates are still high – beginning

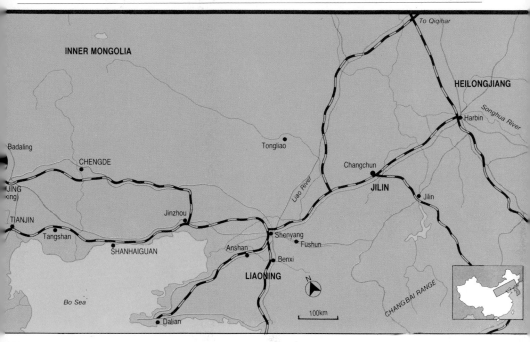

at around ¥400 ($200) a night in most of the top tourist and business class establishments – there are some cheaper budget deals to be had here and there.

At the top of the range you can take your pick of the following prestigious or newly

built palatial places to stay – one of them, the Youyi (Friendship) Hotel, has five main buildings, 48 apartments, 2,630 rooms and

The Ancient Palaces, better known as Beijing's Forbidden City, is the largest surviving cluster of wooden buildings on such a scale in the world.

nine restaurants capable of seating 3,000 people:

Beijing Hotel
Great Wall Sheraton
Jianguo
The Palace
Shangri-La Beijing
International
Holiday Inn Lido
Beijing-Toronto
Heping
Youyi (Friendship)Minzu
Xiyuan
Qianmen
Jingshun
Daguanyuan (Grand View Garden)

Lest the thought of the room rates still scare you, there are a couple of cheaper places which offer comfort, cleanliness and all tourist facilities and don't require a bank guarantee to check in. I found such a place called the **Beiwei Hotel** south of the city center and close to the Temple of Heaven, which offers very comfortable rooms, has a friendly and efficient staff and a good Chinese-Western restaurant that stays open until midnight.

Another comfortable and convenient budget hotel is the **Haoyuan Guesthouse** at 53 Shijia Lane, Dengshikou Lu, near the Forbidden City and Capital Theater. There's also the **Overseas Chinese Hotel** at 5 Bexinqiao 3-Tiao, the **Tiantan (Temple of Heaven) Sports Hotel** at 10 Tiyuguan Lu, and a real budget place that backpackers head for, the **Qiaoyuan** on You'anmen Lu, south of the Tonghui canal.

I found that Beijing became an astonishingly easy and delightful place to cope with once I was in the Beiwei Hotel, with the problem of room rates off my mind, and tripping along each morning to the Beijing Hotel to splurge on good coffee and apple pie and cream in its cavernous West Wing coffee lounge, where you can sit and watch the full cosmopolitan, wheeling-dealing hustle of this huge city pass by.

There is one other hotel I haven't mentioned, the **Chongwenmen,** south of Chang'an Avenue and just west of the railway station (and right around the corner from the rather awful overpriced Maxim's Restaurant). It's also the location of the top-ranking CITS branch, which I found to be the nastiest and most uncooperative anywhere in China.

Restaurants

I'm not going to even attempt to give a full and detailed guide to eating out in Beijing – the hotels are packed with good restaurants offering every regional taste of the Chinese cuisine, along with Japanese and Western fare, and there are dozens more scattered around the city. There's even a Kentucky Fried Chicken outlet on the edge of Tiananmen Square which has been doing a roaring business since it opened in 1987. The most difficult problem, in fact, is choosing what to eat and where to go among the 80 or so eating houses available. That, and watching the clock: people eat early in Beijing, as early as 5:30 pm, and by about seven most restaurants are crammed full. So always be ready to eat by about 6 pm at the latest.

Most visitors, the moment they arrive in Beijing, want to stuff themselves with one thing: Beijing duck. It's a crispy, greasy, fatty, succulent blend of duck skin and flesh with salty plum sauce, fresh scallions and wafer-thin pancakes, and it's blow-out food, the sort you can unashamedly devour with absolute gusto and complete disregard for everything and everyone around you. And then, if you've got the room and stamina, you can tuck into the 50 or so soups and cooked dishes and 30 cold snacks which are prepared from the rest of the duck – every single part of it, in fact, except Richard Nixon's "Quack!"

The most popular duck spot is the **Beijing Roast Duck Restaurant (Kaoyadian)** which is in a sidestreet off to the right of Wangfujing Dajie running north alongside the Beijing Hotel. But you have to get there very early and be quick on your feet to get a table, for the Beijingese eat there, and as you stand and peruse the packed tables, and crowds waiting for the lucky diners to finish and give up their seats, you'll hear hungry whimpers coming from somewhere and realize it is you.

There's another packed roast duck palace, the **Bianyifang,** right opposite the Chongwenmen Hotel, and a "western branch" of the same restaurant on Qianmen Dajie, the north-south main street that approaches the Qianmen Gate and huge traffic circle and bus station just south of Tiananmen Square.

I chose another branch of the Beijing Roast Duck Restaurant (Quanjude) chain a few doors from the Bianifang and had a sumptuous orgy with a half-duck with duck soup and a side-dish of peanuts and chili for just ¥29.30. I enjoyed it so much that I went back the next night and did it again. I was insatiable.

Elsewhere, you can feast on Mongolian roast mutton and beef dishes and the famous **Mongolian** hot-pot in the **Donglaishan** and **Kaorouji Restaurants,** both close to Tiananmen Square. There's also the famous **Sichuan** just to the west of the Great Hall of the People, and a particularly ornate eating establishment in Behai Park called the **Fangshan (Imperial Kitchen)**

Mule power in the ultra-modern shadow of Great Wall Hotel OPPOSITE in Beijing. Alfresco dining ABOVE in Beijing backstreet.

Restaurant which serves the imperial cuisine that is another legacy of Beijing's illustrious past and is set in what is said to have been the dining hall of the wicked witch of the Qing dynasty, the Empress Dowager Ci Xi.

For something a little different you might try the **Russian Restaurant** in the Exhibition Center, near the zoo, or the **Yanji (Korean) Restaurant,** or the **Beijing Vegetarian Restaurant.** Then there's always **Maxim's** right next to the Chongwenmen Hotel, if you want to eat French and Italian in Beijing. Other than that, you're on your own. And may the sauce be with you.

Sightseeing

The perfect start to any sightseeing in Beijing is morning coffee in the **Beijing Hotel** followed by a short stroll west to the cultural center of the city, and indeed all of China – **Tiananmen Square** with its **Gate of Heavenly Peace** and **Palace Museum (Forbidden City).** This one combined destination alone will probably fill an entire day.

The square itself, expanded to its present vast dimensions after the communist revolution, is a central place of congregation for the people of Beijing and a particularly popular spot for spring and summer kite flying – the colored paper and silk butterflies and various other designs darting and swooping against a backdrop of huge red revolutionary flags billowing across the front of the **Monument to the People's Heroes.** The 36 m (118 ft) granite obelisk commemorates the revolution itself and was the focal point of that other "revolution of 1976" – it was where a gathering of thousands to mourn the death of the highly respected moderate Zhou Enlai was harshly broken up on the orders of the Gang of Four, and the campaign to turn China away from the revolutionary socialist path reached flashpoint.

Close to the monument there's a huge and graphic stone sculpture that is now almost an epiphet of the Maoist era – soldiers, peasants, workers and women in a dramatic revolutionary tableau, breasting the tide of the future.

Beside this big statue, the memory of the Great Helmsman remains revered in the **Mao Zedong Mausoleum,** open to the public as a museum, where the leader who is now accredited with being "70-30" – of having been 70 percent right and 30 percent wrong during his tumultuous reign – lies in state in a crystal coffin. Two other sacred institutions flank Tiananmen Square, the **Museum of the Chinese Revolution,** to the east, presenting what is in fact a history of the formation, development, struggle and victory of the Chinese Communist Party, and the **Great Hall of the People** to the west, which is where the Chinese parliament, the National People's Congress, meets and where you can take a look at the 5,000-seat Great Banqueting Hall where Richard Nixon is said to have quacked up.

The Forbidden City

Everything in Tiananmen Square focuses on one point – the **Gate of Heavenly Peace** and the mecca of all pilgrims to China, the renowned portrait of Chairman Mao. Rallies of a million or more people took place before this gate, from where the communist leader and his party lieutenants acknowledged the thunderous slogan-chanting adoration and acclaim – standing where the dynastic leaders before them, going back to the great Ming reconstruction of the fifteenth century, had occasionally emerged from their divine seclusion to exhort and review the mood of their common subjects. Now, tourist parties are invited to stand where Mao and his lieutenants presided over the masses.

The Gate of Heavenly Peace opens the way into the huge Forbidden City (The Great Within), the largest complex of antique wooden buildings of such scale left in the world, and, all in all, a fascinating but daunting tourist challenge of

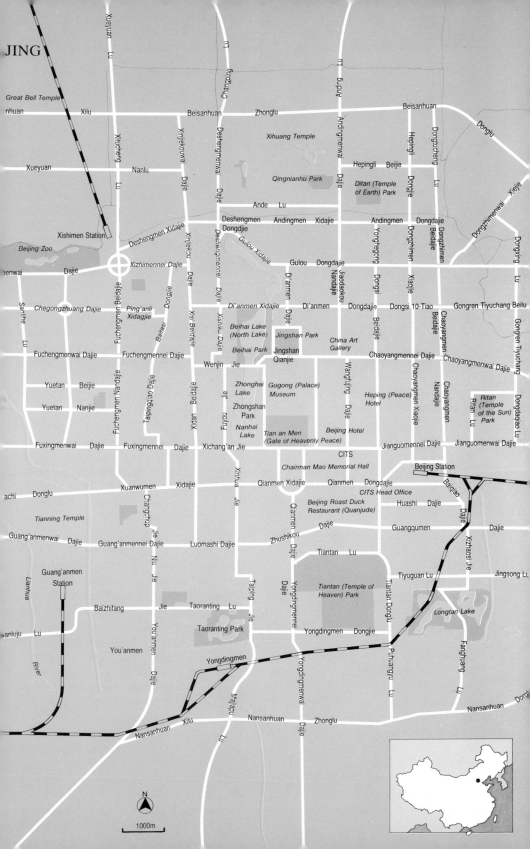

800 palaces, halls, shrines and pavilions and no fewer than 9,000 rooms. This vast museum, formerly the seat of power and isolated inner sanctum of the rulers of the Ming and Qing dynasties, is far too big to cover in fine detail unless you have a week or so in which to do it. Quite frankly, all that you can achieve in one half-day or so is to identify its main halls and relics and contemplate the ghosts of autocracy, pride, wrath, folly, intrigue, debauchery and murder moving restlessly about you.

Beyond the Gate of Heavenly Peace lies a sweeping courtyard leading to the massive **Meridian Gate (Wumen)**, the exclusive gateway of the emperors and where, at the stroke of noon on certain days, they issued edicts, had miscreant mandarins publicly flogged and common criminals were executed. To one side of it you'll see what I consider to be one of the most interesting modern-day spectacles of the Forbidden City – an old black Chinese copy of a 1950s Russian saloon car. It has absolutely nothing to do with the Palace

Museum, but it says a lot about Chinese society now.

One thing that the Four Modernizations will almost certainly not bestow upon the Chinese people is the right to own private cars. There are simply too many people, and you only have to look at the bicycle traffic in the main cities to imagine the chaos if they were all cars. So the old black car, standing on its rims before the entrance to the Forbidden City, is very much a forbidden dream – it's where old peasants, young soldiers, groups of giggling maidens and whole families have their pictures taken, hands resting on the weather-beaten paintwork of its hood and fenders, so that they can imagine, and show the folks back home, what real modernization must be all about.

Beyond the Meridian Gate, five marble bridges lead across the bow-shaped **Jin (Golden) Stream** to the **Supreme Harmony Gate**, which in turn opens on to the ceremonial quarter of the palace complex, a huge courtyard that could hold 100,000 people at imperial audiences and the three **great halls of Supreme Harmony, Complete Harmony** and **Preserving**

ABOVE Monument to the people's Heroes evokes the bold futuristic vision of the 1949 communist revolution.

Harmony, each of which played a particular role in the most important imperial rituals – coronations, New Year's observances, imperial birthdays, court banquets and the awarding of degrees to lucky would-be mandarins in the imperial examinations.

North of these halls you step into the inner palaces or living quarters of the Forbidden City and reach **Qianjing Hall (Palace of Heavenly Purity)** which is surrounded by more than 40 mansions, libraries, medical consulting rooms and quarters for servants, concubines and palace eunuchs. Qianjing is where the emperors chose their successors. Each ruler would write the name of his intended successor on two slips of paper, one to be kept in his personal possession and the other hidden behind a plaque inscribed with the words "Upright and Bright". Upon his death his advisers would compare the papers, and if the names tallied the new ruler would be announced.

One tragic aspect of the Forbidden City is that while it's big on imperial architecture it's surprisingly light on imperial relics and treasures. For that the world can blame Chiang Kaishek and his nationalists, who ransacked the palace of its most precious ceremonial artwork and shipped it with them to Taiwan, where a lot of it is now on display in the National Palace Museum in Taipei.

What's left in the Forbidden City isn't much, and some of it has been brought there from other parts of the country, but it includes the fabulous Suit of Jade and a collection of terra-cotta warriors on display in the **Hall of Preserving Harmony**; Qing dynasty sedan chairs in the **Hall of Middle Harmony**; an old water clock and several mechanical clocks presented by Western rulers in the **Hall of Union**; a magnificent collection of traditional paintings in the **Palace of Peaceful Old Age**; a **Treasure Room** filled with costumes, jeweled ceremonial swords, gold Buddhas and stupas encrusted with precious gems, a five-ton block of carved jade, bronzes,

flowers fashioned from semi-precious stones and arts and crafts of both dynasties in the aptly named **Palace of Mental Cultivation**; murals from the celebrated Ming dynasty novel *A Dream of the Red Mansions* in the **Palace of Eternal Spring**; and other palace halls displaying silks, furniture, jewelry, gold and jade artifacts and the personal possessions of some of the supreme rulers and the many concubines and high officials of their courts.

You re-emerge, slightly dazed and footsore, by way of the Palace Museum's north gate, **Shenwumen (Gate of Divine Military Genius)** to face a climb up **Coal Hill Park**, directly opposite, where the last Ming ruler, Zhong Zhen, hanged himself after murdering his family as the Manchus hammered at the city gates. From there, the path leads to **Behai Park** which was the site of Kublai Khan's grand palace and now features the distinctive **White Dagoba** and the **Temple of Everlasting Peace**, both built on an islet in Behai Lake in 1651 in honor of the visiting Dalai Lama.

On the southern side of the lake, the **Chengguan Dian (Light Receiving Hall)** has a beautiful jade Buddha presented by the Burmese to the Empress Dowager Ci Xi, but shorn of one of its arms when British and "allied" troops stormed and occupied much of Beijing in 1900 to put down the anti-European Boxer Rebellion.

Temple of Heaven

While the Ming and Qing emperors sat enthroned in the "Great Within" at the very center of the Chinese civilization, and that meant the entire universe to them, the firmament itself was represented by four temples beyond the palace walls, one at each of four points of the compass. To the north stood **Ditan (Temple of the Earth)**, to the west **Yuetan (Temple of the Moon)**, to the east **Ritan (Temple of the Sun)** and to the south, close to the canal on the edge of the inner city, the most architecturally inspiring and spiritually significant of all

three-decked marble terrace, it ranks with the Great Wall and Tiananmen Square as a visual symbol of Chinese history and culture, and features a sensational carved, gilded and decorated domed ceiling as complex as a mandala, with a dragon set in the center of it. In fact, the temple is relatively "new." Built originally in 1420 it burned down in 1889 and was rebuilt in he following year in the Ming design and using the construction techniques of that age – supported by 28 cedar pillars with not one cross beam, nail or dab of cement anywhere in the structure.

The Lama Temple

This beautiful Tibetan Buddhist lamasery, the third most remarkable cultural attraction in Beijing, can be found to the northeast of the Forbidden City at the intersection of Andingmen and Dongsi Beidajie, and the best way to get to it is to bicycle north from the Beijing Hotel. A former palace of the Qing emperor Yong Zhen, it was established as a Tibetan monastery in 1744, largely as a symbol of Chinese suzerainty over Tibet, and assumed a spiritual significance as important as that of the Jokhang Temple in Lhasa. It has several halls featuring some of the most splendid Tibetan Buddhist artwork and relics found anywhere in the Chinese "lowlands," including a 26 m (85 ft) high Maitreya Buddha carved from a single block of sandalwood, a large bronze statue of the founder of the Yellow Hat Sect, Tsongkapa, a host of other Buddha images representing the various stages of Buddhahood and a bronze mandala portraying the Buddhist "Western Paradise."

There are many other temples around the city, some of them in reasonably good shape and others derelict or destroyed all but for their pagodas. The most attractive are the **Biyun** (**Azure Clouds**) in Xiangshan Park in the Western Hills, a Yuan dynasty temple extended in the Qing reign and noted for its striking white marble pagodas in the early Indian architectural

style; the **Sleeping Buddha Monastery**, also close to Xiangshan Park, with a giant bronze statue of Sakyamuni Buddha in the reclining position which is said to be the pose he took when discussing with his disciples his impending departure from all earthly matters; the **Da-zhongsi (Big Bell) Temple**, two kilometers (one and a quarter miles) east of the Friendship Hotel, with an immense 46-ton Ming dynasty bell with Buddhist sutras inscribed on it; the **Guangjisi (Temple of Universal Rescue)**, just west of Beihai Park, with many good Buddha statues; and the **Mahakala Miao** at the southern end of the Forbidden City, which is one of the centers of Mongolian lamaism in Beijing.

Other Sights

As you go east on Chang'an Avenue, heading toward the huge Friendship Store, you'll find on the right the ancient

feared nuclear attack by the United States or the Soviet Union, or both.

The **Military Museum** on Fuxing Lu, the western extension of Chang'an Avenue, has exhibitions recounting the history of the People's Liberation Army, its role in the Korean War (and American jets that it shot down) and captured weapons and documents of its most recent military foray, the 1979 military "lesson" that it attempted to teach Vietnam.

At the **China Art Gallery**, just east of Beihai and Jingshan Parks, you can study China's current political switch through the eyes of its artists – the gaudy heroic poster color "mass campaign" art of the revolutionary years giving way gradually to a return to the softer, more harmonic landscapes, birds, animals and life studies of the traditional schools of painting.

The **Former Residence of Soong Ching Ling** on the northern bank of Shisha Lake, just north of Beihai Park, is worth a visit for the symbol that it now represents of the chaotic republican era after the collapse of the Qing dynasty. Soong Ching Ling was one of three daughters of "Charlie" Soong, a wayward Hainanese Chinese who became a Methodist preacher in the United States and was sent back to China to convert the "heathen" nation with American-style holy rolling evangelism. Charlie decided to get rich instead, backing Sun Yatsen and his republican cause and becoming, in the process, the wealthiest magnate in China.

Of his three daughters, Chingling, the "thinking" one, married Sun Yatsen and this placed her in the annals of the revolutionary heroes, while Mayling, the "clever" one, became Madame Chiang Kaishek, thence to use her particular talents for power, guile and false piety to hoodwink the Americans into one of their biggest ever diplomatic blunders, their dogged, shortsighted support of Chiang's corrupt military regime. If you go to the Soong Chingling museum, take along a copy of the book that exposes it all –

Observatory, built in the Ming dynasty and now notable for its collection of Chinese maritime maps and instruments and astronomical gadgets built by Jesuit priests. These scholars, headed by Father Matteo Ricci, were employed in the Ming court to work on a Chinese calendar, and in return were given the freedom to seek Chinese converts – not many of whom ever turned up.

CITS operate daily tours of **Underground Beijing**, a network of subterranean defenses and shelters throughout the capital, some of which have factories, shops, restaurants and even, it's said, some 100 "hotels." They're a legacy of the Cold War and Yellow Peril period when the Chinese

ABOVE Four views of the Temple of Heaven – CLOCKWISE festival flags at marble bridge, renowned Temple of Prayer for Good Harvests, sweeping Echo Wall and detail of temple's decorative gilding and tile-work.

Sterling Seagrave's epic *The Soong Dynasty*. It makes incredible, illuminating reading.

The Summer Palace

This Qing dynasty summer retreat, about 12 km (7 miles) northwest of the city center, was built in the early years of the Manchu reign but has since become more popularly associated with its most famous, or infamous, resident, The Empress Dowager. She put a great deal of money into the place – most of it, as already mentioned, grabbed from funds established to mod-

ernize the antique Qing navy – and had a great deal of trouble keeping it in one piece.

It was torn apart by an Anglo-French force in 1880, damaged again by foreign troops in the Boxer Rebellion in 1900, and, each time, the Dragon Lady put it all back together again. Nowadays it's a public recreational spot, perhaps the most popular around Beijing, reclining along the shore of Lake Kunming and featuring splendid gardens, pavilions, mansions, temples and bridges – and the remarkable **Long Corridor,** a 7,000 m (7,655 yards) covered gallery full of frescoes with mythical themes. And in the lake itself there's the ultimate in imperial kitsch, the Empress's white marble paddle-steamboat. In winter time the lake is the place to go for one of Beijing's favorite seasonal recreations, ice-skating.

The Great Wall

The greatest man-made barrier in the world, the only concrete sign of human existence that can be seen from outer space, the world's longest cemetery, the abiding symbol of membership of the Chinese civilization, the scene of incredible bloodshed, the wall that ultimately faced the wrong way... . All this, and more, you can stand and reflect upon atop the sweeping, crowded **Great Wall** at **Badaling**, 75 km (46 miles) northwest of Beijing, the main section of the 6,000 km (3,720 miles) wall that is open for tourism. It's the ultimate

and, in many respects, the final destination of the China pilgrimage. See the Great Wall, and die.

It is everything that you can imagine it to be – monolithic, magnificent, sweeping and snaking up and over steep hills as though a blind man's blundering had directed its path. In fact, when the great Qinshihuangdi built the ancient first sections of it, the surveying technique followed by his engineers was to send ponies dragging saddles behind them over the hills and peg out the path they chose.

Along its full length, much of the wall has fallen into disrepair, its watchtowers left standing like tombstones in the desert wastes and on the loess hills of the west. You can see decrepit sections of it north of Lanzhou and follow a reasonably intact winding section on the railway ride between Beijing and Datong. The section at Badaling was repaired and turned into a tourist mecca in 1957, and since then other renovations have been going on in Liaoning province. In 1986 a campaign was launched to fund the reconstruction and renovation of the wall's dramatic eastern

terminus, **Dragon's Head** at **Shanhaiguan** on the Bo Sea.

There are various routes to the wall, by direct daily train (except Wednesdays) from Beijing Station, by organized CITS and hotel tours, or by going to Xizhimen Station at the northwest corner of the Circle Line of the Beijing Subway, north of the Exhibition Center, and taking a three-hour hard-seat train ride from there. Trains leave at 7:45 am, 8:30 am and 9:15 am.

Alternatively, there are daily tours from the major hotels and one bus that leaves at

7:30 am from Chongwenmen Dajie, right opposite the Chongwenmen Hotel. Tickets are booked the previous day at the tour office right at this spot. The trip gives you a good two hours at the wall. The only trouble is, it goes on to include a tiring stop-start tour of the **Ming Tombs (Shisanling)** – and from my own impression and that of many other travelers that I discussed it with the Ming Tombs are really not worth the long hot hours of travel and the trudging that it takes to get around them. They may be the resting places of 13 of the 16 Ming emperors, but nowadays

they are virtually empty of relics and artwork and are little more than decorated concrete blockhouses surrounded by tourist restaurants, tea gardens and souvenir stalls. I honestly think it's more satisfying to spend a whole day at tthe wall.

The Radial Route

Beijing has access by air and rail to all parts of China and to the Mongolian Plateau to the north and the former Manchurian territory of the northeast. For rail travelers, **Beijing Station**, with its cavernous halls, crowded concourse and unusually decorative clock towers, is one of the most convenient in the country. No booking struggles here – you simply make your way to its International Traveler's section,

Temple of Virtue OPPOSITE LEFT in Qing dynasty Summer Palace, and detail RIGHT of opulent architecture. The Great Wall ABOVE LEFT and detail of nearby sculptured gateway.

through the central hall and down along the left of the escalators, to find a CITS-style reservations room, just for foreign guests, with two big boards listing destinations all over China, train numbers, departure times and ticket prices.

Outside the reservations section this VIP inner sanctum has a large waiting room, with comfortable furnishings and a Friendship desk, where you can await your train far from the madding crowds and even be escorted to it by an attendant when it's time to go. By average rail travel standards in China it's so comfortable and efficient that it's almost decadent.

THE NORTHERN TRAIL

There are two main northern routes, the "over the top" Beijing-Lanzhou run to Datong and across Inner Mongolia, and the northeast Beijing-Harbin route with major intermediate tourist destinations at Chengde, Shenyang and Changchun.

The region itself is one of the most physically dramatic in all of China, bounded to the north, east and southeast by four great rivers, the Heilong, Wusuli, Tumen and Yalu (where, in its eastern reaches, Chinese forces stormed into the Korean War), and featuring four principal mountain ranges. The most beautiful of these, the Changbai Range, includes **Mount Baita,** the tallest peak in the northeast, capped with snow all the year round. On its upper slopes lies the pristine but moody **Sky Lake (Tianchi),** a huge volcanic crater lake surrounded by 16 lofty peaks, that can be beautifully placid and serene one day and a maelstrom of crashing wind-whipped waves the next.

The Changbai Range also produces the Songhua River, the major tributary of the Heilong, which flows through the region's two most interesting and attractive "river cities," Harbin, completely iced in and a popular resort in the winter months, and Jilin, famous for its frozen "tree hangings," a riverside filigree of ice formed by warmer moisture on banks of willow trees.

Culturally, Shenyang and Chengde have magnificent buildings and relics reflecting the region's former status as the cradle of the Manchu expansion that overran China in the seventeenth century and established the last of the nation's imperial dynasties. The founding emperor of the Qing reign established Shenyang, now the capital of Liaoning province, as the imperial capital before moving triumphantly to the Forbidden City in Beijing. That brief moment of glory has endowed the city with the Imperial Palace, the mausoleums of two Qing emperors and some 70 courts and administrative complexes that rank in architecture with Beijing's "Great Within."

Chengde features the Imperial Summer Villa, the traveling lodge of the early Qing court at Shenyang, northeast of which lie several interesting monasteries and the world's largest wooden Buddha statue. At the region's farthest edge, the city of Mohe, the northern most inhabited point in China, is called the Arctic City for its bitterly cold winter climate as low as 50°C below freezing point (minus 58°F) and the City of the White Night for its spectacular summer displays of the Aurora Borealis.

DATONG

At first sight, this is a rather unspectacular industrial and coal mining center, situated in the north of Shanxi province close to the Great Wall and the Inner Mongolian border and eight hours by train from Beijing. But it has a surprisingly interesting monastery and another major cultural attraction that makes it an important place of pilgrimage – it lies close to the **Yungang Grottoes,** one of the three greatest examples of Buddhist cave art in China, started by the Toba rulers of the Northern Wei when they made Datong their capital in 398.

OPPOSITE Bicyclist and bystanders at Ming dynasty guardian statue on triumphal route to Ming Tombs.

Access

There's only one way to get to Datong, by train. And there are two ways of doing it – stopping off on the west-to-east Lanzhou-Beijing route, or taking the overnight express north from Beijing. After your visit there, you can take a daytime train to Beijing, riding hard-seat, and enjoy a remarkable view of the Great Wall snaking around and right over the hills to the east, and old walled towns along the way.

Hotels

Datong has two hotels. One is the rather run-down **Datong Guesthouse** to the south of the city center, which had very basic double rooms with awful bathrooms when I was there. Then there's a new tourist-class hotel, the Yungang, which opened in 1986 offering comfortable and clean doubles at ¥55 a night. You can double that rate now. CITS immediately moved there from the Datong.

Restaurants

There isn't much in the way of eating out in Datong, but the two hotels have good dining rooms offering set menus with four or five courses that will keep the wolf from the door. Other than that, there's a **Beijing Roast Duck** establishment in the city center on the north-south main street, Renmin Beilu, and a place just across from the Yungang Hotel which had a sign proclaiming "Welcome to All Friends of the World With a Smile!" I walked in and not one person smiled, so I can't vouch for it at all.

Sightseeing

In Datong itself, the main cultural center is the huge, brooding twelfth century **Huayan Monastery,** set on two levels right in the center of the city. Although it's under renovation the monastery looks a bit derelict and drab, until you enter the main hall and are immediately stunned by the fantastic Buddhist artwork crammed into it. Not only does it feature five huge Ming dynasty Buddha images, gilded and flamboyantly decorated and seated on lotus thrones, but they are flanked on either side by honor guards of 31 Liao dynasty statues of soldiers, officials and Bodhisattvas. Around them, the walls are decorated with murals and paintings of Sakyamuni Buddha, arhats, thousand-eye Bodhisattvas

and other deities added by the artist Dong An in the late Qing reign.

To the south of Huayan, the **Shanhua Monastery** dating back to the Tang dynasty features another five splendid Buddha images and many murals. And there's a far more modern, yet antique, attraction in Datong that should not be missed – the **Steam Locomotive Factory** where, on visits arranged by CITS on Tuesdays and Saturdays, you can watch the last of China's beautiful early industrial thoroughbreds being assembled.

Yungang Caves

This dramatic Buddhist grotto, carved into the northern slope of **Mount Wuzhou** more than 1,500 years ago, lies 16 km (10 miles) north of Datong in the heart of the region's coal mining communities. To get there you can either organize a minibus or taxi through CITS or take the public bus, or rather two buses – bus No. 2 from a terminal west of the city's main square, connecting with bus No. 3 on the western outskirts of the city for the direct journey to Yungang.

There are 53 caves covering about one kilometer of the cliff-face and containing about 50,000 Buddhist statues and bas-relief carvings. Along the western face, the whole complex is dominated by a marvelous sitting Sakyamuni Buddha, 13.7 m (44 ft) high, with a slightly amused expression that is said to be typical of the Northern Wei style.

To the east, three ornately decorated wooden pavilions with double eaves and several galleries, built right into the cliff, form the entrance to caverns containing immense Sakyamuni and Maitreya statues and wall carvings and niches reaching right up to the ceilings. These depict the life of Buddha and also include flower motifs, altars, musicians and instruments, and some were added there as recently as Qing times. Although three different

OPPOSITE French tourists dwafed by huge Sakyamuni Buddha image at Yungang Grottoes, Datong.

periods of Buddhist art are represented at Yungang, each grotto contains a Buddha image at least 13 m (43 ft) high that is said to have been modeled on a Northern Wei ruler.

HARBIN

This, the capital of Heilongjiang province, 385 km (238 miles) northeast of Beijing, was a sleepy fishing village – its Manchurian name meaning "where the fishing nets are dried" – until the Russians obtained parts of Manchuria as a concession in 1896 to give themselves access to the east, and built the railway line through to Vladivostok. They then lost the entire region to the Japanese as a result of their humiliating naval defeat of 1905 but continued to have a cultural impression on the area after the 1917 Bolshevik revolution, when Harbin became a refuge for White Russian escapees. And that's largely what Harbin is famous for today, its surviving Russian character, particularly the architecture of its old Orthodox churches. That, and the city's harsh winter climate, when the temperature plummets as low as minus 30°C (86°F) and when the city becomes not only a winter recreation resort but also the venue of a spectacular festival of ice lanterns and sculptures.

Access

There are direct air services to Harbin from Beijing, Guangzhou, Shanghai, Changchun and Shenyang, and daily express trains from Beijing.

Hotels

Being a summer and winter resort, for the top echelons of the Chinese administration as well as foreign visitors, Harbin has no shortage of mainstream hotels and private *dasha*-style villa hotels for overworked party officials. For tourists, the **Guoji (International) Hotel** is about the top of the range with a relatively new nine-story wing, good restaurants and amenities and double rooms. The **Harbin Hotel**

has comfortable rooms but poor bathrooms, and the **Swan Hotel**, remembered for the major fire that it suffered in 1985 – and the American tourist who was subsequently charged with dropping off to sleep with a lighted cigarette – will put you in a refurbished double room for about ¥100 a night.

Other comfortable, renovated establishments are the **Overseas Chinese Hotel**, and the dramatic Kremlin-style **Beifang Dasha (Mansions)**. There's also the **China International Travel Service Hotel,** the **Heping Hotel** and the **Friendship Palace** to choose from.

Restaurants

Outside its many hotel restaurants and dining rooms, Harbin is noted for its Beijing duck, Mongolian hot-pot, shish-

kebab, Korean dog soups and other less orthodox dishes, Russian bread the size of pillows and its glacé ice cream, all of which can be found in its eating houses and its streets. For roast duck try the **Jiangnanchun** at 316 Fendou Jie and the Futailou at 19 Xi Shishandao. The **Beileishun** near Zhuolin Park features local beef and mutton dishes and Mongolian hot-pot in the winter; the **Huamei**

Canting at 142 Zhongyang Dajie has a Western menu with Russian borscht; and the **Jiangbin Fandian (Riverside Restaurant)** is the place for Han Chinese cuisine and seafood.

ABOVE Yungang Grottoes near Datong date back to Northern Wei region and feature about 50,000 Buddhist statues and bas-relief carvings covering three great dynasties.

Sightseeing

Harbin is more of a recreational spot than a cultural center. And while it's a big summer resort, with boating, swimming, hunting, trekking and cruises on the Songhua River, its most exciting season is midwinter. The Songhua freezes over and becomes an ice skating rink and a winter white playground for ice yachting, ice hockey, sledding and sleigh-rides. A long runway of ice for sledding sweeps 150 m (159 yards) down the riverbank and on to the ice at Stalin Park. Elsewhere you can take rides around the toown on donkey and

horse sleighs, clad to the eyeballs in fur fashions bought at the **Fur Product Shop** and **Harbin Fur Factory** at 88 Zhongyang Dajie, catching a glimpse here and there of a surviving cupola or onion-shaped dome and quietly humming the theme from *Doctor Zhivago* in your partner's frozen ear.

But the big attraction is the **Ice Lantern Festival** from January 1 to the end of February, when Zhuolin Park and other areas are decorated with fantastic ice sculptures of animals, plants, temples and pavilions, tableaux from Chinese legends and literally anything that strike's the ice

artist's fancy – all lit up from the inside at night. The festival is already attracting 16,000 visitors a year, and the city plans to promote it to become a major international attraction, with ski resorts to go with it, by 1990.

Of Harbin's Russian architecture, the **Dongzheng Church** is really the only surviving structure in any reasonable shape. It was built in 1899 and was regarded as the finest of some 17 Orthodox churches that were eventually established throughout the short-lived Czarist concession.

SHENYANG

This industrial hub of Liaoning province was a trading center for the nomads beyond the Great Wall a thousand years ago. In the seventeenth century it became the capital of the Manchus, and after they fought and connived their way to the imperial throne in Beijing it remained as the secondary seat of power known by its Manchu name, Mukden.

The city has changed hands several times since then. The Russians controlled it as a center of their Manchurian enterprise until the Japanese booted them out in savage warfare in 1904-5. The Russians took it back after the World War II defeat of Japan, and then Mao Zedong's communists marched in and established it as a key northern base from which they launched their nationwide campaign that led to the triumph of 1949.

Nowadays, Shenyang is a huge industrial and manufacturing city supported by the region's coal and steel, and would be a venue for the joint-venture businessman rather than the tourist, were it not for its magnificent footprint of the Manchu march to power, the Imperial Palace.

Access

Shenyang has direct air connections with Beijing, Guangzhou, Shanghai, Harbin, Nanjing, Wuhan and Xi'an. It is also the junction of six major railway lines in the northeast, and lies on the route of the Beijing-Harbin express trains.

Hotels

With its industrial and manufacturing capacity in the process of modernization and expansion, several new business-class hotels are planned for Shenyang and may already be operating by the time you venture there. Otherwise, the **Liaoning Dasha (Mansions)** is the main tour hotel, another monolithic throwback to the era of Sino-Soviet friendship and cooperation. The **Friendship Hotel,** just to the north, is a villa-style establishment, formerly for Chinese VIPs but now taking up the overflow from the Liaoning, and the **Overseas**

Chinese Hotel, close to the railway station, is where CITS are based and has the same room rates as the Liaoning.

Sightseeing

There are a couple of Manchu tombs in Shenyang, but they're hardly worth going all that way just to see. The main reason for going there is the **Imperial Palace** in the eastern section of the city, which was the Manchu court and seat of power until the takeover of China was completed and the first Qing emperor, the warrior Shunzi, moved the court to Beijing in 1644.

In scale and architecture this palace rivals the Forbidden City where the Qing emperors continued their long and dramatic reign. It was built in three sections, beginning in 1625, and expanded by successive rulers until it comprised some 70 pavilions and halls dominated by the octagonal **Dazheng Hall,** where Emperor Shunzi was crowned before being borne triumphantly south. It has a militaristic design – rows of five pavilions on each side, extending north to south, that give the effect of two lines of tents guarding the commander-in-chief.

The nearby **Shiwang Pavilion** is a series of administrative centers where the Manchu ruler's 10 most important lieutenants – two princes and eight ministers – met each day to plot the combination of political intrigue and military strategy that was to win them the empire. It's now a museum of Manchu armour, carriages, military costume, campaign banners and weapons – and a sword that was worn by the eighth century ruler, Emperor Qianlong, and today, more than two centuries after his reign, is still untarnished.

CHENGDE

This Hebei provincial city, 250 km (155 miles) northeast of Beijing, was a fairly insignificant backwater called Jehol until 1703 when the Qing emperor Kangxi took a good look at its surrounding natural beauty and hot springs and transformed it into his imperial summer retreat. He called his palace **Bihushanzhuang (Fleeing the Heat Mountain Hamlet)** and his successors expanded it until it reached such magnificent proportions that it covered an area the size of the Forbidden City and Summer Palace combined. It is still the biggest garden palace complex in China.

ABOVE Two views of the magnificent early Qing Imperial alace in Shenyang – seat of the manchu warlords.

Emperor Qianlong, who succeeded Kangxi, endowed the palace with three Tibetan-style temples, one of them, the **Putuo Zhoncheng,** a smaller version of the Potala Palace, to bind his authority to the Tibetan Buddhist rule after bringing the mountain stronghold under imperial control. Today the palace's gardens and temples, surrounded by a 10 km (6.2 mile) long red wall, are in varying states of neglect and disrepair, awaiting renovations that will obviously have to be carried out if it is to become a major tourist drawcard.

Its main **Central Palace,** now a museum, is in reasonable shape; so too are its **Misty Rain Mansion, Pine and Crane Studio** and **East Palace.** Of the temples, only five of an original 11 remain standing, but they still present a striking reminder of the power and artistry of the dynastic age. The **Puning Temple,** featuring a beautiful five-story Mahayana Chamber, houses an impressive 22 m (72 ft) wooden Buddha image – A Thousand Hands and Thousand Eyes Bodhisattva – fashioned from five different timbers and the largest image of its type in the world.

The **Pule Temple** has a main building which is almost a carbon copy of the Temple of Prayer for Good Harvests in Beijing, and inside you'll find a three-dimensional mandala, at the center of which is set a bronze sculpture of the Maitreya Buddha. The Potala-style **Putuo Zhoncheng** features a huge statue of the Buddhist Heavenly Mother, mounted on a horse, while the Xumi Fushou Temple, built in 1780 to accommodate the sixth Panchen Lama on a visit from Tibet, is a near-replica of the Tashilhunpo Monastery in Xigaze.

Hotels

The tourist-class **Chengde Hotel** has double rooms and also offers cheaper dormitory accommodation. There's another establishment called the **Jiaodaichiu (Resort Guesthouse)** close to the Summer Palace.

SHANHAIGUAN

This dramatic coastal location, six and a half hours by train out of Beijing, is where the Great Wall terminates in the Dragon's Head on the shore of the Bo Hai (Sea) – tumbling down from the hills to the remains of a walled garrison. It's an opportunity to view the wall without the tourist hassle of the conventional visit to Badaling, and even though the structure at Shanhaiguan is in relatively poor shape, it still has a great deal of physical and romantic appeal. Perhaps more.

"If the head of this great dragon is not restored in our time," says a promotional poster beside the wall, "he will stand shamefaced before our ancestors, our descendants and the whole human civilization."

Shanhaiguan also offers a temple commemorating one of the many romantic legends associated with the Great Wall, or rather its reputation as the "World's Longest Cemetery." The **Temple of Menjiangnu,** six kilometers (four miles) from the town, deifies a lady of the same name who went in search of her husband who had been pressed into service along with thousands of other conscripts during its initial construction in the reign of the ruthless Qinshihuangdi. "Suddenly there was a great rumble," so the story goes, "and a gaping hole appeared in the wall. The bones of not one but thousands of dead workers were exposed to the icy winds." And those of Meng's husband were among them. But life, generally, was pretty cheap in the struggle it took to build the defensive barrier. It's also said that a sorcerer told the Iron Emperor that the wall would not be completed until 10,000 men had been buried in it. Qinshihuangdi immediately tracked down a worker whose name included the character meaning "ten thousand" and had him slain and buried in the foundations instead. In its present decayed state, Shanhaiguan offers only one reasonably comfortable guesthouse, the **Trade Service Hotel**, with a restaurant, bicycle rental service and double rooms for around ¥40 to ¥50 a night. But with the town's civic fathers planning to make it an international resort, there'll obviously be more hotels springing up in the coming years – and the first is the **Sheraton Old Dragon Head Hotel** near the wall – the international chain's first resort hotel in China.

This appeal has been considered strong enough for a Shanhaiguan organization to launch a campaign to to renovate the wall and turn it into another Badaling, and the town itself into an "international tourist resort" attracting five million visitors a year. The Shanhaiguan Great Wall Research Institute hopes to pay for the work by offering two meter-high (6.5 ft) tablets, erected alongside the repaired wall, inscribed with tributes to donors who come up with at least ¥50,000. For ¥100, more modest contributors can have their names recorded on a roll of honor in the town itself.

ABOVE Poplars line boulevard TOP of Chengde, home of imperial summer retreat rivaling the Forbidden City in grandeur and BOTTOM landscaping and architecture of its palace gardens.

Shanghai
and the
Yangtze
Cities

SHANGHAI AND THE YANGTZE CITIES

This dramatic east-west stretch of the long China trail offers an exciting and quite refined gateway to the heart of the nation for travelers starting out from Shanghai – and for those, like me, who may be following the clockwise grand tour, it provides relative comfort, good cuisine and sophistication at the closing stage of the China adventure.

The Yangtze River route is the central axis on which all travel in China swings. On the rail route north from Guangzhou it provides access to Shanghai, Suzhou and Hangzhou in the east and Chongqing, Chengdu, Lhasa and Xi'an in the west. It offers the same east-west access coming, of course, south from Beijing. And from whichever direction you approach it, the two pivotal junctions are Zhengzhou and Wuhan.

ZHENGZHOU

This busy and quite prosperous industrial city, once a Shang dynasty imperial seat and now the capital of Henan province, is one of the two most strategic railway junctions of south-central China – the other being Hengyang on the east-west rail corridor to Yunnan and the west. It's also one of the most difficult cities in China for foreigners to deal with – very few of its people speak English, and its tourist facilities haven't yet been developed enough to provide smooth access to its main cultural attracttion, the Shaolin Monastery, 80 km (50 miles) to the west, considered to be the birthplace of Zen Buddhism and the martial art kung fu.

Access
Zhengzhou has an airport with four direct air services a week with Guangzhou. It also has direct connections with Shanghai, Beijing, Xi'an, Lanzhou and Guilin. For access by train, it's on the main north-

south Guangzhou-Beijing express route, the cross-country Beijing-Xi'an-Lanzhou service and the east-west route between Shanghai and Xi'an.

Hotels
Zhengzhou has a number of hotels and guesthouses ranging in comfort and convenience – and, most importantly, communication – from the tourist-class **Henan International Guesthouse,** to two down-market "mansions" across from the railway station, the Zhongyuan and Zhengzhou, which should be avoided at all costs. Although it's more expensive, the Henan Guesthouse has a CITS desk, some English-speaking staff and transport facilities.

Sightseeing
There's really only one place to go around Zhengzhou, and that's the **Shaolin Monastery.** Built in the time of the Northern Wei dynasty, it was established in tribute to Bodhidharma, the Indian monk (also featured on a mural in the Guangxiao Temple in Guangzhou) who brought the message of Zen to China and is said to have been the first champion of the martial arts – teaching his disciples boxing and unarmed combat for self-protection in those unstable and dangerous times. Legend has it that he was so transcendental that he was able to cross a river on a flimsy reed.

In the monastery's most glorious age, during the Sui and Tang dynasties, it sported 5,000 shrines, halls, pagodas and pavilions. Only four major buildings remain – the Bodhidharma Pavilion, Thousand Buddha Hall, White Robe hall and Bodhisattva Kitigharba Hall – but they offer surviving artwork and relics that echo the monastery's martial role. In the White Robe hall, for example, there are stunning murals depicting scenes and techniques of kung fu, including the epic "Thirteen Monks Rescuing the King of Tang" – a celebrated punch-up that took place when the monks of Shaolin acted as imperial retainers in the Tang dynasty. In the **Thousand Buddha Hall** you can study rounded hollows in the tiled floor – worn there over the centuries by daily kung fu training.

To get to the monastery you either take a CITS tour or a daily bus that leaves from outside the Zhongyuan Mansions opposite the railway station. You buy the tickets at a small white booth on the edge of the station concourse. But you would be well advised to take along a ticket request written in Chinese.

Aside from the monastery, Zhengzhou provides easy access by train or bus to the cultural jewel of central China, Luoyang.

imperial court and also the site of no fewer than 1,300 Buddhist temples.

Access

There is no airport at Luoyang (as yet), and the only way to reach it is by train. There are various approaches, from Lanzhou in the northwest via Xi'an on the express run to Beijing or Shanghai; from Beijing on the same east-west rail loop; from Wuhan via Zhengzhou after the Yangtze River journey west from Shanghai; and from Zhengzhou, heading west, from the Guangzhou-Beijing express.

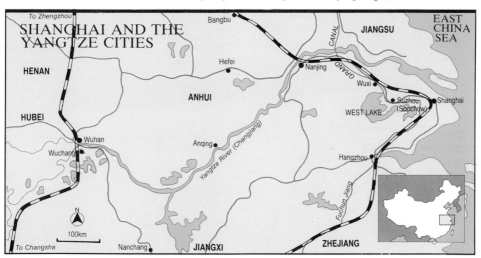

LUOYANG

Luoyang, west of Zhengzhou, is another city whose modern industrial facade obscures its long, illustrious history. Not only was it the founding center of Buddhism in China – the site of the Han dynasty White Horse Temple, built to celebrate the arrival of the first sutras from India – but it was the imperial capital of 10 dynasties until it was destroyed by the armies of the northern Jin reign in the twelveth century.

Its most magnificent legacy of all that history is, of course, the **Longmen Buddhist Grottoes,** first excavated and decorated in the time of the Toba Northern Wei dynasty when Luoyang was the

Hotels

There's only one establishment worth considering, the **Friendship Hotel,** which unfortunately is located on the western edge of the town and which has double rooms that have shot up in price in recent years. The hotel also has the best restaurant in town, and houses the Luoyang branch of CITS. By and large, it's quite acceptable considering the cultural treat that awaits you 16 km (10 miles) south of the city on the bank of the Yi River, and a new tourist hotel should be in operation by the time you read this guide.

Longmen Caves

The **Longmen (Dragon Gate) Grottoes** were dug and carved around the year 493 in the time of the Northern Wei and added

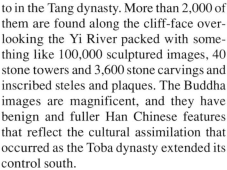

to in the Tang dynasty. More than 2,000 of them are found along the cliff-face overlooking the Yi River packed with something like 100,000 sculptured images, 40 stone towers and 3,600 stone carvings and inscribed steles and plaques. The Buddha images are magnificent, and they have benign and fuller Han Chinese features that reflect the cultural assimilation that occurred as the Toba dynasty extended its control south.

The two most impressive galleries are the **Pingyang Caves** at the entrance to the complex, featuring 11 large Buddha images of the Toba period, and the **Fengxian Cave,** now without its protective roof and actually an open-air grotto, which was built in the Tang era and is dominated by nine huge Buddha statues, the biggest of them 18 m (59 ft) high. One of them supports a pagoda in the palm of its hand and is in the act of crushing a demon underfoot. Aside from the Buddhas and attendant statues, there are sculptures throughout the grottoes of emperors, princes and nobles of the 400-year period over which the immense tableau was completed.

WUHAN

This Hubei provincial capital, one of the largest cities in the interior of China, is actually made up of three cities clustered on both sides of the Yangtze River which provide a striking contrast of past and present. Hankou, on the Yangtze's west bank, is a former fishing village that became a major Treaty Port in the days of British and European military and trading pressure, and its architectural character is similar to that of Shanghai.

Hanyang, to the south, is a largely industrial center connected to Hankou by a bridge over the Han River which meets the Yangtze here. Although it doesn't have the narrow teeming streets and old Victorian commercial buildings of Hankou, it features the city's most historic attraction, the Ming dynasty **Guiyuan Temple**.

Wuchang, on the Yangtze's eastern bank, is the oldest of all these urban centers, its site dating back to 221, but is now more representative of modern China – wide boulevards and streets and high-rise administrative buildings – and

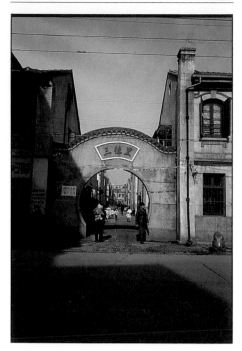

includes the huge **Wuhan University,** the **Hubei Provincial Museum** and the popular recreational resort, **East Lake.** Wuchang is linked to **Hankou** by the spectacular Yangtze River Bridge, built in 1957 and the first to span the great river, its eastern expressway sweeping under the beautiful multi-winged roofs of the city's most remarkable historic landmark, the renovated Ming dynasty **Yellow Crane Mansion.**

Wuhan's contemporary history centers on an accidental bomb explosion on October 10, 1911 that triggered an anti-Manchu army rebellion and in turn became the long-awaited flashpoint of the republican campaign to sweep the Qing dynasty from power.

Access
Wuhan is China's central rail and Yangtze River access. It lies on the main Guangzhou-Beijing express route and the east-west routes from Shanghai to Kunming and Xi'an. The Yangtze River ferries ply east to Nanjing and Shanghai and west to Chongqing. Both the main railway station and river ferry terminal are in Hankou.

There are also direct air links with Beijing, Guangzhou, Chengdu, Chongqing, Nanjing, Shanghai and Shenyang.

Transport
There are good taxi services from the main railway station and the major hotels, and motorized and pedal rickshaws operate around Hankou. There are ferries that run back and forth between Hankou, Hanyang and Wuchang, but they looked so crowded that I preferred to lash out for a taxi ride or take the dramatic stroll across the Yangtze River Bridge.

Hotels
Top of the range, and at a very reasonable room rate, is the new chain-style **Qing Chuan Hotel** on the Hanyang bank of the Yangtze right next to the bridge. It has comfortable, well-furnished double rooms, a splendid dining room, a well-stocked Friendship desk, magnificent views of the

Three faces of Wuhan — sensuously rounded gateway OPPOSITE LEFT to restored pavilion at Guiyuan Monastery CENTER, Hanyang. Same classic architecture is repeated ABOVE in gateway to residential backstreet.

bridge and river and is the center of social life for the large university-based foreign community in Wuhan.

The most romantic establishment, if you can afford it, is the old **Jianghan Hotel,** near the railway station in Hankou, right in the middle of the busiest section of town and featuring an old run-down pre-war decor of polished mahogany balustrades, red velvet curtains and rooms and suites with enclosed latticed verandah sections and old-fashioned valve wirelesses that conjure up images of cabin trunks, ceiling fans, gins-and-tonic, malarial sweats and news of the latest Japanese military advances. The Jianghan charges through the nose for a double room, but gets so packed with VIPs and business groups that it often has nothing but full suites available at ¥120 a night. I stayed in one for one night, just for the romance of it – and hurried the next day to the Qing Chuan.

Restaurants

Around the Jianghan, on Zhongshan Lu, the **China Restaurant** and basic but popular **Laotongchang** are cheap, friendly eating establishments offering a very tasty and nourishing chicken soup in clay pots and *jaozie* for around ¥1.20. Other than that, the only really good place to eat is in the huge dining room of the **Qing Chuan Hotel**.

Sightseeing

Hankou is the most exciting side of Wuhan for street-life – crowded, noisy, bustling, friendly, a cultural clash of old Chinese and Treaty Port Victorian architecture and, here and there, bizarre signs with big crimson lips and white tombstone sets of teeth advertising backstreet dentists. The big department stores are here too, along with an interesting, remarkably friendly and efficient but decrepit branch of the Bank of China, housed in the crumbling shell of an old European banking establishment and so neglected that the cashiers and clerks were working by the light of neon tubes hung by strings from the high ceilings when I was there.

Down on the waterfront, where the Yangtze River shipping agents, warehouses, open markets, drink stalls and the booking office and terminal for the river ferries are located, the scene is like something out of Lord Jim and that line that goes something to the effect that "He sought to lose himself, and his shame, in the teeming mass of humanity."

The city's prime cultural attraction, the **Guiyuan Temple,** is close to the waterfront in Hanyang – a Ming dynasty monastery, extended in the Qing reign, now springing back to life after the repression of the Cultural Revolution. It billows with joss-stick smoke and features a gloomy but fascinating main hall full of Buddha images, sculptures of arhats and a looming, moon-faced guardian deity, all staring from dark and dusty glassed alcoves. Its most treasured relic is a Burmese jade Buddha presented to it in 1935.

Around the Qing Chuan Hotel you can take an interesting riverfront stroll and enjoy views of the Yangtze Bridge, shop at a well-stocked antique store housed in a former temple, and study a vivid contrast of old and new China – low-roofed stone and tiled dwellings sprawling along the riverbank under the city's proud new symbol of modernization, a soaring pencil-tipped communications tower with a revolving observation platform that's as dramatic as the famed CN Tower in Toronto.

As for the **Yangtze Bridge,** you can climb up its stone towers and right on to its top traffic deck and cross the 1,156 m (3,800 ft) span enjoying a bird's eye view of the river traffic and the packed city ferries disgorging hundreds of commuters and their bicycles along the Wuchang waterfront – the crowds streaming like hordes of ants up the ferry ramps, the chrome of their bikes flashing in the sun. Ahead of you, on the Wuchang side, you can also marvel at the towering, golden,

multi-eaved **Yellow Crane Mansion.** It's really a rebuilt pagoda – the original Ming dynasty structure burned down in 1884 – and although completely new it's a popular recreation spot for Chinese and foreign visitors alike. The view from its upper balconies is a dramatic panorama of the bridge, its huge expressway, the Wuchang riverfront and the Hanyang foreshores.

East Lake

Out on the eastern fringe of Wuchang, East Lake is one of the largest freshwater lakes

in China and a long-established recreational resort that has interesting pavilions, boating, good bicycling paths, a botanical garden and three lakeside restaurants, the **Renmin, Liyuan** and **Tingtao.** It's also the site of the small **Hubei Provincial Museum** with a remarkable exhibition of bronze tripods, lacquered furniture and trunks, carvings, sculptures, jewelry and gold bowls and ornaments unearthed in 1978 from the tomb of the Marquis Yi of Zeng, one of the nobles of the Warring States period of 475-221 BC, just before the rise to power of the Iron Emperor Qinshihuangdi.

OPPOSITE Retired workers play cards on Wuhan's Yangtze waterfront CENTER while "liberal era" young show off latest fashions TOP and suburban housewife heads off to stores BOTTOM. ABOVE Crane sculpture and pagoda at newly renovated Yellow Crane Mansion in Wuchang.

But the most splendid relic from the tomb is a huge ancient musical instrument, a bronze bell chime – 65 ornately decorated bells set on a heavy three-level frame and, as the museum's brochure explains, "They were played by five musicians. Each bell has two different pitches. The whole set has a range of five and a half octaves, so the instrument is capable of modulation. Ancient and modern music, both Chinese and foreign, has been played on it, and the sound is melodious and beautiful." You can buy a small souvenir replica of it for a mere $10,000.

There's another notice that strikes more of a chill in respect of this important tomb excavation. It explains the "immolated remains" of concubines and attendants found in 21 plain wooden coffins around the duke's sarcophagus. "Skeletons found in the coffins are those of young females, the oldest being about 25 and the youngest 13. Obviously they were immolated for the master of the tomb. This is an indictment against the feudal exploiting class for their cruel oppression of the laboring people."

Yangtze River Run

The ticket office for the Yangtze River ferries lies on the Hankou waterfront down an alleyway opposite the main terminals under a sign which says "Tic et Office." It may well say "Ti t Off" by now. Anyway, there's a small booking hall in there from which an attendant will take you to an English-speaking reservations counter for foreigners. There you can book a ferry berth west to Chongqing or east to Nanjing or Shanghai.

I would recommend you go second-class two-a-cabin, because the third and fourth class berths are not only packed with people but dozens more crowd aboard at each stop along the river and bed down along the decks and corridors until there's hardly room to move. Because of the vessel's constant hot water supply, the passengers all wash their clothes the moment they step aboard and the decks become festooned with flapping shirts, dresses, underwear and long johns. But it's a restful run, with an occasional stop to pick up cargo and passengers along the way, and, now and then, a passing moth-winged sailing junk thrown in for excitement.

NANJING

Nanjing (Nanking), the old Southern Capital of the dynastic age, now the capital of Jiangsu province, is typical of the Yangtze River cities – well ahead of most of the rest of China in the move to develop out of the stagnation of the Cultural Revolution and regain some of their old sophistication. It has a long and significant history, dating back to 473 BC in the time of the Warring States, and in the ensuing dynastic reigns it was the capital of the Song rule, temporary capital of the early Ming dynasty and a city always regarded as an alternative to Beijing as a seat of power.

In 1842, British troops and gunboats laid siege to Nanjing in the first Opium War, forcing the Qing dynasty to sign the historic Treaty of Nanking which opened up the five Treaty Ports to free trade. In the Taiping Rebellion the city was again besieged, conquered and established as the rebel headquarters. In 1911 it became the republican capital for a brief period and was where Sun Yatsen was declared president of the provisional government. In 1937 it was the headquarters of Chiang Kaishek's government until the Japanese advance drove it up the Yangtze to Wuhan and then to Chongqing. In April 1949, Mao Zedong's communist forces poured across the Yangtze and raised the red flag over its rooftops.

OPPOSITE Two view s of Yangtze riverfront in Wuhan – morning on the Wuchang promenade TOP and evening ferry disgorges rush hour commuters BELOW.

The city is now a leading center of culture and higher education, and a power-house for joint-venture business projects in Jiangsu. It is, in fact, a business city, but its strategic position on the Yangtze River ferry route and its cultural attractions make it well worth a stopover.

Access

You can fly directly to Nanjing from Bei-jing, Guangzhou, Chengdu, Chongqing, Lanzhou, Shanghai, Wuhan and Xi'an. It's also a major port of call on the river route west from Chongqing and east from Shanghai. Your ferry announces its arrival by playing Strauss waltzes, French can-can and German polkas on its PA system.

Coming from Wuhan, this is the place to disembark for the trains on the Shan-ghai-Beijing-Xi'an route to Wuxi and Su-zhou. The city also has a direct bus service to Hangzhou, which otherwise can be reached only by train from Shanghai.

Hotels

The **Nanjing Hotel** at 259 Zhongshan Beilu reflects the rising standard and cost of tourist-class accommodation in Nan-jing – but is well worth the cost if you're only staying long enough to book the river ferry or train. The magnificent 37-story **Jinling Hotel,** with its revolving res-taurant on the 36th floor, reflects the city's modern-day preoccupation – business – and charges business rates too. Luckily, there are three other guesthouses in the budget range, the **Sheungmenlou**, **Sheng-li** and the **Dingshan**.

Restaurants

All the hotels have good dining rooms and restaurants, and there are three other popular eating houses that I can recom-mend – the **Sichuan Restaurant** at 171 Taiping Lu, the **Luliuju Vegetarian Res-taurant** just up the road, and, for Nanjing

duck, try the **Jiangsu Restaurant** at 26 Jiankang Lu.

But no visit to Nanjing is complete without a good blow-out in the pride of the Jinling Hotel, its **Plum Garden Restaurant,** where the food is wonderful, the decor so sophisticated that you'd swear you were in a high-class restaurant in Hong Kong, and the waitresses wear exotic traditional cheong-sams with the skirts split up to the thighs – and not only chat with you but help you with the menu too. And the food isn't really that expensive, either.

Sightseeing

Much of Nanjing's most interesting street life and shopping are found in the Jinling Hotel area and at the intersection of **Zhongshan** and **Hanzhong Roads.** There's another big traffic circle to the north at Zhongshan and Beijing Lu which has an adjacent small park where, each afternoon, the old comrades bring their caged birds to show them off, and, each Sunday, students flock for English-

ABOVE Majestic approach to Sun Yatsen Memorial, the key revolutionary landmark in Nanjing.

language conversation practice. They call it **English Corner.** The city's biggest antique and arts and crafts stores can be found opposite the Jinling and east on **Beijing Lu,** heading toward the southern entrance to **Xuanwu Lake Park**.

This park offers an interesting stroll in well landscaped surroundings, and a chance to watch the Chinese at play, but otherwise is really nothing to write home about. The city also makes a great fuss about its **Linggu (Soul Valley) Park,** about three kilometers (two miles) further west, the home of the **Sun Yatsen Memorial, Tomb of (Ming) Emperor Hongwu, Plum Blossom Hill** and the **Linggu Temple and Pagoda**. Quite frankly, I wouldn't go out of my way to spend time there either: I found the Plum Blossom Garden strewn with rubbish, the Ming Tomb simply another crumbling and quite depressing blockhouse, and the Linggu Pagoda dates all the way back to the 1930s.

The two most interesting cultural attractions in Nanjing are the **Zheng He Memorial Hall** and park and the **Qixia Monastery**, 20 km (12 miles) east of the city, which includes a series of Buddhist grottoes. The Zheng He Memorial Hall commemorates the Ming dynasty eunuch admiral who led the seven great oceanic voyages to the African coast between 1405 and 1433, almost a century before Columbus discovered the New World. The hall and surrounding pavilions are packed with relics and exhibits of life in the Ming reign, graphs, maps and models depicting the Moslem seafarer's expeditions and the total 1,456 sailing junks that were under his command, and a brass bell that was cast to announce his safe return from the last of these "Silk Road of the Sea" odysseys.

The Qixia Monastery has more than 200 grottoes, or **Thousand Buddha Caves**, containing many carved images, but like most of the other historic attractions in and around Nanjing they're something of a disappointment – rendered with cement during a "renovation" carried out by monks in 1924. However, there's a stupa in front of them containing images and relics dating back to the Sui dynasty and decorated with carvings of the life of Buddha.

WUXI

On the eastward run down the Yangtze River, Wuxi is the first major city featuring the maritime clamor, color and excitement of the **Grand Canal.** It lies between Nanjing and Suzhou and can be approached two ways – directly from Nanjing by train, or by doubling back by rail from Suzhou for a quick day-trip. While the city is now a key silk producing center and industrial hub, and a very busy canal port, it has very little of historical importance and one day's sightseeing is really enough.

Other than the Grand Canal, its main attraction is **Lake Taihu,** which in the summer is a-flutter with picturesque square-sailed fishing junks and offers recreational cruises and "convalescent" tours and is being developed as a big tourist resort. But the area around the lake bears all the scars of redevelopment, and I would recommend waiting a couple of years for them to heal before considering it a place to settle into for a few days. At the moment, the city and the lake can be appreciated quite adequately on a day excursion, taking a taxi out to the lake.

Hotels

Of the three main hotels in the city itself, the **Wuxi Hotel** has been renovated to suit the tourist trade, the **Liangxi Hotel** downgraded to provide budget accommodation, and the brand new 342-room **Wuxi Grand**, a Sino-Japanese joint venture, has come in with business rates in the $60 to $150 a night range.

The main tourist hotels are out around the lake, headed by the **Taihu (Lakeside) Guesthouse** with a recently completed new wing, the nearby old East China Sanitorium, now the **Brocade Hotel,** and the **Hubin** and **Shuixiu (Clear Water) Hotels**, around the lake to the east.

Sightseeing

Wuxi has a CITS office at the southern end of the north-south Zhongshan Lu which was recently voted the top branch in the nation, and which I found to be very efficient and accommodating. It also has an aggressive policy aimed at putting Wuxi up on the tourist map, and grand plans for Lake Taihu, most of which translate into high-priced resort attractions.

However, at the moment they will get you on to a tour of a silk farm and factory and a lake tour and banquet aboard their remarkable "Dragon Boat" – a cruising restaurant with a huge dragon's head at its prow. Tour boats also ply the city's teeming waterways, the Grand Canal which flows north-south through the western precincts, and the Liangxi River and Gengdu Canal which loop around the inner city area.

SUZHOU (SOOCHOW)

This city is the undisputed pearl of the Yangtze River and Grand Canal – vibrant, exciting, beautiful, historic and a place that once you settle into for a couple of days you don't really feel like leaving. Marco Polo was entranced by the city, and so too were many wealthy retired mandarins of the Ming and Qing dynasties who spent their last years there and are largely responsible for its greatest cultural drawcard – its famous villas and gardens.

Suzhou really rose to prominence when the southern stretches of the Grand Canal were completed in the Sui dynasty 1,300 years ago. The city became an important trading and shipping link in the water transport chain, particularly for its most valued produce, silk. With its network of canals and waterways feeding off and into the grand Canal, it was later hailed as the Venice of the East, a place of heaven on earth, the home of the most beautiful and accommodating women in

China, a place of pleasure and sophistication, an ideal place, in fact, to spend one's waning days in the idyllic, meditative pursuit of higher thoughts and base instincts.

Not that it didn't have its upheavals. In the 1880s most of the city was destroyed and 70 percent of its population killed – and its silk industry devastated just as Japan was emerging as the major challenger to Chinese silk – by horrific fighting in the Taiping Rebellion. But Suzhou somehow survived the carnage and has since weathered the Japanese military occupation, the civil war, the 1949 revolution and the excesses of the Cultural Revolution, not to mention its latter-day industrialization, to maintain much of its old-world refinement and charm.

Access

Suzhou has no airport, but lies on the Nanjing-Shanghai express rail route. It also has Grand Canal ferry services to and from Wuxi and Hangzhou.

Transport

There's really no other way to enjoy Suzhou than by bicycle, and there are plenty of rental shops in and around the main hotels, the **Suzhou** and **Nanlin.** There are taxis available from both hotels for errand runs to the railway station, and you can also hire pedal-rickshaws for an average ¥6 to most parts of the city.

Hotels

The **Suzhou** and **Nanlin Hotels** are both "garden" establishments located on either side of a canal that runs along Shiquan Jie, and both have comfortable and reasonably priced double rooms, depending on whether you choose the new or old wings. The Suzhou is also connected to the rather noisy, more crowded **Guzou Hotel** which also charges similar rates but has a ground floor dining room which is all pink decor and cheap frills and where foreigners are stuck in a sideroom away from the locals

and overseas Chinese. There's also a cheaper hotel, the **Lexiang,** with dormitory accommodation in the central tourist district on the edge of the Guanqian Bazaar. A new hotel, the 386-room **Bamboo Grove**, operated by Hong Kong's Lee Gardens group, features very picturesque "village dwelling" rooms, a piano bar, disco, business center and health center – and charges for it.

Sightseeing

To go sightseeing in Suzhou you simply rent a bicycle, buy an English-language

Three views of Wuxi – duck farm OPPOSITE, fishing junk TOP and traditional arrangement of pool and ornamental bridge BOTTOM on Lake Tai.

tourist map and cruise gently along the city's spiderwork of canals, through streets lined with beautiful old low-roofed whitewashed housing, under the high cooling dome of dappled foliage of the huge plane trees along each route, amidst great streams of bicycles and official jeeps and alongside the raucous bellow and blaring horns and loudspeakers of the cargo boats and long convoys of barges on the canals.

The people of Suzhou are particularly relaxed and quite genial, especially the canal folk, and the first stop on any tour should be one of the bridges that cross the city's **Outer Moat** where you can stand for hours watching the concrete-hulled boats and barges cruise through hordes of sampans and moored craft. The **Renmin Bridge** to the south is a good spot, and there are other bridges, Wannian, Wumen, Hongqi and Guangji on the city's west side that offer interesting vantage points.

The main tourist hub is the **Guanqian Bazaar** area on Guanqian Jie, running east off the main north-south thoroughfare Renmin Lu. Part of the district has been closed off to traffic and turned into a pedestrian mall, and it's surrounded by arts and crafts and antique stores, bookshops, cinemas, the Suzhou Story Telling House, Kaiming theater, confectionery stores and a series of old, popular and incredibly crowded restaurants headed by the 200-year-old Songhelou.

The **Suzhou Antique Store,** on Renmin Lu just up from the Lexiang Hotel and close to the new Friendship Store, is one of the best in all of China – crammed with ceramics, porcelain, scrolls, paintings, jewelry and other artwork. Whether this is significant or not, it has one floor of particularly refined porcelains and other art that's not for sale – it hasn't been given the government's wax seal of approval for export.

On the northern side of Guanqian Lu you'll find the **Daoist Xuanmiao (Temple of Mystery),** a big wooden barn of a place with a main hall, **Sanqing,** supported by 60 pillars and a sweeping double roof with "winged" eaves. The temple was founded in the Jin dynasty, around 275, but the main hall was built in 1181 after the original structure burned

down. What makes the temple more than just another temple is the bazaar that spreads through its courtyards and grounds – so much buying and selling going on that the "religious" section, the altars and images, are roped off to prevent them being overrun by base commerce.

North of Guanqian along Renmin Lu, you can't help but notice the city's second most famous religious institution, **North Temple (Bei Si)** with its soaring, beautifully decorated nine-story pagoda. It's Suzhou's oldest Buddhist temple, built 1,700 years ago, and the 72 m (236 ft) high brick and wood pagoda was one of the first erected south of the Yangtze River. Close by is another particularly well preserved temple, the **Avalokitesvara Hall**, built in the Ming reign, and to the southeast of the city center, just south of a small canal that runs alongside Ganjiang Lu, you'll find the elegant **Twin Pagodas,** erected in the time of the Southern Song.

For a fascinating study of Suzhou's silk industry, CITS arrange visits to silk farms and spinning mills, while the **Suzhou Museum,** set in the former mansion of Prince Zhongwang, a leader of the violent and ill-fated Taiping Rebellion, has some very good exhibitions of sample silks, brocades and *kesi,* a combination silk and gold thread, of the Song, Ming and Qing ages. The raising of silkworms is one of the most remarkable processes known to man – a batch of 700,000 silkworms weighs only half a kilo at birth, and no less than five tons when they are fattened up on mulberry leaves and ready to spin their cocoons.

The Suzhou Gardens

These landscaped works of art, designed for harmony, meditation and tranquillity in the golden years of retired court officials, merchants and property owners, are the pride and joy of Suzhou. Many of them were built in the Ming reign, and at one stage there were about a hundred of them scattered all over the city. Now there are only six, and thankfully they have been

Two views of Suzhou, "garden city" of the Grand Canal – canal-side homes OPPOSITE and softly rounded bridges BELOW add ancient charm to the spiderwork of waterways.

preserved for posterity. The one that's considered to be the most splendid is **Zhuozheng (Humble Administrator's) Garden**, to the north of the city adjacent to the Suzhou Museum. The name itself has an interesting history to it: the garden was built by a Ming dynasty official who fell from imperial grace and was bundled off to Suzhou as a punishment. Among its most beautiful aspects are an ancient tea-house, a large ornamental pool with a bridge that becomes crowded with visitors photographing each other, and beyond it **Mandarin Duck Hall,** a lovely pavilion that was once a small theater and has latticed windows with blue-glazed glass overlooking a smaller pond.

The most fascinating garden is **Wangshi (Garden of the Master of the Nets),** which lies to the west of the Suzhou Hotel off Shiquan Jie. It is a very small place, less than half a hectare, but somehow its gardens, rocks, halls, pavilions and ponds have been artfully arranged to give the illusion of far greater space.

Of the other gardens, perhaps the **Xiyuan (West Garden)** is the most interesting because it combines landscaping with temple architecture and Buddhist artwork. Lying to the northwest of the city beyond the Guangji Bridge, it includes the **Jiezhuanglu Temple,** originally called Guiyuan and built around 1271 in the Yuan dynasty. In the Ming reign it became the residence of a high court official named Xu Shitai and was given its present name. In 1860 it was destroyed in the Taiping Rebellion, but was restored in the latter years of the Qing dynasty.

The temple has several well preserved halls, including the **Hall of Celestial Kings, Main Shrine Hall, Avalokitesvara Hall** and the **Hall of the Arhats,** containing a striking display of 500 gilded clay statues of these immortals, along with several Buddha images and a statue of a guardian deity whose face is friendly on one side and severe on the other.

HANGZHOU

Like Suzhou, Hangzhou rose to prominence and flourished as a trading center, key food supplier and a hub of the rich silk industry of the Yangtze city region when the Grand Canal was built in the Sui reign.

The canal began at Hangzhou, eventually to link this southern city with Beijing, and this imperial bonding was not by trade and commerce alone. The Song dynasty, pushed southward by the "barbarian" Liao and Jin dynasty challenges from beyond the Great Wall, settled and established its capital in Hangzhou, and it was here that the most renowned age of refinement in China was born. It lasted until the Mongol armies of Kublai Khan marched south to put Hangzhou to the sword and destroy it in the campaign to bring the whole of the country under their heel.

The industrious Ming emperors restored the city, and in the Manchu Qing reign it became a popular imperial summer retreat rivaling that of Shenyang in the northeast. Then the Taiping rebels marched in and destroyed most of the city again in 1880, and much of its historic and cultural architecture and character went with it. But somehow it remains today one of the most renowned and beloved cities of China, famous for its balmy climate, its teas and silks, regarded as a place of romance and a mecca for honeymooning couples, still paid homage to in an old

saying that has been applied to it, and its Yangtze sister Suzhou, for many centuries: "Above there is heaven, below there is Suzhou and Hangzhou."

Today, as in the past, Hangzhou is famous for its nearby recreational resort, **West Lake,** formed in the eighth century when an emperor ordered the dredging and diking of a lagoon off the Qiantang River and landscaped and decorated with palaces, halls, temples, pavilions and gardens during the later dynastic reigns. It is now packed each summer with Chinese tour groups from Shanghai and the Yangtze cities and thousands of foreign visitors. Among its most distinguished contemporary visitors was Richard Nixon in 1972. His sudden move to end years of Sino-American hostility was considered so momentous that the new airport 24 km (15 miles) from Hangzhou was built especially for his historic touch-down in Air Force One.

Access

There are five flights a week to Hangzhou from Hong Kong, and regular serices with Beijing, Guangzhou, Guilin and Shanghai. You can also get there by bus from Shanghai and Nanjing. By train, you travel from Shanghai, and that means that if you approach eastward down the Yangtze River cities you've got to go to Shanghai first.

Hotels

Two new hotels, the **Shangri-la Hangzhou** and **The Dragon**, have claimed the top of the accommodation range in Hangzhou, with prices to match. Otherwise, the **Overseas Chinese Hotel** has opened up to "round-eyes" to help fill the budget gap, offering doubles and dormitory accommodation. The **Hangzhou Hotel,** comfortable, well-equipped with all the amenities

ABOVE Bamboo and delicate latticework in Suzhou's Garden of the Master of the Nets recall idyllic beauty of its renowned villas and gardens. OPPOSITE Elegant Song dynasty Twin Pagodas rise to city's southeast.

junks and sampans were specially designed over many centuries to withstand the force of it and ride it out.

For the rest of the West Lake, you can walk around it and above it, paddle a boat on it, sit and contemplate it, visit its islands, bridges, dikes, pavilions and the mansions that formed part of the Summer Palace in Qing dynasty times, but otherwise it is best summed up in the words of an American expatriate teacher who visited it from the Tongjie University in Shanghai. "It's not the lake itself," he said, "but what's around it."

SHANGHAI

Shanghai is a booming, teeming time-warp, a step back into a strange evocative combination of Manhattan, the Hong Kong waterfront and the Liverpool docks, all in the 1930s. It is a city where the art deco neons that glow at night along the antique skyline have probably been there since the last Japanese Zero buzzed over the city more than 40 years ago.

It's where the British and their European rivals, the French, Germans and Italians, and the Americans, gained not

Hangzhou Hotel lies in idyllic setting on bank of West Lake. City's most historically renowned products, silk ABOVE, is still a key export.

so much a toehold as a colonial throat-hold, backed up by military force, on the Chinese economy and society – turning a small insignificant fishing town on the Huangpu River close to the Yangtze's wide estuary, into one of the richest, most frenetic, most desperate, most exciting, free-wheeling and most wicked cities on earth.

In its heyday as the Treaty Port and International Settlement of China, it had a foreign population three times bigger than the expatriate business community of 20,000 in Hong Kong today. Huge trading and financial houses built out of the nefarious "foreign mud" of opium rose up on The Bund, over the wharves, smoke-stacks and derricks of the Huangpu waterfront alongside branches of some of the most respected, distinguished, and just as sharp, financial institutions of the West. Based on cotton textiles, an immense low-paid Chinese manufacturing workforce and its position as a natural Yangtze River conduit of trade goods from the interior of China, Shanghai reveled in its wealth, flamboyant materialism, snobbery, vice and a kind of swaggering modernity compared with the rest of the country while an epic power struggle took place around it between the nationalists, communists and the Japanese.

In the late 1930s, when the Japanese blitzkrieged their way down into the south of China, the entire Shanghai dream collapsed into a nightmare of military repression, starvation and atrocity that cannot be imagined unless one was there at the time, imprisoned, or takes the time today to read accounts like J. G. Ballard's disturbing *Empire of the Sun,* brilliantly portrayed in the 1987 movie by Steven Spielberg. When it was all over – World War II, the Japanese master-plan, the struggle for supremacy between Mao Zedong and Chiang Kaishek – it was as though only a city as wicked as Shanghai could have been punished with such suffering.

And it is perhaps because of that legacy of suffering that one of the most crucial power-struggles of the revolutionary years was played out chiefly in Shanghai – the city was the hot-bed of radical socialism, the power base of the Gang of Four, the place where the barricades of the People's Commune went up in the violent and ill-fated campaign to head off the "rightist tendencies" in Chinese society who wanted to nudge the nation on to the capitalist path.

Today, Shanghai has little to show for its past notoriety except its early Manhattan-style skyline along The Bund, its neon signs, and a faint echo, or a feeling, here and there of what it might have been like in the pre-war boom. But it is still an industrial and manufacturing giant, a huge, teeming metropolis with a wider municipal population of 11 million people, a city with more stores, more consumer goods, more private businesses and a far more fashionable character than any other in China. And, for the foreign visitor, it is the perfect place to start, or finish, the grand China tour.

Hotels

With the new 40-story Shanghai Hilton International open, along with the Nikko Longbai, the Hua Ting Sheraton, the five-star Portman opening up in the huge new Shanghai Centre - and some 60 other top-class hotels on the drawing boards - it's obvious that any review of accommodation in Shanghai is going to outdate itself very fast. The best that can be done is to point out that room rates are as much a nightmare in Shanghai as they are in Beijing, though one sign of things to come is a 30 percent rate reduction by the Hua Ting Sheraton because of the intense competition. In the business/tourist class you can choose from the following places:

Hilton International
Peace Hotel
Shanghai Mansions
Jinjiang Hotel

Park Hotel
Jing'an Guesthouse
Shanghai Hotel
Hua Ting Sheraton
Nikko Longbai
Portman Shanghai

For budget rates, you can try your luck at the following:
Seagull (Seaman's Club)
Pujiang Hotel
Shenjiang Hotel
Dahua Guesthouse
Hengshan Guesthouse

bus or coastal liner out of Shanghai, and help anyone find a hotel room or dormitory bed at a rate that suits them.

Restaurants

All the major hotels in Shanghai have good dining rooms, along with coffee shops that serve real coffee (an indescribable luxury when you've been riding the rails around China for nine and a half weeks). The **Peace Hotel** used to offer a good solid meal at a reasonable price and in that haunting Art Deco atmosphere of neon and velvet curtains, but

If it all looks a little depressing, there's one thing that Shanghai has got that Beijing definitely hasn't – and that's a good, helpful, reasonably efficient and sympathetic CITS branch. You'll find it in the ground floor lobby of the now-renovated and Hong Kong-managed Peace Hotel, with English-speaking staff who will handle all transport bookings by air, rail,

ABOVE Two views of Shanghai – bustling Nanjing Road OPPOSITE, the city's main shopping street, and Waibaidu Bridge with the old Manhattan-style Shanghai Mansions Hotel.

since its remodelling this one vivid aspect of Shanghai's physical and culinary time-capsule has changed and gone distinctly upmarket.

For a really special treat, go to where I ate the next night – the **Gong De Ling (Forest of Good Merits) Restaurant**, which is a Buddhist vegetarian restaurant just around the corner from the Park Hotel, is packed to the rafters any evening after 6 pm, closes at 7 pm sharp, and serves wonderful mock meat dishes in which beancurd, mushrooms and other vegetables are prepared to the texture and taste of chicken, duck, pork, crabmeat and other meat dishes. There's a similar vegetarian place serving similar imitation dishes at the **Longhua Temple and Pagoda** on the southwest side of the city but it's open only for lunch, or rather brunch, and, would you believe it? It closes at 11:30 am.

There are many other restaurants in Shanghai, most of which are listed on the back of the English-language *Shanghai Tourist Map,* along with the sort of cuisine they serve. One thing to look for if you're visiting the city between October and December is the Shanghai specialty, hairy crab, a small freshwater delicacy that packs the city's eating houses the moment it appears.

Sightseeing

With very little notable history beyond its Treaty Port days, Shanghai doesn't have much in the way of cultural attractions, but it is still a wonderful city to be in and to stroll around. It's the time-warp that makes it interesting – the feeling that this is probably the last place in the world where you can actually get an impression of what a Victorian port looked like in the days of maritime power, what parts of Chicago may have looked like when Al Capone and his mobsters ruled supreme, what a Chinese city looked like in the days when Guomingdang generals and Shanghai textile magnates packed and fled in the path of the Japanese war machine.

There are those who have a fetish about identifying every aspect of the **Shanghai International Settlement,** where the famous hotels, nightclubs, brothels, restaurants and great homes were. Most of it is a waste of time. It isn't there any more. And the Shanghai of today has 11 million walking, living, breathing realities that are far more relevant and interesting than all the ghosts of its past.

Every day, they crowd along **The Bund** and into the tiny **Huangpu Park,** overshadowed by the immense bulk of the

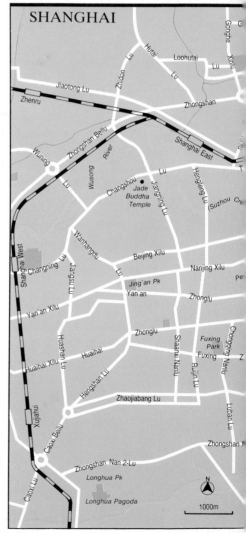

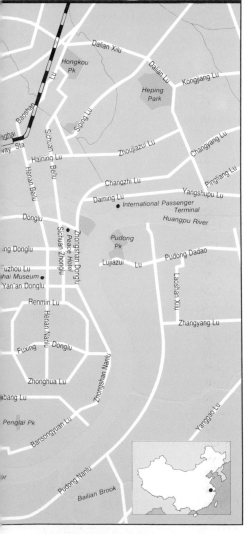

Shanghai Mansions Hotel, strolling, chatting, picnicking, taking pictures of each other amid gardens that were once forbidden to all "dogs and Chinese." Among them are English-language students who actually operate in teams along the waterfront, working on every foreigner who comes their way. They'll waylay you while you're watching Shanghai's past gliding down the Huangpu – beautiful full-sailed junks tacking under the towering hulls of the modern container freighters.

They pack the sidewalks down the long east-west shopping thoroughfare, Nanjing Road, where you can find the **Shanghai No. 1 Department Store,** dozens of small boutique-style silk shops, bookstores, arts and crafts centers and, just before the Shanghai Exhibition Center, another of the finest antique stores that I found anywhere in China, the **Friendship Store Antique and Curio Branch.** Along Nanjing Road you'll also find the **Shanghai Acrobatic Ground,** an auditorium where on certain days you can go in and watch the rehearsals. CITS will book tickets for the shows themselves.

South of this area, in what was once the Frenchtown of the treaty port days, the **Site of the First National Congress of the Communist Party of China** commemorates the city's role in the revolutionary ground swell during the chaotic republican years. Shanghai was where the communist party was founded in July 1921. To the south of the commemorative hall, you'll find more of the former residences of **Sun Yatsen** and **Zhou Enlai,** and, on Fenyang Lu, a mansion housing the **Arts and Crafts Research Institute** and another where the **Conservatory of Music** is based.

On the religious side, Shanghai offers the **Jade Buddha Temple,** in the city's northwestern Puto District, not very old –

ABOVE The cultural Shanghai – Buddha Temple TOP LEFT and Yuyuan (Mardarin) Garden RIGHT which features a pleasant tea-house and the Temple of the Town Gods.

it was originally founded in 1882 – but
featuring a good collection of gilded Buddha figures, scriptures and paintings representing the major dynasties going back
to the time of the Northern Wei. The **Longhua Temple and Pagoda,** on the city's
southern riverbank, goes back a little further, to 247 and has an arhats hall, bell and
drum towers and several other interesting
buildings – along with its vegetarian early
luncheon restaurant. For a garden that
ranks with anything in Suzhou, go along
to the **Yuyuan (Mandarin) Garden,**
south of the Shanghai Museum and The
Bund. It's another compact garden, covering only two hectares (5 acres) and was

built in the Ming reign. Its central feature
is its **Temple of the Town Gods,** which
failed to safeguard it when it was attacked
in the Opium War of 1842, virtually
destroyed by the French when it was
used as a command base for the Taiping
Rebellion, and then clobbered again by
the European forces in reprisal for the
Boxer Rebellion of 1900. It also has a very
pleasant tea-house, the **Wuxinting**.

Another attraction is a three and a half
hour, 60 km (37.2 mile) river boat cruise
on the Huangpu. You can get tickets for
this at CITS or at the ferry dock on The
Bund close to the Peace Hotel. If you want
an aerial view of the waterfront and the

194

busy **Suzhou Creek,** the best place is from the 18th floor of Shanghai Mansions, going up in a surprisingly new-fangled "speaking elevator" – a robot American female voice announcing "Fifth floor. Going up" to the amused grin of an attendant still employed to operate the thing.

If you're starting your China tour from Shanghai, it's the place to catch your breath, find your legs, test yourself for the challenges and surprises to come. If you're ending there, as I did, after many weeks of pilgrimage, you haul yourself wearily aboard the *MV Jinjiang* at the International Passenger Terminal near the Seagull Hotel, and you gaze across the waters to the old prehistoric skeletons of The Bund, and you have this sudden thought that is not relief and not regret, not love and not indifference – something that is, in a way, a little more bewildering than that. It suddenly occurs to you, with something of a shock, that you are leaving China, and that from this day forth you will be elsewhere, and wherever you are, whatever time it is, one billion people will be struggling to make something that's at least 4,500 years old continue to work.

ABOVE Ferry provides moment to catch up on news on Huangpu River cruise along the skyline of Shanghai's famous waterfront, The Bund.

Travelers' Tips

THE WAY TO CHINA

MAINSTREAM TOURS

For visitors who choose the mainstream or organized tour trail there's a wide variety of package tours and luxury expeditions offered by the leading tour operators and specialized "trailblazer" agencies of Britain, Europe, the United States and Australia. They'll put you on a train in London and deliver you to Beijing via the memorable Trans-Siberian Railway. They'll fly you directly from London, San Francisco, New York, Seattle, Vancouver, Paris, Frankfurt, Geneva or Sydney to Beijing, Shanghai or Guangzhou or to the main staging point for many China tours, Hong Kong. You can take an ocean cruise from Sydney Harbour and call in on Shanghai and Guangzhou, or you can arrive triumphantly in Kashi (Kashgar) or Lhasa aboard a luxury bus.

Organized group tours are obviously the expensive way to visit China, and an average comparison is an 18-day tour costing $4,500 against the $2,400 it cost me for nine and a half weeks. But they are also the most comfortable, convenient and predictable way to do it – you have the advantage of being able to roll along with your group knowing that you don't have to lift a finger on your own behalf except to eat, drink and buy souvenirs and gifts. Most of the big established operators provide escorts with a soound experience of China travel and Chinese culture, and they also take care of everything from visas to a very welcome short stopover in Hong Kong at the end of the trip. Their prices generally include international travel to and from China, all internal travel, full accommodation and meals, cultural excursions, Chinese interpreters and guides and airport taxes.

From the moment you enter China your arrangements are in the hands of the China International Travel Service (CITS), sometimes called *Luxingshe*, which decides how many visitors the international operators can bring in each year, where they can go, where they'll stay and how much they'll pay. CITS also serves as the ground handling agents for all tours in China, mustering the transport, accommodation, guides and interpreters that are needed.

The Conveyer Belt

For all the criticism that is often leveled at CITS, this is where it comes into its own. It was set up specifically to handle the big organized tours and to a great extent it reflects the prevailing government view that official tour groups, easily controlled, unlikely to poke their noses all over the place or try to mix too intimately with the ordinary Chinese – and obviously willing to pay more for comfort and convenience – are by far the most preferable way of admitting foreigners to China.

The trouble is, CITS is not the most efficient or up-to-date tourist organization in the world. It tends to regard tourists as so many bodies on a conveyer belt and so many wallets to lighten as they pass by. Its desk workers and guides are often poorly trained and its resources are also severely stretched, especially in the peak summer periods when it's not only struggling to keep the major tour groups moving smoothly but also to find accommodation in the major cities for hordes of individual travelers, backpackers and resident foreign students suddenly unleashed on their summer breaks.

Consequently, mistakes can be made with transport, accommodation and itineraries, with last-minute alterations. These sort of problems can be ironed out by the tour escorts, of course, but it must be understood beforehand that a group tour means being shepherded through China and being almost constantly on the move, being allowed only a limited amount of time at each cultural venue, being committed to a lot of Friendship Stores, antique stores, souvenir stalls and the harassment of souvenir hawkers at a lot of places that you visit, eating and relaxing as a group and having very little contact with Chinese beyond the guides, dining hall staffs, hotel employees and an occasional factory or commune public relations officer.

In short, a group tour has to be regarded as a relatively smooth sightseeing pilgrimage, aimed more at the physical than the social attractions of China.

THE TOUR OPERATORS

Britain and Europe

Voyages Jules Verne is probably Europe's biggest and most experienced China tour operator, with its own office in Beijing to help smooth out accommodation and itinerary problems, especially in the September-October period when it says China is "fiendishly booked out." The company offers a choice of 20 tours of China and beyond that also take in Tibet, North Korea, the Republic of Mongolia and the USSR and range from one week to 45 days.

It also conducts tours on the Trans-Siberian/China rail route, starting in London and terminating in Hong Kong, and adventure tours by rail and coach along the route of the Silk Road. Prices range from $892 to $5,925. For brochures and detailed information their London office is: **Travel Promotions Ltd,** 10 Glentworth Street, London NW1. ✆ (01) 486-8080. Telex 28441 VJV TP.

In London Voyages Jules Verne, Thomson Worldwide and P&O Air Holidays operate a kind of cooperative on the China tours, the others using the Voyage itineraries. Contact:

P&O, Canberra House, 47 Middlesex Street, London E1 7AL. ✆ (01) 247-1611. Telex 885551.

Thomson Worldwide, Greater London House, Hampstead Road, London NW1 7SD. ✆ (01) 388-7661. Telex 261123.

SCT China Travel, a member of the Premier Travel Group, is another well connected and experienced tour company operating from London with British Airways and Pakistan International Airways as the main carriers. They offer just about everything that the competitors have available, including a range of SCT Silkway tours from Hong Kong and an adventurous Karokoram (Friendship) Highway tour into western China following the route of the Silk Road.

Groups are flown from London to Rawalpindi and cross into China by coach to Urumqi with a tour of the Kungur Mountains and a camping stopover in a Mongolian yurt – the traditional nomadic animal-skin

tents – on the way. The cost: $3,412 for 18 days of what a spokesman assured me is suitable for middle-aged as well as younger travelers – "In fact one of our most enthusiastic customers is a 79-year-old retired British forester." Contact:

SCT China Travel, 10 Rose Crescent, Cambridge CB2 3LL. ✆ (0223) 311103. Telex 818822.

For other reputable operators offering mainstream package tours from London or elsewhere in England, you can take your pick of the following:

Thomas Cook Escorted Journeys, ✆ (01) 629-0999.

National Holidays Ltd, ✆ (01) 924-377122.

Hayes and Jarvis, ✆ (01) 235-9497.
Jetsave, ✆ (0342) 28511.

ABOVE Main pagoda and graceful tiled roofs of Qing dynasty imperial summer retreat in Chengdu.

Kuoni, ✆ (0306) 885044.

Premier Holidays, ✆ (0223) 311103.

SACU Tours (Society for Anglo-Chinese Understanding, ✆ (01) 482-4292.

Wings Faraway Holidays, ✆ (0992) 87211.

The United States

With its direct overland rail access to China and the long experience in China affairs of its major tour operators, London is obviously one of the most convenient starting points for many of the more adventurous tours. And for these reasons many of the British companies have operations in the United States. Voyages Jules Verne can be contacted at their main office:

Voyages Jules Verne, 41 East 42nd Street, New York, NY 10017. ✆ (800) 358-3330 (toll free) or ✆ (212) 953-7720.

P&O Air Holidays have a tie-in with one of America's leading China tour operators, Exprinter, address:

Exprinter, Suite 510, 500 Fifth Avenue, New York, NY 10110. ✆ (800) 221-1666 (toll free) or (212) 719-1200.

ATS Tour World on the West Coast is another leading China travel operator, and arranges itineraries on behalf of the giant **Bayliss International** chain of travel agencies. ATS can be reached at:

ATS Tour World, 1101 East Broadway, Glendale, CA 91205. ✆ (800) 223-9658.

Hong Kong

An alternative to taking a package tour right out of your own backyard is to fly to Hong Kong, enjoy a few days of shopping and sightseeing without tour pressure and then take advantage of China tours organized and operating from there. For the first leg of the trip there are many London ticket agencies offering cheap flights to and from Hong Kong, most of them in the $750 bracket, and airlines such as Korean Airlines, Northwest Orient and China Airlines (Taiwan) offer similar deals from San Francisco, Los Angeles and Seattle in the United States. More on these cheap ticket opportunities a little later in this section.

From Hong Kong, organized China tours ranging from a one-day hop over the border to 19-day grand tours are offered by CITS itself and other agencies. CITS has booking offices on both sides of the harbor at which tours can be arranged and visas obtained in as little as 24 hours:

China International Travel Service (Head Office), 78-83 Connaught Road Central, opposite the Outlying Districts Ferry Pier. ✆ 853 3888. Telex 85222 HCTSF HX.

CITS Branch Office, 1st Floor, Alpha House, 27 Nathan Road, Kowloon. ✆ 721-9826. Telex 40536 CTSKL HX.

Among the other agencies, Silkway Travel, representing SCT China Travel, offer a wide range of China tours and weekly tours into Tibet from May to October. Contact:

Silkway Travel, Silvercord Centre, Tower One, Canton Road, Kowloon. ✆ 724 3322. Telex 36662 SILK HX.

Trinity Express/China Tours, with branches at the Regal Meridian, Imperial and Harbour View Hotels, can take you in on trips lasting from one to 10 days. Their head office address is: **Trinity Express/China Tours,** Basement 1, shop 15, New World Centre, Tsimshatsui, opposite Sheraton Hotel. ✆ 368 3207.

There is also a local office of Voyages Jules Verne in Hong Kong, and can be found at:

Travel Promotions, 2nd Floor Arcade, Lee Gardens Hotel, Hysan Avenue, Causeway Bay, Hong Kong. ✆ 895 3181. Telex 63164.

The Beijing Connection

Information on CITS tours and other China travel matters can also be obtained closer to home by contacting an overseas office of the China National Tourist Office:

China National Tourist Office, 4 Glentworth Street, London NW1. ✆ (01) 935-9427; or in USA, Suite 465, Lincoln Building, 60 East 42nd Street, New York, NY 10165. ✆ (212) 867-0271.

Office du Tourisme de Chine, 7 Rue Sainte Anne, Paris. ✆ (01) 662-142.

China Tourist Office, Eschenheimer Anlage 28, D-6000 Frankfurt am Main-1. ✆ (0611) 555-292.

TAILOR-MADE TOURS

Aside from mainstream package tours, some of the major operators and CITS will tailor a visit to suit particular group or individual requirements. This, in effect, is a more comfortable and predictable form of individual, or lone, travel in which you can set your itinerary and decide what you want to see and do and leave it to CITS to make all the accommodation and travel bookings and other arrangements. They also provide interpreters and guides along the way. But there can be problems: the questions of traveling to someone else's timetable has already been mentioned; also there can be surprises and accommodation changes along the way. On top of that, there have been complaints that some of the CITS guides and escorts know very little about their own culture and history and in certain cases don't care for it very much anyway – particularly the religious aspect, which their Communist Party upbringing has taught them to dismiss as "peasant superstition."

However, these escorted individual and special interest tours, covering Buddhism and other faiths, archeology, medicine, zoology, natural science, agriculture, silk production, Chinese cooking, kung fu and what-have-you can be talked over with the China National Tourist Office nearest you, though from my own experience I would suggest the best route to go would be to contact:

SCT China Travel, 10 Rose Crescent, Cambridge CB2 3LL, England.

The Society for Anglo-Chinese Understanding, 152 Camden High Street, London NW1. ✆ (01) 482-4292.

China International Travel Service, 78-83 Connaught Road Central, Hong Kong. ✆ 853 3888. Telex 852222 HCTSF HX; or 6 East Chang'an Avenue, Beijing. ✆ 557-558. Telex 22350 CITSH CN.

PACKAGED TREKS

After the mainstream package tours and special interest visits come the organized backpack, trekking and overland bus expeditions that are a cheaper, more informal way of touring China. Again, there's a wide variety of operators and agencies offering these trips, and again, many of them operate from Britain. Most can be found in the travel sections of the Sunday newspapers, *The Observer* and *The Sunday Times,* and another good place to look is in the classified section of the satirical magazine, *Private Eye.* The tours either cover China specifically or, with a little sense of adventure, you can take the overland trips to Kathmandu and trek or bus into Tibet and China from there. Contacts:

Encounter Overland Ltd, 267 Old Brompton Road, London SW5 9JA. ✆ (01) 370-6845.

Hann Overland, 185 Streatham High Road, London SW16. ✆ (01) 769-6659.

Explore Worldwide, 7 High Street, Aldershot, Hants. ✆ (0252) 319488.

Trailfinders, 42-48 Earl's Court Road, London W8 6EJ. ✆ (01) 603-1515.

Rightaway Travel, 12 Hanover Street, London W1. ✆ (01) 408-1611.

Dragoman, Framlingham, Suffolk IP13 9A6. ✆ (0728) 724184.

Long Haul Expeditions, 56 Bohun Grove, East Barnet, Herts. ✆ (01) 440-1582.

ADVENTURE TOURS

Finally there are the real adventure trips on which you are advised beforehand that, while everything in the way of international travel, documentation and food are well taken care of, you'll need stamina and the ability and willingness to pitch in with everyone else to keep the show on the move. *Road Rider* magazine in the United States is beginning to organize motorcycle tours in southern China, for example, and has already run some between Guangzhou and Hainan Island. For more information you can write to: **Road Rider,** Box 678, South Laguna, CA 92677.

For information on other trekking, camping and biking tours of China operated from the United States, the following addresses can be tried:

China Passage, 302 Fifth Avenue, New York, NY 10001.

Wilderness Travel, 1760 Solano Avenue, Berkeley, CA 94707.

Ocean Voyages, 1709 Bridgeway, Sausalito, CA 94965.

In Australia there are several tour operators offering adventure tours to centers in China and Tibet and beyond, and one of the leading companies, Australian Himalayan Expeditions, goes further than that with a bicycling tour of the southern provinces. I met one of their riders in Guilin, a middle-aged professional man, who was on a tour of Guangdong and Jianxi provinces – a set itinerary with all hotel bookings taken care of, light-weight 10-speed bicycles and a Chinese backup crew comprising a guide/-interpreter, bus and repair truck following along behind. "This is about the mildest tour the company has organized," he commented ominously, resting over a cup of tea in Guilin's La La Cafe. Address: **Australian Himalayan Expeditions,** 159 Cathedral Street, Woolloomooloo, Sydney 2011. ✆ (02) 357-3555.

Since the opening of the Nepal-Tibet border for tourists, trekking from Kathmandu into Tibet has become one of the few adventure experiences left for travelers who have done just about everything. There are several operators in Kathmandu offering packages ranging in cost

from about \$280 to \$525, for both organized tours and individual travelers. In fact, even individual backpackers have had to buy into a tour to get a visa to cross into Tibet, and in some cases the package is entirely bogus and is simply aan "exit fee."

On the other hand, there are highly reputable and experienced "soft hard slog" operators who run legitimate tours both ways, and among the best of them is Mountain Travel Nepal, also known as Tiger Tops Mountain Travel, operated by two brothers from Britain, who run trekking tours into Tibet through the border at Changmu and by now may have opened up an entirely new crossing in far western Nepal, only 100 km (62 miles) from one of the region's most magnificent Himalayan eyries, Mount Kailas and Lake Manasarova. Many of their two-week tours begin and end in the luxurious Mandarin Hotel in Hong Kong and their guides are veteran British and American trekkers backed up by Nepalese Sherpas. The cost is relatively high: the company warns you can expect to be spending up to \$200 a day, but promises a lesson in self-discipline and self-sufficiency that'll tone up

the physical and the spiritual body. For details: **Mountain Travel Nepal**, PO. Box 170, Kathmandu, Nepal. Telex 216 TIGTOP NP.

Tiger Tops Mountain Travel International Ltd, 3rd floor, Tak Yan Commercial Building, 30-32 D'Aguilar Street, Hong Kong.

In London, Cathay Cycle Tours are running strenuous but wide-ranging and exciting 26-day bike tours in association with the National Sports Federation of China. The tours use the Rumanian carrier TAROM and stopover in Bucharest on the way to Beijing, then cover the Beijing, Xi'an, Luoyang and Yangtze/Shanghai regions by train, with radial bike tours, backed up by support vehicles, from each center. The cost: $2,638. The address: **Cathay Cycling Tours,** 2 Lancaster Avenue, West Norwood, London SE27 9DZ. © (01) 670-9897.

INDIVIDUAL TRAVEL

The latest Chinese guidebook to China, put out by the official publishing agency Xinhua, warns its readers that "usually you need an invitation (from government bodies, organizations, institutions or enterprises) to visit China."This is simply not true, and it tends to reflect the ambivalent attitude of the authorities toward individual visits and the continuing fear of foreigners fanning out on their own all over the country.

Despite what this otherwise quite helpful guidebook, *How to Tour China,* says, China has been allowing foreigners to come in and get around on their own wits and steam since about 1982. The government allows it, but obviously doesn't want it to get out of hand. It'll do nothing to hamper individual travel, but its governing tourist body, CITS, will do the least it possibly can to encourage it.

This ambivalence obviously cannot go on the way it is, and sooner or later the government is probably going to have to decide once and for all what to do about it – whether to give it the official seal of approval and order CITS to take it seriously, or stop it altogether and confine all foreign travel in China to group tours.

In the meantime, while it's getting a wink and a nod, it is certainly the only really satisfying way of experiencing China as a whole – its cultural attractions and the grassroots of its society. In many respects the individual traveler is a temporary resident of China, involved directly with the ordinary Chinese people, traveling with them, competing with them in the booking offices and market-place. Traveling on your own means being simply one in a billion.

Visas

You can get a tourist visa for anything from one week to one year at any Chinese embassy or consulate, or you can fly first to Hong Kong and obtain it very quickly at CITS, or you can simply arrive and get a visa on the spot at any one of nine ports cleared since 1985 to grant them: Beijing,

Towers and apartments of the astonishing Potala Palace are reflected in waters of Cultural Park in Lhasa.

Tianjin, Shanghai, Hangzhou, Fuzhou, Xiamen (Amoy), Guilin, Kunming or Xi'an. It is of course precautionary to obtain a visa before you leave and you may prefer to go to an embassy or consulate of the People's Republic of China. Here is a selection of addresses:

England: 31 Portland Place, London W1N 3AG. ✆ (01) 636-5637.

USA: 2300 Connecticut Avenue NW, Washington DC 20008. ✆ (202) 328-2515.

520 12th Avenue, New York, NY 10036. ✆ (212) 279-1127.

1450 Laguna Street, San Francisco, CA 94115. ✆ (415) 563-4857.

Canada: 415 St Andrew Street, Ottawa, Ontario, KIN 5H3. ✆ (613) 234-2706.

Australia: 14 Federal Highway, Watson, Canberra, ACT 2602. ✆ (62) 412-448.

France: 11 Avenue George V, Paris 8 me. ✆ 270-114.

West Germany: Kurfuerstenallee 12, 5300 Bonn-BAD Godesberg. ✆ 885655.

ABOVE Winter ice glistens on Kunming Lake, the landscaped centerpiece of the Summer Palace in Beijing.

Again, from my own experience, I would recommend flying straight to Hong Kong, spending two or three days there to acclimatize, do some last-minute shopping and preparation, enjoy what has become an exciting fast-paced capitalist funland, and arrange your visa through CITS. It's a simple and efficient process – you go to the CITS head office on the Central waterfront (78-83 Connaught Road Central), fill out the application forms, leave two photos and your passport and 24 hours later you have a visa.

The people there are quite friendly and helpful – I asked for 10 weeks and was given nine and a half and told I could get an extension at any one of the Public Security Offices in China, and there's one in every city. My visa cost me HK$170 ($21) and the train trip to Guangzhou another HK$140 ($18). The only problem with this particular arrangement is that, if you want to reserve accommodation too, CITS will do their best to put you into one of the luxury tourist hotels in Guangzhou – White Swan, China Hotel or Dong Fang. But I feel that even this is a reasonable expense – it helps you ease comfortably into China and enjoy its most modern city in some style before starting out on the tougher sections of the trail. And there are cheaper hotels to be had in Guangzhou, as you'll find in the detailed guide to the city.

The Aerial Route

As for getting to Hong Kong and China, you can take your pick of a large variety of airlines flying to both destinations, and a selection of standard fares, special deals or cheap seats. Qantas and the national carrier, China National Airways (CNAC), run weekly direct flights to Beijing and Guangzhou from Sydney and Melbourne, and for the Hong Kong route Qantas and Cathay Pacific offer cheaper APEX fares from Sydney, Melbourne and Perth. There are also discount ticket agents in all three cities who can fix you up with an even better deal on the Southeast-Asian airlines.

From the United States, Pan Am, China Airways and Japan Airlines fly regular scheduled services from San Francisco to Beijing, Shanghai and Tokyo, and JAL can also deliver you via Tokyo to Guangzhou and Hangzhou. If you want to take a cheaper service via Hong Kong, Northwest Orient Airlines, United Airlines and Korean Air offer APEX and discount fares out of Seattle, and China Airlines (Taiwan) offer similar deals from Los Angeles via Taipei. Korean Air also has reduced fares from Vancouver, providing a cheaper alternative to the scheduled Vancouver-Hong Kong services of Cathay Pacific and CP Air.

But possibly the best deals of all are found in London, where discount ticket agents clustering around the Oxford Street area have for years been finding ways to offer cheaper fares than the major airlines on the Middle East-Far East routes.

At the top of the scheduled fare range, British Airways and CNAC offer an APEX return direct to Beijing (for $1,112) with 14 days advance booking required, and British Airways, British Caledonian and Cathay Pacific also have APEX deals to Hong Kong.

The East European airlines offer even cheaper deals, most flying directly to Beijing. In fact, North American travelers facing the higher fares to the Far East might well find it cheaper to hop over to London on Virgin, or Panam's special transatlantic deals and pick up a good discount fare from there. The main agents to shop around are as follows:

M&J Travel, 130 Regent Street, London W1. ✆ (01) 437-0168.

Clubair Travel, 7 Maddox Street, London W1. ✆ (01) 493-8777.

Golden Jet, 145 Oxford Street, London W1. ✆ (01) 439-0428.

Jupiter Travel, 91 Regent Street, London W1. ✆ (01) 734-1812.

Unijet, 91 Mortimer Street, London W1. ✆ (01) 637-8001.

Flightquest Travel, Radnor House, 93 Regent Street, London W1. ✆ (01) 439-6561.

STA Travel, 74 Old Brompton Road, London SW7; 117 Euston Road, London NW1. ✆ (01) 581-1022.

The Hong Kong Stopover

As for accommodation during the Hong Kong stopover, hotels there are not the cheapest in the world but there are some reasonably good deals available. Rates at the top class hotels like the Mandarin, Regent, Peninsula and Shangri-la commence at between US$150 and US$175 plus 10 percent service charge and 5 percent tax but there's a level of older, well-

run hotels that fits more suitably into the budget category. Examples:

Hong Kong Cathay, 17 Tung Lo Wan Road, Causeway Bay. ✆ 577 8221.

Harbour, 116-122 Gloucester Road. ✆ 574 8211.

New Harbour, 41-49 Hennessy Road. ✆ 861 1166.

Imperial 30-34 Nathan Road, Kowloon. ✆ 366 2201.

ABOVE A rock hangs precariously forming an arch in the Stone Forest, Shilin.

For rates below these there are several places to go, all of them in the guesthouse and hostel category. The most famous of them, **Chungking Mansions,** ✆368-7710, in Tsimshatsui, has been operating for as long as I've known Hong Kong (and that goes back as far as 1966), offering cheap rooms that are clean, air-conditioned and fairly comfortable and certainly acceptable for a few nights as long as you can cope with the building's claustrophobic, coffin-like lifts. You can find Chungking Mansions at the harbor end of Nathan Road between the Imperial and Holiday Inn Hotels.

For students, or those who can pass themselves off as one, the STB Hostel in Kowloon offers 84 beds in air-conditioned rooms with hot showers or a dormitory, a TV lounge and a "nice quiet and comfortable atmosphere" at rates that no-one should pass up. Address: **STB Hostel,** Great Eastern Mansion, 2nd floor, 255-261 Reclamation Street, Kowloon. ✆ 710 9199.

There are also YMCA guesthouses on both sides of the harbor. The **Hong Kong Student Travel Bureau** ✆ 730 3269, Room 1024, 10th floor, Star House in Tsimshatsui close to the Star Ferry, will help visitors find cheap accommodation and also arrange trips into China.

Hong Kong to China

The main route from Hong Kong to China is by rail from the **Kowloon-Canton Railway's** Hung Hom Terminus next to the Cross Harbor Tunnel's Kowloon exit.

CAAC (reservations office, ✆ 861 0288; ticketing, Swire House, Central, Hong Kong, ✆ 840 1199 and 4 Ashley Road, Kowloon ✆ 739 0022) fly directly to Guangzhou, Kunming, Beijing, Tianjin, Shanghai and Nanjing, and cover virtually the entire country from Guangzhou.

Cathay Pacific (main reservations office, ✆ 884 1488; ticketing, Swire House, ✆ 842-5348) run a twice weekly service to Beijing and four flights a week to Shanghai. The new Hong Kong airline, Dragonair, also has regular charter flights to Beijing and Shanghai, and to seven other major Chinese cities.

There are regular overnight ferries to Guangzhou operated by the Pearl River Shipping Company which can be booked through the two CITS offices or Trinity Express, ✆ 368 3207.

Daily hovercraft services also run up the Pearl River to Guangzhou from the Tai Kok Tsui Wharf along the western waterfront of Kowloon. Tickets can be purchased from CITS or from:

Hong Kong and Yaumati Ferry Company, Jordan Road Pier, Kowloon, ✆ 330-5257, or Central Harbour Service Pier, Hong Kong, ✆ 542 3428.

Daily hovercraft services also operate from Tai Kok Tsui to Shekou in the Shenzhen special economic zone, a joint China-Hong Kong manufacturing and trading enclave on the northwestern boundary of the New Territories. From Shenzhen you can hop the Kowloon-Guangzhou trains into China proper. Silkway Travel also operate air-conditioned bus excursions to Shenzhen.

Another interesting route to consider is going by hydrofoil to Macau, the Portuguese-administered enclave and gambling playground across the mouth of the Pearl River. Tickets cost $18 and can be booked through travel agents or at the Macau Ferry Terminal just west of the new Victoria Hotel on Connaught Road along the island harbor front. From Macau you can take a bus trip across the border to the Zhuhai special economic zone in Zhongshan county. From there, buses can be taken to Guangzhou or elsewhere in Guangdong province. There's also a direct jetfoil service from Hong Kong to Jiuzhou, the Zhuhai zone's port, and you can make bookings through CITS and the Hong Kong Hydrofoil Company, Ground Floor, Nathan Center, 580 Nathan Road, Mongkok, Kowloon, or the Tai Kok Tsui ferry pier, ✆ 395 4795.

Yet another hovercraft service from Hong Kong runs from the Tai Kok Tsui pier to Wuzhou in the Guangxi Zhuang Auto-

nomous Region, and from there you can go by public or air-conditioned "tour" bus to Yangshao, the main tourist venue on the beautiful Li River (see **Guilin and Yangshou,** page 67) or on to Guilin. Bookings can be made at CITS or Trinity Express.

Or you can take the relatively luxurious route by ship directly from Hong Kong to Shanghai. There are two companies running these 60-hour cruises from the Tai Kok Tsui wharf in Kowloon to the International Shipping Terminal alongside the Seagull Hotel right across from the northern end of The Bund in downtown Shanghai. The luxury liner *MV Jinjiang sails* every five days to and from Shanghai, and the Shanghai Haixing Shipping Company operates two other vessels, the *Haixing* and *Shanghai*.

Each vessel offers luxury staterooms and other cabins and berths ranging from first to third class and costing between $115 and $63, including meals. Amenities include a lounge and disco, bar, coffee shop, swimming pool, barber and beauty salon, video games room and a cinema that

Sampans and river barges pack around ocean liner on Shanghai's Huangpu River, China's busiest port.

screens fascinating Chinese movies, set in Shanghai, in which all the characters wear suits or trendy casual ensembles, are connected in some way with the arts, flash a lot of money around, live in sumptuously decorated modern homees and studio apartments, never spit and raise cigarettes to their lips every time the camera turns on them. Bookings for all three ships can be made at:

Shanghai Haixing Shipping Company, 152-155 Connaught Road Central, Hong Kong. © 544 0558.

Richown Shipping & Enterprises Ltd (agents for Shanghai Jinjiang Shipping Company), Shop 143, World-wide Plaza, 19 Des Vocux Road Central, Hong Kong. © 521 4106.

Lastly, there's another relatively cheap but grand route from the West to China – via the Trans-Siberian Railway. The full route is London – Berlin – Moscow – Ulan Bator (Mongolian People's Republic) – Beijing, and tickets cost around $450. You can book through Thomas Cook & Son or other major China tour operators in London and the USA listed on pages 199-202, or you can fly to Berlin or Moscow and take the train from there. You must have visas for the Soviet Union and Mongolia.

Getting Around China
Travel inside China is surprisingly easy and efficient, largely because of the extensive air and rail networks.

Domestic Airlines
While CNAC operates the international flights into the country, domestic services are divided among China Eastern Airways based in Shanghai, China Southwest Airways in Chengdu and China Southern Airways operating from Guangzhou.

Reservations in any city can be made through CITS or its domestic counterpart, China Travel Service (CTS), or directly at any airline booking office which, until the reorganization of the service is complete, will still be found under the old CAAC sign.

CNAC warn that tickets must be purchased by noon at the latest on the day before a flight, and a no-show for any domestic flight means absolutely no refund. I can also add that the airline system is under tremendous pressure at any time of the year, and outside the major cities you can find yourself waiting for perhaps several days to get a seat. The reservations desks also have a habit of holding blocks of seats for last-minute bookings by important party officials, cadres, military and other VIPs and are known to allow planes to take off three-

this is the direct route to the soul of China. This is where you meet the people, and people from all levels of society, in reasonably relaxed situations in which both of you can spend time with each other on a fairly equal level – you are not the foreign "millionaire" shuttling behind coach windows betweenn the hotels, Friendship Stores and temples, you are traveling with them and it's the one environment in which they can share something of their lives with you. I had some of my most touching, amusing and bizarre experiences aboard the trains. On a trip

quarters full, after telling everyone they're booked solid, rather than risk being on the receiving end of some stranded official's wrath.

Riding the Rails

To my mind, the only way to travel in China is by train, and having done it that way through 20 cities I can promise you that if you can cope with the struggle at most booking and railway departure halls

from Guilin to Kunming I came down with a bad dose of diarrhea and was cured with acupuncture by a Palestinian medical student from Shanghai. On the run from Kunming to Chongqing I gave an English-language conversation lesson to the wife of a military officer, and she gave me, the "teacher," an apple in return. I shared my berth between Xi'an and Xining with another genial military man who joined me in an impromptu show for a little boy with a panda glove puppet that I'd bought for one of my own sons – while he was proudly being described to me as "a high

ABOVE Early industrial beauty and power still in action on China's extensive rail network.

level military officer in China." On another trip from Datong to Beijing a group of young farm workers solved the language problem by giving me a lesson – inducing me to read out the names of all the Chinese provinces in Pinyin from my atlas, and to the entire carriage.

There are three classes of travel on the trains – soft-berth, or "soft-sleeper," hard-sleeper and hard-seat. Soft-sleeper is the top of the range, offering separate four-berth compartments, well serviced by the attendants, equipped with a table and lamp between the bunks, white nylon curtains and carpet slippers. It's the most comfortable form of travel but for that reason it's also reserved for officials, military personnel and VIPs who, in my experience, can prove to be very boring company on a long haul, some of them nervous or too politically cautious to mix too intimatelyy with foreigners.

Hard-seat is at the other extreme – open carriages packed with simple vinyl-covered wooden seating, crammed with peasants, soldiers and workers and their luggage, and anything from crated TV sets to factory spare parts; and while it is a lot of fun it is definitely to be avoided as much as possible on any long overnight runs. The people are the salt of the earth, but hard-seat is very hard.

I tried it on the Beijing Express out of Guangzhou at the start of my trip, riding 10 hours overnight to a junction called Hengyang, and my diary records the scenes of pain and misery that swam before my eyes just before dawn. It's as though a bomb has hit the compartment – bodies everywhere in all attitudes of agony. Just no way to sleep on these seats. People are groaning loudly as they writhe about.Some are on their hands and knees in the cigarette butts and seed-husks on the floor with their heads on the seats trying to catch a moment's rest.

Despite the discomfort and overcrowding hard-seat can be fun, so long as it's taken on short daytime trips. Food trolleys roll up and down the aisles at all times,

there's constant hot water for tea, and you get "in-flight" movies, some of them in English with Chinese sub-titles, on the TV monitors at each end of the carriages. All in all, it's a far more relaxed and convivial ride than soft-sleeper.

But considering that most inter-city journeys last between 10 and 36 hours, the most satisfying class of travel, by far, is the one in between – hard-sleeper. These are carriages lined with open three-tiered sets of bunks, rather like steerage class on a migrant steamer. But they are comfortable, nonetheless, and they combine the attractions of both soft-sleeper and hard-seat travel – you can socialize freely with the people around you but also retreat to your bunk, especially if you take my tip and always choose the middle one (the Chinese prefer the bottom cots) and doze or read in privacy.

Essentials

Whatever class of train travel you choose, you need to carry snack food with you, especially on the long hauls. The dining cars get terribly overcrowded and the food they offer is generally very basic and uninspiring. The standard of cleanliness and hygiene can be also be a rude shock. On most routes the trains stop long enough at main stations and junctions for you to stretch your legs on the platforms and buy hard-boiled eggs, buns, fruit and cigarettes.

There are two other essential items that you need to have with you – a face towel to wash with and an enameled and lidded metal mug, which, as I recall from my notes, performed a wide variety of important functions. One drinks gallons of tea from it, eats noodles from it, cleans one's teeth in it, washes from it, uses it as an ashtray – and you can even fit it over your mouth and scream into it when things get really rough!

Conditions on most trains are quite clean, and the constantly accumulating litter of seed-husks, fruit peels, cigarette butts and sweet wrappings is regularly swept right down the aisles and straight out on to the tracks. But don't expect clean personalized bed-linen. The sheets, blankets and eiderdowns on the bunks are changed about once a week, and the pillows are covered with hand towels to keep the cotton cases reasonably clean – and that means the towels themselves get pretty grubby.

The toilets, marked CESUO, at each end of the carriages are basic hole-in-the-floor conveniences over which you squat and hold tightly to a rail, especially in the vicinity of the main stations where the drivers tend to brake the trains so abruptly that they sometimes actually skid to a halt.

There is one infernal problem on all the trains that Westerners find quaint and interesting at first, and then increasingly aggravating – a constant blare of travel information, public announcements, Chinese pop music and Beijing or Cantonese opera from public address speakers installed up and down every carriage. The racket begins at 7 am and does not stop until 10 pm, and while you can switch the speakers off in the soft-sleeper compartments there's nothing you can do about them in hard-sleeper or hard-seat. Some have very flimsy wiring, if you care to inspect them closely, but otherwise you just have to accept that nothing moves in China without a lot of commotion and noise to help it along.

Reservations

To book seats and berths on the trains you can either go to the CITS office in each city or directly to the railway stations. CITS will often say they need a couple of days, or four days in Kunming, for example, to arrange the reservation, and they often insist they can only get you a soft-sleeper berth. You can either go along with this or go straight to the station booking halls and count on at least an hour or two of struggle with the crowds to get to the booking windows.

But it's not as arduous as it sounds. If you go first to your hotel reception desk and ask them to write in Chinese what class of travel you want, on what day and to where, and then show this around the booking hall, someone will point you into the right queue. If there are any serious language problems, you can count on arousing enough interest and excitement around you to attract a guardian angel – someone with enough English to help you get what you want.

As for the struggle to get to the trains, you'll find that at most of the major stations right down the east of China there are special segregated waiting rooms with soft chairs and sometimes even a coffee bar and souvenir counter for Chinese VIPs and foreign travelers (as long as you're not traveling hard-seat), and attendants who will escort you to the right train. At others you are pitched in with everyone else, and even with the station police and attendants controlling the crowds you can expect a rough free-for-all getting through the ticket barriers.

After being jostled, crushed and very nearly trampled at a couple of stations, notably Chongqing, I learned to avoid the mob by staying back behind it as we went through. This worked quite well until one instance at Beijing station where I followed calmly on the heels of about a thousand people heading for the overnight express to Datong. As the crowd surged and pushed before me toward the gates, an announcement blasted over the public address system. The mob immediately wheeled around – ordered to another waiting hall behind me – and, like a flash flood, engulfed me and virtually carried me all the way to the train.

The Buses

The same sort of free-for-all occurs on virtually all the public buses in all the towns and cities, and you would be well advised to stay right off them unless there's no

OPPOSITE Packed trolley buses and bicycles are the main form of peak hour transport on frigid Beijing morning.

alternative way of getting somewhere. There are some places where you have to ride them, usually to get to a cultural attraction just outside a city, and in those cases it is best to get them from the start of their route – you have a better chance of getting a seat, and the conductors will sometimes put you, the foreign guest, aboard firsst. If this happens, don't fight it: it is an honor. And besides, you'll need to conserve your strength for the struggle to get off.

Taxis

Major hotels in the big cities have taxi services, which I would recommend for the shorter, crucial hops, usually back and forth between the hotel and the railway station or CNAC. They're not expensive – and are usually booked at the hotel reception desk or a facility outside. They also operate from most of the railway stations, and at all times of the day or night, and even if they're not available you can always find a variety of other forms of transport including tiny pickups powered by motor-cycle engines, motor-cyclos, pedal-cyclos, pedal rickshaws and even bicycles with open goods trays on the back. I rode one of these with all my luggage into downtown Xi'an, in a driving snowstorm, and fouund myself alternating between laughter and the inevitable question that crops up in everyone's mind every now and again as they travel individually through China: "What am I doing here?"

Pedal Power

The most convenient and enjoyable form of transport in any city is the Chinese answer to the Western family car, the bicycle. And you can rent one at most hotels or at rental shops prominently advertised in English in the main streets. The bikes are the standard proletarian Chinese models, all of them based on the design of the old British workhorse, the Raleigh, and they come equipped with the two most vital accessories of bicycle travel in China, a security lock and a bell. They have no gears, but then they're not widely available in cities – Chongqing for instance – that are uncomfortably hilly.

You can rent a bicycle by the hour or full day, paying an average ¥1 an hour or ¥5 for eight hours, with orders to be back by nightfall. You pay in advance and firmly resist any attempt to hold your passport as security. You then wheel out into the streets and find that biking in China is initially like venturing in a rented car into the Los Angeles freeway system. It takes some nerve and eyes in the back of your head to learn to flow along smoothly in the creaking, jingling floods of chrome, steel and rubber. You need a good English-language street-map showing you how to get to the main tourist attractions, and you can find these at any Friendship desks in the hotels. You also need to check the bicycle over first for loose components or tire leaks and make sure that the saddle is at the right, comfortable height. From there, Chinese society is yours.

WHEN TO GO

The tourist season in China begins as early as March in Shanghai and the provinces to the south, and reaches its peak all over the country in the high summer and as late as September-October. For organized tour groups the peak season means simply a lot of other groups crowding along on the route, but for individual travelers it can

mean transport and accommodation problems so severe that you can find yourself virtually camping in hotel lobbies and corridors in the biggest cities waiting for a bed.

My advice to any individual traveler who wants to travel in reasonably relaxed style is to go in the off-season, from November to March, when you can be sure of a room and a berth on the train wherever you go. It means traveling in the north and northwest in the grip of winter, but it must also be remembered that at this time the southern provinces are still quite warm.

WHAT TO WEAR

In summer, the lightest clothing possible, obviously, and preferably drip-dry garments that can be rinsed through and dried overnight in the hotels, though most of them offer cheap same-day laundry services. In winter, long thermal underwear, thick socks, Chinese-style hat with ear-flaps and good gloves are a must if you're going north. In all seasons, dress for comfort rather than fashion – soft-soled walking shoes, jogging shoes or trekking boots rather than high-heels, for example. If you plan to tour Tibet in the summer, take warm clothing and a light-weight sleeping bag – there have been many instances of trekkers caught without adequate protection on mountains where the temperature plunges to freezing point at night.

WHAT TO TAKE

Individual travelers should travel as lightly as possible if they want to avoid their trip becoming an endurance test. One spacious but comfortable backpack, and preferably not the type with a large aluminum frame – they're too cumbersome in crowded situations and they get snagged in train and bus doorways. Maybe one other soft holdall and a camera case – but no more than that; you'd

be surprised how grueling it is just to negotiate the length of an average Chinese railway platform after a long journey, especially if you're loaded down with too much luggage. There are other basic necessities that should be taken along, and are as follows:

Chopsticks – It's safer in the long run to use your own in most restaurants outside the major hotels.

Chapsticks – In winter, particularly, the climate in the north and Tibet is harshly dry.

Toilet paper – Ransack every hotel bathroom along the way – there's none to be found elsewhere.

Coffee – Outside the main hotels and Friendship Stores there's none of that either.

Vitamin pills – Definitely of supplementary value in Tibet and in the northern provinces in winter.

Swiss Army knife – You won't need to prize many stones out of horse's hooves, but you'll need it to prize the lids off food cans.

Batteries – The Chinese ones are so weak that if you don't have your own you'll have to kick-start your Walkman.

Torch – Optional, but comes in handy in the dead of night on the way to toilets in Tibet.

CURRENCY

The standard Chinese currency is the renminbi (people's currency) or RMB, known officially as yuan but popularly called "gwai." The highest denomination is the 10-yuan note, or ¥10, which means you generally carry a hefty bankroll wherever you go, and it's no wonder the Chinese think you're a millionaire. Exchange rates for major currencies at the time of going to press are:

US$1.00 = ¥3.71
JP¥1,000 = ¥24.74
DM100 = ¥113.77
FFr100 = ¥56.67

shaw drivers if they can get away with it), but in most cases, particularly at the railway booking windows, it's advisable to offer RMB first and then be prepared to switch to FEC if you get back a blast of indignation. The following credit cards are acceptable – Visa, Master Charge, Federal Card, Million, JCB, American Express and Diners Club – but only in the major cities and a small handful of the budget-category hotels.

All currency exchange is handled by the Bank of China, with branches in all cities and major towns or at most large hotels. You are issued with a receipt for each currency transaction, and you must hold on to all receipts until you leave the country or face embarrassing questions as you go through the customs check.

The yuan is divided into 10 jiao, more popularly known as "maou," and there are 10 fen to the jiao. Fen come in two forms – aluminum coins or irritatingly tiny bank notes, and you'll find more notes in the countryside because the peasants are said to melt the coins down and sell the aluminum on the black market.

At first, the currency can be quite confusing, but it follows two simple, if illogical, rules: wherever renminbi is written, it's called yuan and jiao; when you're actually buying something with it, it's "gwai" and maou. As already mentioned, tourists are required to pay for most things in FEC (foreign exchange certificates), or "wu hai," which have the same official exchange rate as the Renminbi but are also of great value to those Chinese who can get their hands on them (they can use them to buy imported goods) and so they are worth a lot more on the black market. The black market can also be worth arrest, detention and a lot more trouble for foreigners caught dealing on it, and at least two years' jail for any Chinese who's nabbed.

I found that almost all hotels demand payment in FEC, and so do CNAC and some taxi companies (and even rick-

CUSTOMS

When you enter China you are required to fill out a form declaring how much money you're carrying and in which currency. When you leave you must declare what you have left and be prepared to show all Bank of China exchange receipts. You're also required to declare all jewelry, watches, cassette players, radios, cameras and lenses, typewriters and all other valuable personal items; and in case there is any temptation to sell any of these to the Chinese during your tour, you are asked to produce your copy of the declaration on the way out and all effects are checked against it.

You must also declare for inspection any gold and silver antiques bought on your tour, and produce a sales receipt which shows they have been cleared for export. Some other antiques may also be checked for a hard wax seal which shows they have been similarly cleared.

ABOVE stilted, ornately costumed dancers add color and excitement to massive Spring Festival parades throughout China.

HEALTH

You don't need to show a vaccination certificate on arrival in China unless you've traveled from or through an area where there's been a recent outbreak of smallpox, cholera or yellow fever. Inside China you'll probably come down with colds, chest and sinus congestion and a persistent cough if you stay any real length of time, largely from a combination of damp and industrial pollution in the bigger cities. You'll also suffer a bout or two of stomach trouble from the change of diet,

and so should take along a supply of Lomotil or any similar anti-diarrhea medicine. If you get caught without Western pills I can recommend a widely distributed Chinese medicine with the formidable name of SUXIAOSHANGFENG-JIAONANG which comes in coated pill form and does a good speedy job. Consider acupuncture only as a last resort.

Hepatitis is the main illness to worry about, because of the general lack of hygiene at eating houses, noodle and soup stalls and even some of the hotel kitchens. It's advisable to have a gamma-globulin shot before you go to China. Once there, always be careful where and what you eat on the streets, use your own chopsticks wherever you can, always drink only the boiled water supplied in the hotels and on the trains for tea, and if you're unlucky enough to come down with extreme lethar-

gy, nausea, fever, loss of appetite and a yellowing of the whites of the eyes, get right out of China, fast. Go to Hong Kong, and straight to hospital.

FOOD

The Chinese cuisine has developed over many centuries from two overriding pressures – pure survival and limited fuel for cooking. Consequently, it's fundamentally a famine cuisine in which a vast range of domesticated, wild and exotic animal and aquatic life and vegetation has been gathered to the kitchen table and then refined and developed into a culinary tour de force by aristocratic tastes and whims and the responding creativity of the greatest chefs of the various dynastic reigns. The Chinese have a wonderful saying that sums up their attitude to food: "If its back faces heaven, you can eat it." The scarcity of fuel for cooking has meant that much of it is quickly stir-fried in small bite-sized portions – hence the use of chopsticks.

China's climatic contrasts, sub-tropical south and temperate-frigid north, have varied the staple foods on which the cuisine subsists – rice and rice noodles, buns and meat – and prawn-stuffed *won tons* in the south, heavier wheat breads, flour noodles, buns, dumplings and meat-filled *jiaozi* in the north. Regional tastes and innovation, along with a kind of movable feast of contributions from the chefs of the imperial courts, have given Chinese cooking four fairly distinctive regional characters:

Beijing food is spiced, relies on bread and noodles for bulk and embraces two universally known dishes, Beijing duck and Mongolian hotpot. **Shanghainese** food is noted for its seafood and poultry dishes, and its seasonal hairy crab, and is not only spiced but is heavier and oilier

ABOVE Bank notes reflect image of new semicapitalist era in modern mural in bank in Guilin.

than Beijing fare. **Sichuan** food is the spiciest of all, specially developed to ward off the damp chills of this mountainous, often foggy western province, and it also includes a smoked duck which rivals Beijing duck for innovation and taste. **Cantonese** food, known everywhere the Cantonese have emigrated around the world, is lighter, more sophisticated and less oily than the other regional cuisines, shows great flair with sauces and condiments, is based on rice and seafood, pork, poultry, fish and vegetables and includes the renowned *dim sum* luncheon savories that pack out the restaurants at midday in Hong Kong.

To go any deeper into the details and philosophy of the cuisine would be purely academic at this stage because it no longer exists as such in China. Until the society's culinary skills and tastes are developed again, and new restaurants crop up, the food will remain as it has been since the revolution – nourishing but basic fare in most areas except Beijing, Shanghai, Guangzhou and sophisticated business-class hotels like the Jinling in Nanjing. The best of the existing eating places can be found in the guide section of this book, and for a deeper insight into the full splendor of the cuisine as it once was, and no doubt will aspire to again, I can recommend any books by the world's two most popular experts on Chinese food, Emily Hahn of the United States, and Britain's Kenneth Lo.

"TAXI CHINESE"

Mandarin is the official language of China, and again there are distinct regional variations – Cantonese is the dialect in Guangdong province and much of the south, and there are eight other major dialects elsewhere. On top of that, there are the Turkic tongues of the Moslem northwest and Tibetan in Tibet. Unless you're prepared to invest in a crash language course before you go to China, it's virtually impossible to even begin to master it in a hurry – there

are complicated tonal nuances, for example, that can turn a perfectly innocent but poorly pronounced statement orrequest into a cause for shock or gales of laughter.

However, there are several good English-Chinese dictionaries and phrasebooks on the market from which you can cobble together a smattering of "taxi Chinese" and get what you want, but make sure you buy a reference in Pinyin, the new Romanized form of Chinese, as distinct from the old Wade-Giles system. It is Pinyin that has changed Peking to Beijing, Mao Tse-tung to Mao Zedong, Soochow

to Suzhou and Chungking to Chongqing. From the tourist's point of view, the language is governed by five letters which can draw a blank if they're not pronounced properly:

"X" – pronounced **"sh,"** as in **"Shian"** (Xi'an).

"Q" – turns inscrutably into **"ch,"** as in the **"Ching"** (Qing) dynasty.

"C" – sounds like **"ts,"** as in **"it's"** or **"cang"** (tsang).

"Zh" – as in **Guangzhou** or **Lanzhou,** is pronounced with a **"j"** as in **"Joe."**

There are two universally useful terms, **"Ni Hao,"** which means "Hello. How are you?" and **"tongzhi"** (pronounced **"tongjie"),** which means "comrade" and which

ABOVE Chinese ciagarettes on sale in Shenyang, their cover artwork a blend of ancient and revolutionary motifs.

The safest way to conduct yourself in China is the way you'd do it in any country or city – don't flash a lot of money around, don't take in too much in the way of valuables and consign those that you happen to buy along the way to your hotel safe-deposit.

ELECTRICITY

The voltage is 220 all over China, and the sockets are mostly two-pin. It's best to take battery-operated shavers, dryers and other gadgets.

TIME

Despite the size of the country, there are no time-zones. When it's 12 noon in Beijing it's 12 noon everywhere else. However, you'll find there's a strange, unofficial 10-minute time difference wherever you go. Wherever I went and no matter how many times I reset my watch, it was always 10 minutes fast or slow.

ACCESS

Just about every area of tourist interest is now open to packaged and individual travel – Tibet and the Xichuanbanna minorities' area south of Kunming being among the last great bastions of special permit travel to fall in early 1986. If there are still any towns or areas that still require a permit it is because they haven't yet been brought up to the level where they can cope with an influx of foreigners, or are places of top security; and to my mind, this is a good enough reason to avoid them.

There are good reasons to avoid certain other areas. Some have cultural attractions but are just not worth the expense and trouble it can take to get through to them. As I've already stated, the paramount consideration that should be given to any itinerary or travel plan in China is the question of enjoyment versus endurance.

Selected Reading List

JACQUES GERNET, *A History of Chinese Civilization*, Cambridge, Cambridge University Press, 1986.

HARRISON E. SALISBURY, *China: 100 years of Revolution*, André Deutsch, 1983.

ALAN SAMAGALSKI & MICHAEL BUCKLEY, *China: A Travel Survival Kit*, Hong Kong, Lonely Planet, 1984.

ROBERT K. G., China: Land of Discovery and Invention, Weldingborough, (UK), Patrick Stephens, 1986.

ANTHONY LAWRENCE, China: The Long March, London, Merehurst Press, 1986.

DANIEL P. REID, *Chinese Herbal Medicine*, Hong Kong, CFW Publications Ltd, 1987.

Classical Chinese Architecture, Hong Kong, Joint Publishing Co.

BLUNDEN & ELVIN, *Cultural Atlas of China*, Phaidon Publications, 1983.

CHENG DALIN, *The Great Wall of China*, Hong Kong, South China Morning Post.

DAVID BONAVIA , *Seeing Red*, Harrap, 1987.

HARRISON E. SALISBURY, *The Long March*, Pan, 1986.

LYNN PAN, *The New Chinese Revolution*, London, Hamish Hamelton, 1987.

The Rough Guide to China, London, Routledge & Kegan Paul, 1987.

STERLING SEAGRAVE, *The Soong Dynasty*, Sidgwick & Jackson, 1985.

The Psychology of the Chinese People, Oxford University Press, 1986.

ZHU JIAJIN, *Treasures of the Forbidden City*, Viking Press, 1986.

Quick Reference A – Z Guide
to Places and Topics of Interest with Listed Accommodation, Restaurants and Useful Telephone Numbers

Photo Credits

Adrian Bradshaw: Cover, 3, 4, 5 right, 6 left, 7, 10, 13, 17 middle, 18, 19, 24-5, 27, 28, 30, 37, 38 top, 43, 45, 46, 47, 50, 55, 62 right, 65, 66, 78, 80 middle, 81 bottom, 82, 83, 85, 86, 96, 97, 99, 100, 101, 104-5, 106, 107, 108 top, left and right, 110, 111 left, 112-3, 120 left, 122, 125 top left, bottom left and right, 132, 134, 135, 138-139, 141, 143, 145, 147, 152 top right, 154, 155 bottom, 159, 162-163, 164, 165, 166, 167, 169, 172-173 center, 173, 174, 175, 177 top, 184 bottom, 187, 194-195, 196, 197, 199, 202-203, 205, 207, 211, 212, 213, 214, 215, 217, back cover-top right, left top and center, bottom left.

Michael C Hall: 88

Nik Wheeler: 5 left, 6 right, 11, 14, 17 top, 17 bottom, 20, 22-23, 32-33 bottom, 34, 38 bottom, 62 left, 63, 70 top, 71 bottom, 72-74, 75, 116-117, 118, 119 bottom, 120 right, 121 left, 126-127, 128, 129, 130-131, 133, 137, 140, 146, 152 top left and bottom, 156, 157, 168, 178, 180, 181 top, 182, 183, 186, 188, 190, 192, 193, 204, 208, back cover-center and bottom right.

The Author: 32 top, 33, 48-49, 51, 57, 59, 60, 68, 69, 70 bottom, 71 top, 76, 77, 80, 90, 91, 92, 94-95, 98, 108 bottom, 109, 111 right, 114, 115, 119 middle, 121 right, 125 top right, 142, 150, 153 top, 155 top, 160, 162, 172 left, 177 bottom, 181 bottom, 184-185 top, 191, 216.